PENGUIN BOOKS

DID THINGS GET BETTER?

Polly Toynbee is a political and social commentator for the *Guardian*. She is a regular broadcaster and was the BBC's Social Affairs Editor. Educated at Oxford, she began her career on the *Observer*, and has won many awards, including the George Orwell Prize and *What the Papers Say* Commentator of the Year. Her books include *Hospital*, *A Working Life* and *Lost Children*. She is a member of the NHS national screening committee and has four children.

David Walker is Analysis Editor and a leader writer for the *Guardian*. He has also worked for *The Times*, the *Independent* and the BBC, where he continues as a regular presenter of Radio Four's *Analysis* programme. Educated at Cambridge and Sussex universities, he was a Harkness Fellow in the United States. His books include *Sources Close to the Prime Minister* (with Peter Hennessy), *The Times Guide to the New British State* and *Media Made in California* (with Jeremy Tunstall). He is a director of People for Places, one of the country's largest social housing providers.

Polly Toynbee and David Walker

Did Things Get Better?

PENGUIN BOOKS

PENGUIN BOOKS

Published by the Penguin Group
Penguin Books Ltd, 27 Wrights Lane, London w8 5tz, England
Penguin Putnam Inc., 375 Hudson Street, New York, New York 10014, USA
Penguin Books Australia Ltd, Ringwood, Victoria, Australia
Penguin Books Canada Ltd, 10 Alcorn Avenue, Toronto, Ontario, Canada m4v 3b2
Penguin Books India (P) Ltd, 11 Community Centre, Panchsheel Park, New Delhi – 110 017, India
Penguin Books (NZ) Ltd, Private Bag 102902, NSMC, Auckland, New Zealand
Penguin Books (South Africa) (Pty) Ltd, 5 Watkins Street, Denver Ext 4, Johannesburg 2094, South Africa

Penguin Books Ltd, Registered Offices: Harmondsworth, Middlesex, England

First published 2001
2

Set in 10/12.5 pt PostScript Monotype Imprint
Typeset by Rowland Phototypesetting Ltd, Bury St Edmunds, Suffolk
Printed in England by Clays Ltd, St Ives plc

Contents

Preface: Did Things Get Better?

We decided to write this book not because we already knew the answer to that question, but because we did not. We wanted to find out just what had been done and what left undone by the Labour Government in its term of office.

The more we looked into the evidence, the more this book seemed necessary. Many of the programmes, much of the money dispensed – perhaps most of it – have barely registered with the public. That could mean that Labour's schemes have been singularly ineffective, or that people do rely on press reports in which, unless a policy becomes a battle, a scandal or a joke, it vanishes into thin air. There is a puzzle here. Labour published glossy annual reports and sought to mobilize Government public relations. Yet a government famous for its capacity to 'spin' failed to project so much of what it did: the reason may lie with its own ambivalence. What was the message – tough or tender, prudent or eager to spend, unafraid to tax or tempted to do good by stealth?

Even we who get paid to follow policy pronouncements were surprised by the sheer extent of Labour's doing. This was an exceptionally busy government – fidgety, some said. Departments poured out programmes, new deals, targets, bits of money here and there to address particular problems. Ah, the sneerers said, 'initiativitis'. The truth is that many of the schemes may work to transform housing estates, young offenders, the life of poor older people, but measurable results may not emerge for years. Come an election, Labour will no doubt be making exaggerated claims for programmes that are barely off the ground.

Labour deserves better than spin-doctoring. We have tried to give as fair and accurate a progress report as the available figures allow. Here at least is an accounting of what the Blair Government began, acknowledging that reliable measures of its achievements and failures may be years ahead.

Polly Toynbee
David Walker

Introduction

Early in the morning of Friday, 2 May 1997, outside the gates of Downing Street crowds were singing and hugging and dancing. Strangers embraced: 'Where were you when Portillo lost?' A seventy-year-old woman brought a red rose for Tony Blair – 'If I live to be a hundred there'll never be another day like it!' One man had jumped in his car and driven all the way from Liverpool. In their wild euphoria they even talked of the night the Berlin Wall fell, of Nelson Mandela's release. It was the day the country exulted – even the sneering editorial writers at Wapping.

Within hours pollsters had trouble finding anyone willing to admit voting Tory. Millions, including the many who had not bothered to turn out that Thursday, pretended they too had willed this change. But Blair's Commons landslide was deceptive. John Major had a higher proportion of the vote in 1992 than Blair won in 1997. Less than three-quarters of the electorate had felt the urge to mark their ballot paper at all. May 1997 saw no resounding endorsement of Labour, rather the collapse of the Tories. That glorious morning showed no deep-rooted desire for change. Perhaps it was just one of those moments of madness that swept the country from time to time: the death of Diana, say, or the September 2000 petrol price revolt.

Inside Downing Street caution was the watchword from that first morning. Millbank and Number 10 periodically liked to terrify themselves over any fluttering sign of Tory revival. They did not believe what had happened, despite the extraordinary unbroken run of popularity that lasted for the whole of the first three years. They were gripped by almost superstitious fears that the plainly vanquished Tory foe would rise from its grave unless they stood guard over it night and day.

In the weeks leading up to the election Labour had tried to run a restrained campaign. Did any government sweep to such power on such small promises? Those five easy pledges on the party's little election cards promised no revolution – just a bit more here, a bit better for hospitals, schools, youth crime. And, between the lines, much of the Thatcherite inheritance. Even the campaign song was chosen for its unambitious theme, D:Ream's 'Things Can Only Get Better'. But who reads manifestos, let alone background policy documents? That morning black night was at an end: eighteen years of Tory rule came crashing down and in that moment great inchoate expectation was stoked up.

One promise shaped so much of the term that followed – the freeze on public spending for two years at the level set by the Tories in their last budget, plus a pledge not to increase income tax at all. Deposed Chancellor Kenneth Clarke chortled: this was madness, of course he had never intended to stay within that spending straitjacket. But Gordon Brown wore the garment with pride. The key question is whether that pledge was right or necessary. Spending more, Labour could have seized the popular imagination with its programme. If new budgets for schools, hospitals and transport had been struck on day one, voters would surely have seen the practical results – well in time for the next election.

Instead, in spring 2001 they see much less than they expected. For public services a large significant improvement has yet to come. Great sums of money were eventually announced but not till July 2000, and even then the cascade would only flow after April 2001. By then, sadly, Labour had devalued the currency. It promised too much, too soon. Billions were talked of but did not appear. And meanwhile, overall spending decreased as a proportion of GDP. Under Tony Blair the public sector actually shrank.

The over-claiming was shrillest in Gordon Brown's Comprehensive Spending Review of July 1998. Once exposed to scrutiny, it emerged that the Chancellor had craftily triple-counted what were modest sums. That encouraged a general scepticism:

telephone-book numbers were discounted by the public who waited to see visible change in schools and surgeries. In their response to public impatience it was as if the Blairites believed that clever presentation could paper over people's practical experience.

In a sense Labour government did not start till April 1999 when Tory spending ended and Brown's own spending plans came in. This meant that by the time the next general election was held, voters would be lucky to see the result in better services. They would just have to trust. But trust in politicians, waning for decades, was frail. Cynicism and indifference settled back in after that fleeting May dawn. The UK was no different from other countries where confidence in government had been also falling for decades. Yet lessening faith in politics may be a rational public response to the decline in government's importance in people's lives. In a post-Cold-War world where big corporations determine where investments and jobs go, the very stuff of government matters less; why bother watching daily political news, reading newspapers or voting – all in decline? Add to this prevailing mood across the West some specifically British elements, such as the control of mass-circulation newspapers by a right-of-centre reactionary camp bent on fostering cynicism. There remained a deep British history of individualism, making government a hazardous enterprise: progressive government was even more difficult.

Labour tied itself to that pledge on taxing and spending partly as a concession to the Zeitgeist, partly as a straightforward electoral calculation. Politicians, like old generals, often refight the last war. For Labour the last war was the 1992 campaign and it had been a bloody disappointment. Neil Kinnock, now credited with having brought Labour back from the brink after the abysmal defeat of 1983, had gone. (His resurrection as a tough, managerialist Euro commissioner is nothing short of miraculous.) John Smith, who is now blamed for the tax-and-spend commitments that helped Labour lose in 1992, had scant time to change the party and was perhaps not much minded to.

The Blair–Brown team abandoned Clause 4, which had committed the party to nationalization, back-pedalling from Labour's heritage of promises to raise income tax in order to boost spending. The transformation was not all plain sailing. The shadow cabinet split in 1996 when Robin Cook objected to Brown's welfare-to-work scheme and his insistence that young people who refused a training place be denied benefit. Brown had his eye partly on spending, partly on 'credibility' – creating the ineffable trust that Labour could govern safely. This became a cult of toughness which they carried into office: when necessary we think the unthinkable (such as the privatization of air traffic control) and do the unspeakable (cutting single mothers' benefits).

Pollsters say the Tories lost it the day sterling crashed out of the Exchange Rate Mechanism (ERM), never to recover their lead in the polls (until briefly in the September 2000 petrol crisis). But that did not mean Labour had won the people's trust. Labour's Goulds and gurus were forever warning that the strong economy might tip voters back towards the Tories, and then there was Europe. Among the scars of previous defeats was the antagonism of the press. For Rupert Murdoch, Thatcher's friend, Europe was a touchstone issue. Labour's pledge to hold a referendum if it decided on joining EMU was partly designed to reassure him. Blair's notorious article in the *Sun* on 21 April 1997, waving the flag of St George – 'We'll see off the euro dragons' – was part of the implicit (or explicit?) deal. It seemed a necessary compromise, for as polling day approached evidence mounted of a turn of opinion in a Eurosceptic direction evident among those who previously said they were likely to switch away from the Tories. Then and since, one of Labour's postures on Europe has been avoidance.

Labour memories were long and anxious, plagued with insecurity and nightmares. They remembered how the City and international markets had panicked before, when Harold Wilson arrived in Downing Street. They feared another run on the pound, a flight of capital and spiralling inflation. But above all, branded on all they thought and did was the memory of 1992 when victory should have been theirs.

What was left of the left hated the Blairites' analysis, that 'Middle England' was where they had to win votes. The shrinking manual working class was no longer a reliable base for the centre-left. Political success depended on winning support from the broad middle class – Mondeo Man. The ideological fit for this class was low taxes and weak trade unions. At this point the left fissured. Some said if that analysis holds, there is no point in a Labour Party. Others accepted the sociology but still denied that the electorally successful coalition Labour needed to build in Middle England required these Blairite policies. Middle England did want good comprehensives and hospitals. As to whether Middle England would pay for them, the left shrugged its shoulders and said Labour would win anyway in 1997 because of the mood for throwing the Tory rascals out – an act of faith the leadership eschewed.

Labour HQ took a darker view. Thatcher's legacy was a fundamental shift in attitude and lifestyle, leaving England an essentially conservative country. The psephological facts of life said you had to win not just England but specifically the Tory southlands. In 1992 the Saatchis' double-whammy last-minute Tory posters successfully accused Labour of wanting to disturb Middle England's comfort. So, said the Blairites, never again would Labour be carried away by their own rhetoric into believing there was much of an appetite for taking from comfortable Peter to ensure poor Paul had a reasonable standard of living. A country that could return the Tories four times in a row was not much concerned with the plight of the poor, who had trebled in number during those years. Good must be done quietly, taxing by stealth. That was why they had to take the pledge on tax – shocking Labour's supporters but the Tory electioneers even more. Their 'Demon Eyes' posters did not work because the old redistributionist devil was dead. Labour's past now looked as if it had been transformed into something remarkably like a Tory present.

Keith Joseph, once Thatcher's policy mentor, lived on in much New Labour thinking. He had talked of 'remoralizing the working class', transforming it into a new self-reliant bourgeoisie. What else, the stupefied Tory Ferdinand Mount asked, is Labour engaged in, with its desire to educate and train single mothers, stamp out truancy and smarten up the unemployable? But the Tory language was cruel, their methods heartless. On the principle of Nixon in China, only Labour could effect this tough kind of social policy while genuinely believing in social inclusion.

Labour outdid the Tories in its apparent trust in the benignity of private enterprise. How else do we explain the curious faith – shared by Brown, Blair and even by John Prescott, erstwhile standard-bearer for Old Labour views – in 'partnership' between the state and the private sector? 'This new partnership meant we had to put the ideology and dogma of the past behind us. We will not be judged on what we own or how much we spend. We will be judged on what we deliver. Our focus in all that we do must be on outcomes rather than inputs.' That comes from Labour's National Policy Forum of 2000, the essence of the Third Way. Was Blair, some wondered, a 'corporatist' who did not really like combative politics, preferring instead a nirvana where business lions would lie down with public sector lambs, as if their interests and the national interest were the same?

But the minds of voters in 1997 were on concrete issues. Labour had promised not to raise taxes yet also to make widespread improvements – that was its abiding fiscal problem in office. This financial tension was covered up. Labour's manifesto and attendant commitments were a work of art, gaudy and voluminous, verging on the casuistic.

The written document contained some 177 commitments, three-fifths of which were to be accomplished within three years. Labour was to police itself by means of annual reports and, in addition, building on the league table enthusiasms of John

Major, long lists of Public Service Agreements to which government departments would in theory be held. This was a targeted government.

But some of the 1997 pledges were pretty vacuous, such as the promise to hold a Commonwealth summit in 1997 or to maintain 'strong defence through Nato'. Some forty-four of the commitments were about processes rather than outcome. Of the original commitments, only fifty were specific enough to be measurable and they have all been achieved. But that is not necessarily to say a great deal – just as when Chief Secretary to the Treasury Andrew Smith told MPs in 2000 that 90 per cent of the 1998 Public Service Agreement targets had been met. The obvious response was, so what?

Labour would be about 'the delivery of policies that will make a difference to the lives of millions of real people out there in the country at large: shorter hospital waiting lists; smaller classes and better education; relief from the seemingly inexorable rise in crime and disorder; a release from poverty for millions, through an opportunity for breadwinners – mothers as well as fathers – to work; caring welfare for those who really cannot work and therefore cannot exploit that new-found opportunity'.

The famous Five Pledges were written on a card. They were:

- Cut class sizes to thirty for 5–7-year-olds.
- Fast-track punishment for persistent young offenders by halving the time from arrest to sentencing.
- Cut NHS waiting lists by treating an extra 100,000 patients.
- Get 250,000 under-25-year-olds off benefit and into work.
- No rise in income tax rates, cut VAT on heating to 5 per cent and inflation and interest rates as low as possible.

They have all just about been realized, without too much equivocation. But they are only part of the picture. Despite the official caution, Blair stoked the fires of hubris with his subsequent and extraordinary promises on child poverty. To match him, Brown announced he would achieve full employment. Had anyone suggested either pledge as part of the 1997 manifesto, they would have been hurled into outer darkness as backwoods Bennites. Those promises blaze like beacons – no poor families? Full employment in Jarrow and Barrow, Knowsley and Middlesbrough?

A long way from Teeside, in November 1999 in the freezing cold magnificence of Lorenzo de Medici's palazzo overlooking the River Arno, we witnessed the apotheosis of the Third Way – that brilliantly vague description of what Tony Blair thought his government was all about. Up there on the dais at the Florence summit sat President Bill Clinton, Chancellor Gerhard Schröder, Premier Massimo D'Alema, Prime Minister Lionel Jospin and President Henrique Cardozo of Brazil. This was a key gathering of the great Western social democratic leaders, a brief moment in time when the United States of America, Germany, Italy, France and Britain all had social democratic executives. In varying terms they talked Third Way, how they had each navigated that same path between market capitalism and old-style socialism to fuse a new political project in their own political traditions.

Here were the ideas on which Tony Blair had forged New Labour. He and Bill Clinton emerged as the intellectual masters of this event. Influenced by Tony Giddens, prolific author and director of the London School of Economics, Blair had found the doctrine's ambiguities politically useful. Yet some of his rhetoric was breathtakingly ambitious. He talked without irony of regenerating democracy while capturing the new century for progressive forces in the way the last had been dominated by conservatism.

A long-term project, surely. Sometimes Blair and Brown acted and spoke as if they had all the time in the world. 'Much done, much still to do' was their slogan, anticipating at least one further parliamentary term. In hindsight they appear both over-ambitious and yet complacent. But how much more could or should they have done? Voters are notoriously ungrateful. The problems solved and the mountains scaled are quickly forgotten. The only thing that counts is the deficit in what is. And – in spring 2001 – it gapes. There are holes, still, in school roofs and nurse shortages in the NHS, unsafe trains (when they run) and gridlocked roads.

It is hard, even with the luxurious wisdom of hindsight, not to ask why Labour did not dare more. The prudence of opposition was carried into office creating a stifling need to command and control even in territories where the very effort was counterproductive (the attempts to foist Alun Michael on Wales and Frank Dobson on London were unmitigated disasters). Little was done to change the hearts and minds of Middle England, much to appease it. Leadership sometimes gave way to craven people-pleasing.

The great disappointment will be if over-caution has squandered an unrepeatable opportunity with such a mighty majority to achieve far more. The fear is that a smaller majority will lead to greater caution. But the money is there, the plans are laid. Now we wait to see if a second victory will convince them that they really are the masters now.

A Fairer Society

What they promised

A month in power, Tony Blair walked up a newly disinfected stairway on Aylesbury Estate, a great urban wasteland in Peckham, south-east London. There he made his first pronouncement on the plight of the poor and what Labour was going to do to – for – them. Supporters were impatient to know, in words from his own lips, whether the Prime Minister's heart still, however erratically, beat to the left.

The estate – there were 1,999 others like it – was only two miles from Westminster, but the pulse of booming London was a world away from the concrete walkways and blocked garbage chutes of these forty-four grey blocks. Here 11,000 people lived in deprivation: high unemployment, 59 per cent of households poor enough to draw one benefit or another, 78 per cent of seventeen-year-olds already out of school with dim prospects. With high crime, drugs everywhere, graffiti, smashed lights and vandalism, this dismal landscape was as good a testing ground as any for the application of Labour's core values.

'No forgotten people and no no-hope areas' was what Blair promised that day. He offered a new social contract between 'comfortable Britain' and the poor. He would tackle 'the dead weight of low expectations, the crushing belief that things cannot get better'. Cheers went up from those hanging out of tower-block windows but also around the country from those who had voted Labour but had been waiting for a clear statement of intent. Here he laid out his plans for bringing the socially excluded back into society. 'Work is the best form of welfare,' he said, but acknowledged there were no quick fixes. Change would take years. His words were listened to by the residents, many of them women with prams standing out in the sunshine that morning, sceptical.

So did life improve for the Aylesbury Estate or Liverpool Speke, Middlesbrough's Pallister ward or Grangetown in Redcar? (England's most deprived wards were chronicled as never before when in 2000 the Government brought out a reverse Domesday Book of ward-by-ward *Indices of Deprivation*.) One indirect answer has to be that in four years Labour did a lot more for the people of the estates than it had formally promised: since 1997 more money and energy went into its anti-poverty programmes, national and specifically targeted, than anyone expected. But did things change in the walkways and blocks where in November 2000 ten-year-old Damilola Taylor met his shocking death? When Blair said there were no quick fixes, was he hinting that he realized inequality is endemic in our kind of society and economy, that being tough on the causes of poverty might require some brutal questions to be asked about the economic system? No, such questions belonged to New Labour's past. Blairite ministers believed poverty could be done away with by means of schemes and tax credits.

An orthodox left analysis might say: not enough. But given the circumstances of 1997, or rather Labour's remaking of itself between 1992 and 1997, what was remarkable was the appetite they still had to try, within the limits, to make a dent on unequal Britain. Did they realize quite what a slow and thankless task they were undertaking, with so little public interest or appreciation?

Blair with a bleeding heart did not fit the conventional picture. Yet as if to affirm his crusading credentials he went on to make a promise remarkable for being so difficult to place within his Third Way rhetoric or the modest little promises of the manifesto.

It came out of the blue at a gathering of poverty experts in the symbolic precincts of Toynbee Hall, a settlement to help the poor founded in the East End last century. Blair arrived to deliver a lecture but instead told the world something profound about Labour, that the new was not so different from the old. Without equivocation, escape clause or weasel words he promised to abolish child poverty in twenty years. He later embellished the pledge by promising to reach half his target within ten years. *Abolish child poverty!* Was backward Britain, near the bottom of EU social scales, to transform itself into another Sweden in just twenty years? If poverty is defined as lacking a set proportion of an average household income, he was talking about a major shift in income distribution in a progressive direction. Egalitarianism, it seemed, lived after all.

The size of the problem

Labour genuinely wanted to know what worked. Whitehall research budgets grew; the Department for Education and Employment set up a new unit of its own and established the London Institute of Education as a 'what works' centre outside (though the UK still had one of the lowest spends on official statistics as a proportion of GDP). John Hills and other experts from the London School of Economics became welcome and regular visitors in both the Treasury and the Department of Social Security. Under Labour, government became better informed than ever about the effectiveness – or otherwise – of what it did.

Early on, Labour's dismal inheritance was set out in a New Policy Institute audit which serves as a benchmark. Some 4 million children, one in three, lived in poverty (defined as households living on less than half of average incomes). A third of all the poor children in the EU were born in the UK. Since 1979 average incomes had risen by a handsome 40 per cent in real terms, while the incomes of the poorest stayed static. Some 8 million more people had fallen into poverty. The number of households where no one had a job doubled. The health of the poor was bad and getting relatively worse, as measured in premature birth, infant mortality, adult life expectancy, accident rates, obesity, smoking and bad diet. The gap in life expectancy between rich and poor was rising. Single mothers were among the poorest, 30 per cent less likely to be working and earning than married mothers.

The plan

Poverty was more than just a matter of income, the Government declared, and its new definition – 'exclusion' – gained general recognition. In December 1997, the Social Exclusion Unit was set up at the heart of the Whitehall machine designed to work under the Prime Minister's direct patronage. Seven of its eleven members were women, and it included experts and outsiders from the police and probation. Its analysis was first-rate, in a series of reports on truancy, school exclusion, rough sleepers, teenage pregnancy, children leaving care, failed housing estates, juvenile crime and many more, confidently prescribing what to do. But on how to do it, civil-service conservatism often married with Labour's failure to think afresh about councils and committees and the nuts and bolts of delivering programmes to the doorsteps of the run-down estates.

At first ministers were frenetic. Area-based initiatives abounded, since the excluded usually lived cheek by jowl in estates and identifiable city wards; employment, health and education action zones were begun. In the first two years so many schemes flowed from hyper-energetic new ministers that almost at once there were no control zones where *nothing* was happening that researchers could use to compare. Soon the media lost count – and sadly lost interest.

As the manifesto promised, the centrepiece, to be financed by the £5 billion windfall tax on the privatized utilities, was the New Deal for the young unemployed. The target group was 250,000 18–25-year-olds neither in a job nor in education. The New Deal summoned each of them to meet civil service advisers who would spend four months assessing them and helping them get jobs. If that failed then New Dealers had to take one of four options: education (up to a year), a job with an employer paid £60 a week to take them on, work on an environmental project or helping a voluntary organization. It was the first time the unemployed had been given intensive personal help with one adviser to see them through the whole process and pick them up if things did not work out.

Later the New Deal was extended to single mothers. (Work was never made compulsory for them, but an annual interview to show them what was on offer was made obligatory from April 2001.) Another scheme, New Deal Plus, was launched to help the unemployed aged over fifty, with another for disabled people and another for the over-25s.

As unexpectedly as Blair announced his poverty pledge, Brown followed up with a declaration that full employment was now the goal. It was a radical departure. However well employment trends were going, the idea that all job-seekers in Liverpool or Barrow or Paisley would find work seemed far-fetched. New Deal policies alone would not work. Action Teams for Jobs were formed in 2000 to go into the hardest areas with extra money for retraining and to encourage employers to take people on. But the Government adamantly refused to do what most experts agreed would eventually be necessary – the state (local authorities) deliberately creating jobs through new public works and expanded payrolls.

So how well did Labour do? By 2001 with over 1 million new jobs created since 1997 and unemployment at around 4 per cent, one unemployment count put the total out of work at less than 1 million. But headline figures disguise the picture in the worst areas. The Indices of Deprivation showed a reserve army 85,000 strong in Birmingham which might be at work. In the Durham coalfield, in niches in the south such as Great Yarmouth as well as in the traditional blackspots of Liverpool and Middlesbrough, rates were double the national average and sometimes 10 per cent higher.

Launched into a booming economy when more jobs were

becoming available, the New Deal was open to attack as a waste of money – surely a lot of those young people would have got jobs anyway? The New Deal did well, with 75 per cent of its graduates in work three months later: the rest disappeared, many presumed to have been claiming fraudulently. Objective evaluation showed that by mid-2000 some 160,000 more young people had been found jobs at least six months faster than they would have done had there been no intervention. For the over-25s, longer unemployed, assessors said the New Deal had doubled the number who would have found work. It all cost £800 million, and that worked out at £4,000 a job, a modest price compared with time on benefits.

Brown had a long-term strategy – perhaps too long-term for modern politics. He seized on research showing how by the age of just twenty-two months children from the top two social classes are already 14 per cent higher on the educational/developmental scale than children in social classes D and E – and the gap widened thereafter. Destiny starts at birth. But American programmes seemed to provide a remedy. The Perri High Scope scheme, part of the American Head Start programme, had shown how intensive teaching and support for the poorest families with very young children delivered lifelong results. Two years of teaching pre-school children how to learn and think ultimately saved the state $7 for every $1 spent. By the time those children were thirty they were more likely to go to college, have a good job and own their own home, less likely ever to draw social security or commit crime. That is why the Sure Start programme was founded in HM Treasury, led by Norman Glass, a Whitehall economist who never expected to devote his senior career years to bringing up babies.

Labour had pledged a nursery place for every four-year-old, but this was something else. Sure Start became an administrative model for other Labour interventions: a small central unit setting targets for local committees, often made up from but not led by councils. Some 250 Sure Start schemes, with £580 million to spend, were set up in areas of greatest poverty, working with midwives and health visitors to identify mothers straight after birth who were struggling, depressed and in need of support. There might be children's day centres, home visits for depressed mothers, mother and toddler groups, all kinds of experimental attempts to give the poorest young children a better family life. Targets were set, for example to cut infant mortality. After Sure Start came a pledge on expanding nursery education, then the promise to cut class sizes in primary schools to ensure that every child at least learned basic reading and writing.

All this was intended to 'join up' with designated health, education and employment zones, each of which had its packet of new money for projects such as after-school and holiday clubs, which were paid for by the Lottery's New Opportunities Fund. Alongside this ran a host of targets for local social services. Half the children in council care were to pass one GCSE – a shamefully low benchmark which, by 2001, had not been hit. *One Healthier Nation*, from public health minister Tessa Jowell, bravely announced a target to reduce the number of teenage pregnancies, both a symptom and further cause of poverty for girls – promising to halve the rate by 2010. Targets sprouted everywhere, hundreds of them, trying to measure and force improvement as never before – but often dreamt up in Whitehall with too little regard to local delivery.

One imaginative approach to the delivery problem came in November 2000, when Brown put £450 million into a Children's Fund to be dispensed to charities and voluntary organizations – Barnardo's, Save the Children, NCH, NSPCC and others – already running good projects that worked. The idea was that they would spread the word.

A second wave of spending addressed the problem of children who failed later at secondary stage. Finally, if some escaped, there was the Connexions programme for 11–25-year-olds and then the New Deal to catch them in its last-chance safety net. Taken altogether, assuming it will 'join up', Labour created a preventative social programme for a generation. It would take two decades but if it worked there should be many fewer children leaving school unemployable, many more with the qualifications to lift them above their parents and squeeze poverty out of society – an optimistic, idealistic vision.

The mistakes

An error was the promise in the manifesto of major changes in social security. Tony Blair even called it his Big Idea. His extravagant characterization of the Department of Social Security (DSS) budget as a bloated symbol of political and social failure was a serious misjudgement when progressive ministers should boast that a well-managed social budget is a symbol of a civilized society caring well for its old, sick and poor. Labour had inherited a social security bill of just 13 per cent of GDP, compared with a European average of 19 per cent. In fact the DSS bill for benefits was falling, from just over £100 billion in 1996–7 to just over £99 billion in 2000–2001, with a planned increase for 2001–2. This reflected plummeting unemployment which would have pushed the total down further but for deliberate generosity, mainly in increased pensions, child benefit and income support for children.

Promising some great undefined revolution, Blair brought Frank Field into the DSS to 'think the unthinkable'. Field was a charismatic man with many admirers, most of them in the Tory Party. A loner, he had a great gift for describing the moral perversities of social security, calling it a system designed to encourage people to cheat and lie, where claimants were asked what they could not do and were rewarded accordingly. Re-moralizing the poor had been Field's long-term goal – a Tory inspiration, a century old, that appealed to Tony Blair too.

Trusting Field to come up with a new answer (himself vague about what this might be), Blair embarked on a roadshow round the country to soothe the heartland's nerves after the lone parents' cuts disaster (see page 18), trying to explain why the whole system needed radical reform. Unfortunately, Field's critique was considerably better than any alternative he managed to devise. After hiding away in his room at the DSS, he presented a horrified Prime Minister with a plan for universal contributions and mutual benefits that would have cost a staggering £8 billion. The unthinkable turned out to be impossible. After Field left, quiet incremental reform looked a better bet. The main change was to remove chunks of the DSS budget and hide it away inside Inland Revenue accounts by rebadging benefits as tax credits, another of Gordon Brown's American inspirations.

The Government failed to fire the public with its myriad programmes, but that was due to Downing Street's ambivalence and fear that Middle England might find out how much money was being spent on the poor. Why would its denizens have voted Tory all those years if they had cared about growing poverty? Individual ministers were full of zeal, buttonholing anyone willing to listen to talk enthusiastically of projects, but somehow they never captured the public's imagination. As for Labour's core support, they either did not know, so little was any of this covered in the newspapers, or they did not believe: the rhetoric never rang with the word they most wanted to hear – redistribution. Valuable measures such as an end to disconnecting households unable to pay their water bills won faint praise.

The problem, first, was the spending freeze. Anti-poverty programmes were always likely to move at the pace of a glacier, so they needed to be started at once. But everything except the New Deal began two years late. Two mighty rows soured public perceptions. The fiasco over lone parent benefits was caused by far too literal an interpretation of the promise to stick within Tory spending limits. Labour fell into a trap deliberately laid by Peter Lilley, Major's Social Security Secretary. Brown forced Lilley's successor, Harriet Harman, to push through cuts no one thought just or wise. It was a terrible blooding for Labour's new MPs as they were dragooned through the lobbies to vote, some of them in tears. The episode permanently blackened Labour's name, even though single parents got the money back a year later through other benefits. Stalwarts who hated Third Way fudging and the wooing of Middle England now had ample ammunition. Later Brown's aides admitted it had all been needless panic born of inexperience in the early days.

In an even bigger backbench rebellion over disability benefits in May 1999, sixty-seven Labour MPs voted against the Government and another fourteen abstained: this brought Blair's welfare reforming zeal to an abrupt halt. Despite the lone parents' debacle, the Prime Minister still felt reform must be pursued to prove to Middle England that Labour could tighten the screw on social security. Obeying orders, Alistair Darling searched in nooks and crannies for savings and lighted upon an idea that had dawned on Michael Portillo back in 1993 but which he wisely dropped. It was to turn Incapacity Benefit (IB) into a means-tested benefit. Those who received the £66.75 IB would no longer get it automatically: if they also had an occupational pension above £85 a week it would be tapered away to take their income into account.

Over the Tory years IB had become a resting place for early retired people unlikely to work again. Their doctors signed them on out of kindness, though many were genuinely depressed by unemployment or had a string of minor ailments. The Tories had secretly instructed local employment offices to push unemployed people on to IB to cut numbers on the official register. To Labour it made no sense at a time of rising good health and rising employment: the idea was to bring people back on the jobless register then help them find jobs. A New Deal for the over-50s offered them extra money with a chance of training and advice.

In cool Whitehall corridors the policy may have looked rational. To MPs and the public it was an inexplicable assault upon disabled people. It was a blunder. For the sake of a smallish saving (£350 million) Labour concentrated attention on what it was *not* doing to help the disadvantaged instead of focusing on the very large sums the Government *was* spending elsewhere on the poor. The policy misfired even in Middle England, whose inhabitants believed billions were squandered on 'scroungers' but the disabled were not counted among them. To soften the gesture, more was given to 30,000 disabled children and to the very severely disabled.

Behind this cut – and even more on pensions (see page 23) – there was a single strand of thought that dared not speak its name. Over many years, starting with the last Labour Government but marching ahead under the Tories and tacitly accepted by New Labour, policy-makers in the Treasury and DSS recognized that the old National Insurance (NI) system was gradually falling apart. William Beveridge never envisaged an ever-growing tide of well-off pensioners, nor a large pool of millions living permanently on benefits caused by long-term unemployment and still less a million lone parents and their children. The modern need was less for universal benefits paid as a right from a largely imaginary NI fund, much more for benefits targeted on the genuinely needy. In 1979 half of the DSS budget was spent on National Insurance benefits, but by 1997 this had eroded to only a third – and three-quarters of that was spent on pensions. National Insurance payments were on their way out.

Benefit increases

'Work is the best welfare' and 'A hand up not a hand out' had been Labour's somewhat forbidding mantra. All the evidence showed that the only route out of poverty is employment; long-term exclusion from the labour market is exclusion from society. The rich may manage fulfilling, socially energetic lives without having a job – but most people with nothing find unemployment corrosive and alienating. Labour concluded that any job, however low-paid, however part-time, was the path back. Some found this harsh: what use is a part-time, insecure, badly paid Macjob, they asked? Better than nothing, was the convincing response.

This idea under-pinned Labour's thinking on social security. The new awkwardly titled ONE was to be a single gateway for all benefit claimants, with job-search and claims dealt with together by one adviser, underlining the conviction that work is the first obligation, so extra money was poured into those work incentives. There was already a benefit that topped up wages for working parents with children – Family Credit – but Brown replaced it with a far more generous Working Families Tax Credit. The money was taken out of the DSS budget and paid instead by the Inland Revenue directly into the pay-packet of the main earner in any family. (Virtually no WFTC recipients are from two-earner families.) The reason the social security bill did not drop as a result is to Labour's great credit: not only those in work, but the old and unemployed families with children also got big rises.

There were objections. What about employees' privacy? Once employers were handing out the benefit and calculating how much it was, would it not encourage them to pay lower wages than they might have? However, the minimum wage was designed to stop that. One and a half million people, most of them women, saw their pay rise significantly when the minimum wage came in – it had taken a century and the advent of an explicitly non-socialist Labour Government to realize this great goal of founding father Keir Hardie. It was set at a disappointingly low rate at £3.60, with the young paid less, but it was something no other Labour Government had dared to do. Despite all those Tory warnings about job losses, the Low Pay Commission, which fixed the rate, reported afterwards that no jobs had been lost, though the CBI grumbled and no doubt exaggerated when they claimed it had cost industry £4 billion.

With WFTC, families where one adult worked now saw a huge rise in their incomes – up to £50 more a week, with an average rise of £24 over the old Family Credit system, with more to come in the March 2001 budget. In 2000, no family with children would ever live below £214 a week; they would pay no tax until earning over £12,000 a year. As WFTC paid so much more than Family Credit it brought more families into its net, and 1 million households received it. Nearly 1 million of the poorest workers no longer had to pay NI either. But, critics said,

WFTC was a transfer from handbag to wallet: they were silenced by the sheer amount of extra money handed out. Besides, most families on WFTC are single mothers, where the handbag-to-wallet effect did not apply.

What of the families left reliant on social security? Mainly they were lone parents or families in unemployment black spots. The suspicion was that all extra money had been piled on to in-work benefits, leaving those out of work behind, but that did not happen. Although the talk was all of WFTC and the virtues of work, the income support rates quietly kept pace. Non-working families saw benefits rise more sharply than ever before. Income support for children went up by a huge 72 per cent in real terms between 1997 and April 2000 – from £16.90 to £31.45 per child under eleven and more to come in April 2001. Child benefit for families rich and poor leapt up by 25 per cent in real terms for the eldest child to £15.13, 2 per cent more for subsequent children. It is surprising how little these great leaps forward entered into the political consciousness.

From 2001 a new children's tax credit of £520 a year for most families (for households up to £40,000) replaced the old Married Couples Allowance of £285. In 2003 Brown hopes to reform all this again, binding children's credits and payments into a single tax credit worth the same for families in or out of work. The idea is to create new work incentives with a single block of money families never lose; they can build on it with their own earnings. The poor who benefited least under Labour were those without children or those whose children had grown up, whose benefits only rose with price inflation: if they drank, smoked or drove they tended to be worse off, increases in indirect taxes hitting them hardest.

Under the last Labour Government there was an approved list of items a poor claimant could get a lump sum for – furnishing an empty flat, replacing a broken cooker or a child's stolen winter coat. The list grew and so did the money dispensed, with local officers having to make difficult and inevitably erratic decisions about who qualified for what: there was undoubtedly some fraud.

The Tories introduced a cash-limited Social Fund to dispense mainly loans, not grants. Money owing was always taken off benefit cheques at a sharp rate, making the poor even poorer, though at least they were not in debt to loan sharks. Indignant in opposition, in power Labour could think of nothing better: the sum in the fund fell slightly. All the same the number taking out loans rose, up 760,000 from 500,000, an oddity when more were in work, and benefits had risen. Researchers thought the increasing applications were due to a new less patronizing application form that no longer required applicants to say what they wanted the money for. However, there was much embarrassment when it emerged that the numbers turned away for loans had risen steeply under Labour, from 4,856 in 1997/98 to 362,000 in 1999/2000. The main reason was a new rule, introduced by Labour, under which a poor person who has already received one loan is no longer eligible for a second loan until a major part of the first has been paid off. A promise was made to do something.

The pension

The Government stumbled badly over its handling of pensions. But it ended well, with Labour on the verge of a remarkable success: pensioner poverty to be abolished once and for all. Underfunded ever since Beveridge, pensions were too low, over 2 million old people living below the poverty line in 1997. Labour lifted them above it and index-linked the lowest payments to earnings, so that pensioners should from now on enjoy a tolerable standard of living.

This is how it happened. The basic state pension goes to the most important single group of voters – 12 million older citizens, 25 per cent of those who actually bother to vote, a formidable lobby. Labour was usually accused of bending like a reed before every puff of public opinion, but on pensions Gordon Brown had proved dangerously obdurate. It was right in theory not to increase the basic state pension beyond price inflation. Brown was adamant that any extra for older people should go to the poorest, though it meant the growing numbers of better-off elderly would see their state support shrinking (at least in relation to earnings). However fair, right and brave, the message never flew. All that registered with most voters was the 2000 budget and a pension increase (based on low price inflation) of 75p a week. 75p! How could Labour so insult the old? Anything, even a few pennies over a pound, would have sounded better. Even though by 2001 the automatic uprating would produce an extra £2, still that 75p entered political mythology: miserly Brown.

The clamour from the grey lobby and within Labour's own ranks was for a restoration of the link between the basic pension and average earnings: the link had a brief life between being introduced by Barbara Castle in the mid-1970s and its severance by Margaret Thatcher. But Labour had never said they would restore it and they did not, with good reason. Times had changed. These days a third of pensioners are pretty well off, with every new cohort retiring on better occupational and private pensions. Increasing the basic pension by more than just prices gives all of them more, but barely helps the poorest one-third who rely on income support (the safety-net means-tested benefit) to supplement their state pension.

Pension increments paid to everyone are regressive, not redistributive. But complete consistency is rare in politics, and so as a sop to the universal principle Brown did give a £150-a-year lump sum for winter fuel to all, untaxed. Free TV licences went to all the over-75s, worth £2 a week – more justifiable since older pensioners tend to be poorer. Similarly, a National Bus Pass Scheme for pensioners was to start April 2001, benefiting 5 million by guaranteeing a 50 per cent reduction on their fares: some local authorities will choose to be more generous.

Inequality among pensioners was growing when Labour came in, so there was a clear need to distinguish within the post-65 population. Very poor pensioners had doubled in number while Labour was out of office. By 1997 2.4 million old people were living below half average income – the European poverty line measure. To lift them above the poverty line, Labour introduced a Minimum Income Guarantee (MIG), to be uprated each year with earnings. When first paid in April 2000, it gave an immediate extra £5.45 a week real increase to the poorest. It was linked to a campaign to find the estimated 500,000 who were not claiming all their entitlements: the down-side of targeting is that it always misses some people.

But all this well-targeted spending won Labour little gratitude. The MIG is good old-fashioned redistribution. If the universal pension had been raised, the poorest would have got a mere 4 per cent more instead of 9 per cent in 2000, the year the row broke out afresh at the Labour Party conference. The Chancellor kept saying how much he had done – but was not believed. So then he did something that will stand as one of the great milestones of this government.

At a stroke, Brown increased the MIG so sharply that it pulled all pensioners out of poverty. Age Concern calculated that £90 a week was the least pensioners could be expected to live on decently but 54 per cent of them lived on less. The lobbyists for the elderly were astonished when the Chancellor announced in his November 2000 pre-budget statement that not only would their sum be met, but it would be increased. All pensioners would get at least £92.15 from April 2001. What is more, they would get £100 by 2003 and the money would be linked permanently to earnings. In all he spent £3 billion more on this just distribution of pension cash than if he had simply re-established the old earnings link. It was a bold and right thing to do, for he could have earned far greater kudos and spent a lot less if he had simply given way to the Old Labour pensioners' lobby.

Since by 2000 the idea of the MIG had sadly failed to catch on politically, Brown hammered home the message about his generosity by also adding £5 to the basic pension for all. It was, of course, entirely contrary to his previously announced principles, but that 75p had made it a political necessity: the likes of the Queen Mother got their extra too, alongside the poor.

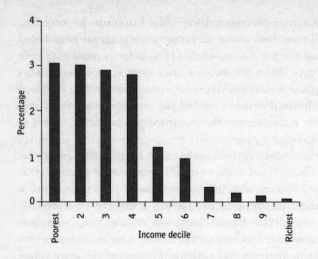

Figure 1: Pre-Budget Report Analysis: measure for pensioners

Source: Institute for Fiscal Studies

(As a thin disguise, it was described as a 'transitional' payment.) Then, another political rabbit out of the hat, he produced an extra £50 for winter fuel: £200 to all pensioners, to be paid in November 2000.

The problem with raising the poorest up was that those just a little above them grumbled that their small savings and occupational pensions disqualified them from this largesse or made their thrift redundant. To meet the point and encourage savings the government promised Pensioner Credits, which will give extra to those with small savings pound for pound, to make sure they are always better off than those on MIG creeping up behind them. Up to a ceiling of £135 a week, the more they saved the more they will get, starting in 2003.

Also with an eye on the baby-boom generation coming up to retirement, Labour ministers made speeches extolling the virtues of older workers and produced a code of practice against age discrimination in employment, which might in future become law.

Moral hazard bedevils social security – the danger here is that if state benefits for the old seem too generous, people will not bother to save. Labour's recipe was a second state pension. This was to replace another of Barbara Castle's inventions, the State Earnings Related Pension which the Tories had partially dismembered. Labour's new version, to be phased in over five years, is intended for low earners (up to £9,000 a year) and offers various entitlements and credits to carers or disabled people who are not earning.

Another innovation was Stakeholder pensions – private products on sale from April 2001. Here the object was the same, to get people on lower earnings (those in the £9,000–£20,000 bracket) who do not save to make provision for their future – so that they would not be dependent on the state. The incentive was to be rebates on National Insurance payments. The policy was prompted partly by Tory mistakes, when a great Government-encouraged pensions mis-selling scandal had made people suspicious of private pension snake-oil merchants. Now the Government gave a kite-mark to stakeholder pensions with very low administration charges. Whether people on lower earnings can afford to save much using this or any other vehicle is disputed: there is a danger of the Government itself mis-selling to those who may never save enough to get them above state provision. But then people may rightly worry that future Conservative Governments might not keep up with the level of pensions guaranteed now to the poorest. For example, the Tories have refused to promise to keep MIG earnings-linked.

These were all clever pension and poverty policies from a clever Chancellor. They were well targeted, tackled problems and wasted little money on those who did not need it. But just try explaining them snappily on a billboard or in a soundbite. Brown was too much an experts' Chancellor. The Minimum Income Guarantee hit the spot financially but not politically. Brown's thrust was egalitarian, but he had to compete with the Tories' crowd-pleasing calls for 'more on the basic pension for all'. Yet he gave Labour one clear and resounding boast – for the first time in history, there should be no more pensioners living below the breadline.

The disabled

Had it not been for the Incapacity Benefit row, disability groups would have declared themselves on the whole pleased with Labour's first term. The manifesto made just one pledge and they implemented it at once: 'comprehensive and enforcible civil rights for disabled people at work and in society'. In 1995, amid passionate protest at its feebleness, the Tories had introduced a Disability Discrimination Act. Labour gave it teeth with the Disability Rights Commission, which opened its doors in 2000: its first test case established the right of the long-term clinically depressed to be registered disabled. A Special Educational Needs and Disability Rights in Education bill was tabled late in 2000, to give fairer access to education.

The New Deal for Disabled People was widely welcomed, started with pilots and rolled out nationally in April 2000, with advisers trained in the complex and varied barriers to getting work for disabled people.

Disabled people are a big lobby – a government taskforce estimated in 1999 that there were 8.6 million, two-thirds of them over sixty-five. Labour had inherited from the Tories the hated Benefits Integrity Project, which sent inspectors off to investigate whether those on higher rates of Disability Living Allowance were really disabled enough. There was no corresponding test to see if some of those on the lower levels had become more disabled and qualified for higher payments: the only possible effect of this 'integrity' was to make savings. It was degenerating into farce, as newspapers highlighted cases of severely disabled people suddenly cut off from benefit, or one case where someone with Down's Syndrome was asked how long they had suffered from it. Gordon Brown demanded that the new tests remain for a whole year, still trying to prove Labour was as tough as the Tories, souring what would otherwise have been a good record on disability. But it was eventually abandoned.

Great Britain has an estimated 5.7 million carers and one in six households – 17 per cent – contains a carer; of them 1.7 million devote at least twenty hours a week to caring. Tory legislation allowed them to request an 'assessment' with a view to getting help. Labour increased council powers to help and extended the definition of carer to include sixteen- and seventeen-year-olds. In 2001 the carers' premium rose by an extra £10 a week and the disabled children's premium also rose. By 2001 the most severely disabled people had seen their guaranteed income rise significantly: by April 2001 none would have to live on less than £142 a week.

Fairer to women?

Labour swept in with 101 women MPs who will forever be haunted by that embarrassing picture of them adoringly surrounding the new man in their life, Tony Blair. The 'Blair babes' came under fire thereafter, as if they should have been a bolder, more rebellious group than the men: they were hardly a more coherent group than any other random sample of backbenchers. Women MPs were still only 18 per cent of that Westminster men's club, yet they were treated as if this were some kind of revolution.

Women benefited most from Labour reforms because many more women – mothers and pensioners – are poor: minimum wage, part-time workers' rights, WFTC, targeting the poorest pensioners – they all had a disproportionately good effect on women. Divorced women for the first time won a right to a share of their ex-husbands' occupational pensions. The ambitious target of ensuring women get 50 per cent of public appointments reached only 34 per cent, but it was still an improvement. Paid maternity leave was doubled, to eighteen weeks, but remained the lowest in Europe. In late 2000 more was promised.

Basic inequalities remained. The gap between the pay of women and men remained wide – with an average of £326.50 a week for women and £442.41 for men which, allowing for differences in hours, meant a 19 per cent pay gap. It is narrowing slowly, more through market forces than government action. A Women's Unit in the Cabinet Office found that women start to earn less from their first day in their first job whether they leave school young or with degrees, long before motherhood alters their career path. But here, as so often, Labour's anxiety to appease employers stymied their other egalitarian goals and no prompt action followed this report.

The single most important project for women was the National Childcare Strategy, with the grand goal of eventually finding good, affordable childcare of one kind or another for all 0–14-year-olds who needed it. The wonder is not that the strategy was brilliant – far from it – but that it happened at all. For decades the UK lagged far behind most of the rest of Europe in providing any state-aided childcare, adding to the stress and difficulty of women who worked. Large numbers did. By 2000, 73 per cent of mothers with children under thirteen were in work while 66 per cent of the rest said they wanted to be, but could find no suitable childcare.

The Tories had been divided between moralizers who thought women should stay at home and Treasury ministers who thought the soaring numbers of single mothers living on income support should be urged out to work. American-style compulsory Work Fare was considered, but the expensive state-funded childcare that had to be built into any such scheme put them off. Labour came to office with light baggage on this and the same arguments went on. This time it was Harriet Harman who lobbied the Treasury, with plans to float dependent single mothers off benefits. Childcare, she argued, was the most effective instrument for reducing the DSS budget in the long term. Women who did not work while their children were young were unlikely ever to work again; research confirmed that children brought up in workless households did worse on all scores, including their own chances of employment. Gordon Brown was convinced, and in speech after speech he quoted the key importance of childcare as part of children's emancipation from poverty.

In 1998 Labour gave itself the target of providing places for 1 million children by 2003. By April 2000 the National Childcare Strategy spent £88 million from the DFEE and £17 million from the Lottery's New Opportunities Fund (NOF) to provide after-school, holiday and breakfast clubs for children with working parents needing care beyond school hours, plus 8,000 homework clubs. More money came in the 2000 spending review, which released £163 million from April 2001 with £155 million extra from the NOF, rising each year.

A government starting from virtually zero with hardly any existing state nurseries could only scrape a beginning. By June 2000 there were still only 256 not-for-profit nurseries, all with shaky hand-to-mouth funding. The private sector was booming in both nurseries and nannies but they charged up to £180 a week, beyond the pockets of most mothers. Places expanded, but by early 2001 there was still only one place for every seven children under the age of eight, and that included the private sector. There was only one out-of-school club place for every fourteen children aged five to thirteen. Childminders were low paid: as job opportunities increased, the number fell, dropping by 8 per cent in 1999. DFEE minister Margaret Hodge brought in new start-up grants of up to £500, with heavy advertising to encourage women into childminding, and new recruits started coming forward.

Universal access was still a long way off. Sure Start and new Early Excellence Centres offered intensive nursery education for deprived children but there was still only one free or subsidized childcare place for every fourteen of the 600,000 poor children under three who needed it most.

Under Labour, women with children were in the money, up to a point. In 1999 Brown brought in a generous Childcare Tax Credit, allowing people to buy their childcare from any registered provider. Parents earning up to £20,000 a year could claim help with 75 per cent of their childcare costs, up to £70 a week for one child, £105 for two. There were, however, relatively few takers – 120,000 by autumn 2000 – partly because even this sum still fell too far short of the £150–£180 a week cost of nurseries or a childminder's £120. There was also a lack of any childcare to spend it on in many poor areas. Most working mothers use a hotch-potch of relatives, friends and a little paid unregistered (black economy) help. Labour's love affair with employers again prevented ministers picking a public row over the fact that barely 4 per cent of employers offer crèches (and they are mainly in the public sector) and only 2 per cent offer cash help.

In childcare the Government ran hard, did very well, but once again earned little kudos. A year after the National Childcare Strategy was launched, 83 per cent of parents had still never heard of it. There had been a serious spin-deficit. Perhaps no one will notice until greater change is actually delivered – a nursery as a hub for children's services for all in every community.

Family values v. Teen pregnancy

'Family' was one of those totemic issues, barely mentioned in opposition but in office a great separator of the men from the women. The Blair cabinet was a fair reflection of society at large: the Lord Chancellor had run off with his best friend's wife, the Home Secretary was on his second marriage, the Secretary for Education and Employment was divorced; it was muddled life as usual, despite an extravagantly uxorious Prime Minister. But whatever their personal circumstances, some ministers were tempted by moralism or at least the need to nod in the direction of the noisy hypocrisies of the tabloid press. First came arguments about sex education and the necessary involvement of school nurses in contraceptive advice. David Blunkett, Education Secretary, eventually conceded that, as part of sex education, every school ought to inform its pupils where the nearest contraception clinic was and its opening times. Teenage pregnancy rates in England were shamefully high, 90,000 getting pregnant in England, 8,000 under sixteen.

A powerful report from the Social Exclusion Unit led to the Government's adopting the tough target of halving teenage conception by 2010. But the report also showed how many girls get pregnant almost deliberately, lacking any higher ambition. Poor girls are ten times more likely to become teenage mothers – so the worst areas were given extra money. Sure Start Plus pilots were designed to keep teenage mothers in education to break the cycle of deprivation for them and their children. One hundred and fifty specialists were dispatched to make sure special contraception clinics were open everywhere at times and in places teenagers could reach them. School nurses were to give out easy information on how to get the morning-after pill. From 2001, despite an outcry, it became available over the chemist's counter. But teen pregnancy figures remained stubbornly high and even rose slightly in 1999, in the wake of a minor scare over the pill.

At the Home Office a different note was struck. Jack Straw and his junior minister Paul Boateng pandered to the *Daily Mail*. In speeches they proclaimed that the ideal family had two parents in a stable marriage. Blair said it too, as if happy marriage were a matter for governments to arrange. Unsurprisingly their inter-departmental committee on family policy accomplished little: of the many levers governments can control, sex is not one of them. Strip away the *Daily Mail* rhetoric and Labour's actions were generally sensible. The Tories clamoured for a tax and benefit system that would reward marriage, claiming the current system undermined it. Pressed to explain, all they could them-selves promise was a restoration of the Married Couples Allow-ance, which Gordon Brown – who joined the ranks of the married in 2000 – had abolished. The Married Couples Allowance had been worth only £285 a year when Labour came to power, so it was hardly a big wedding incentive at a time when 40 per cent of marriages were ending in divorce at colossal cost to both parties. In its place, Labour gave money for children, not marriage certificates, introducing the far more generous Children's Tax Credit from April 2001, worth £520 a year. While Labour spoke the empty words of marriage, the money went to children.

A misshapen monster of a divorce law had passed through the Commons just before the 1997 election. Intended to reduce warfare between parents on divorce, it was littered with bizarre amendments appended by the moral lobby who feared divorce was being made too easy: in their pre-election funk Labour had approved it. The new law brought in 'no-fault' divorce – a liberal reform to stop parental battles over blame in the courts. But to appease the moralists curious provisions had been added such as the requirement that couples attend 'information meetings' to see if they might reconsider. The attempt to channel couples into divorce negotiations conducted by professional mediators rather than expensive lawyers was sensible, but the pilot experiments proved that intervention was very tricky and deeply disliked by couples who had already reached the divorcing stage. The whole law was quietly and wisely dropped by Lord Chancellor Irvine.

Problem children

The backwash of successive reports into horrific abuse of children 'in care' hit Labour amidships, prompting efforts – far from complete – to rework children's services and the rest of social work. Labour half answered the question whether councils could any longer be trusted to run social services; local authorities were regarded with suspicion and hedged about with inspectors. In the archipelago of local authority children's homes dreadful things had happened, and it fell to Labour to sweep up. The effects of 'care' last long afterwards: children leaving care formed 0.5 per cent of the population yet 25 per cent of rough sleepers and a grotesque 39 per cent of prisoners were aged under twenty-one. Labour answered with the Care Leavers Act 2000, which placed a duty on councils to act like normal parents and go on supporting people after the age of eighteen.

Councils, however, were seen as part of the problem more than the solution. The Tories had virtually ignored social care, costing some £9 billion a year and employing 1 million people; they passed the innovative Children Act 1989 in a fit of absence of mind – some 330,000 children came under its auspices. Labour said it wanted to reshape social services around the people who used them, especially children. This meant more uniform standards across the country ending the discretion of councils, giving better training for social workers and care staff (at least four-fifths of whom had no qualification) under a new social care council and, at last, considerably more money – nearly £300 million extra up to 2004.

Labour's plans envisaged the number of local authority social workers rising from 53,900 in 1998 to over 63,000 in 2004 – considerably more than the 43,500 in post in 1991. But some ministers, notoriously Paul Boateng, started emulating Chris Woodhead, the schools inspector, by barking at social workers for their incompetence: not a wise move when staff shortages were being reported all round the country – vacancy rates running at 10 per cent and applications for training dropping. Controversially, the Government thought about employing South Africans but backed off the idea.

Gaps in one field exposed others. Labour's ambitious plans for nurseries and childcare upped demand for staff yet council pay rates were low – care assistants, responsible for lifting and changing elderly and disabled people, were paid only £3.80 in 2000. Pay in the public sector was a growing problem. Here was another of the 'joining up' problems Labour failed to resolve: if homes could not take infirm people they would 'block' hospital beds, exacerbating bed shortages when a flu epidemic struck. Costs in private homes might rise as a result of Labour's Care Standards Act, which set up a national commission (from 2001) to enforce regulations on private and voluntary sector homes, for adults as well as children. The Department of Health's Social

Service Inspectorate embarked on an intense examination of local authority establishments. Quality Protects was a rubric under which more lower-grade staff might get training and social workers acquire some pride in their profession.

In the light of the inquiry by Sir Ronald Waterhouse into homes in the former counties of Clwyd and Gwynedd, Labour sought to restrict the employment of people suspected of abuse. But a proposal for a children's commissioner was watered down into a children's rights officer in the (English) Department of Health. The Prime Minister's principal contribution in this area, inspired as much by the *Daily Mail* as by a legitimate wish to minimize the number of children being cared for by councils, was to talk up adoption and pressure social services to provide a quicker service for parents seeking children. He proposed a national register of children seeking adoption and of couples eager to adopt. It was a side-show, with only 1,267 applicants and 2,400 children, many of them in care, not at all the blue-eyed untroubled babies beloved of the propagandists and moralizers, from whom sadly Blair did not always distinguish himself.

Labour's impulse to seize social problems that had not been sorted out locally coloured its approach to rooflessness. It was another concern which, like adoption, hit the headlines but was tiny in comparison with other social issues. In June 1998 there were 1,850 people sleeping rough in England on any single night. The Government solemnly promised to cut the number by two-thirds by 2002. It is well on its way to being realized.

For many, an abiding symbol of Thatcherism was the sudden eruption of large numbers of beggars and rough sleepers – out of prison, or care, or the armed forces. Many had serious mental illnesses. Their problems were not just lack of physical accommodation. Blair appointed a 'tsar' with an impressive budget – £145 million over the three years to 2002, that is £24,100 per person, per year – enough to buy half a terrace of prime property in Blair's Durham constituency. Louise Casey, formerly at Shelter, turned out to be tough-minded and effective. She took flak for asking the public not to hand out soup and sandwiches or give money directly – it fed addiction and discouraged change – but to support efforts such as the foyer movement, where young people with problems might get sorted out and eventually be found employment. Deeper questions were avoided, such as the geographical imbalance in affordable property. But due either to Ms Casey or to the all-round growth in jobs as the economy expanded, in 1999 there was a 28 per cent drop in rough sleeping and some of the homelessness charities even whispered that their work was at an end, in terms of providing places to sleep. A stubborn rump of beggars and street people remained, in need of treatment and intense casework for their drug and health problems. Meanwhile the 'official' homeless – families accepted by local authorities as being in dire need – rose slightly in England over the three years from 1997, but they were less noticeable than the rough sleepers.

Poor communities

In opposition Labour had been attracted by American ideas about community reconstruction. The sociologist Amitai Etzioni became a guru figure as the author of the new 'communitarianism'. A caring, sharing, geographical group of people was fine – if you were not too concerned about liberty. It implied reimposing old lace-curtain social disciplines or hounding out alleged paedophiles without evidence or trial.

The practical question was how to regenerate run-down, economically deprived areas; the theory was that down there, at the grass roots, communities could be revived or had to be invented. There was a vogue for 'social entrepreneurs' – a dynamic headteacher or vicar perhaps. Councillors were viewed as obstacles but usually turned out to be the only people reliable enough or with the time to handle the vast additional sums of public money Labour started pouring into poor places.

The Social Exclusion Unit used the data from the new Indices of Deprivation to identify the poorest estates and councils with highest concentrations of deprivation. Labour took over a model for remedial action invented by Tory Environment Secretary Michael Heseltine, the Single Regeneration Budget (SRB). This was a way of forcing disparate local groups and public sector bodies to work together to bid for money in partnerships, proving they could pool resources and expertise instead of working against each other. Once, the focus had been physical refurbishment of estates blighted by changing patterns of trade and industry. But research sponsored by the Joseph Rowntree Foundation confirmed how 'despite thirty years of short term urban regeneration programmes, many areas are still characterized by deprivation'; too often there was no link between physical development, economic regeneration and benefit to people who remained socially excluded. The Coalfields initiative – Tory conscience money for the collapse of mining – was faulted for its lack of impact in, say, South Yorkshire.

Labour reshaped the SRB to concentrate money and schemes on deprived people, leaving physical regeneration for the regional development agencies and dedicated quangos such as English Partnerships – though it was hamstrung by a European Commission ruling restricting subsidy to firms in run-down areas. The *Indices of Deprivation*, published in August 2000, became a kind of bible. Four-fifths of total SRB resources were to be spent in the most deprived local authority areas, with at least one new project up and running in each target area by March 2002.

Labour's £800 million New Deal for Communities worked along similar lines, reserving grants for projects based on designated areas of deprivation. Starting in 2000, it was concentrated first on a score or more neighbourhoods of 1,000–4,000 people, offering £20–£50 million each for programmes that had to show they were genuinely grounded in the local community, pulling in every local service – school, health, social workers, police, housing departments and the Employment Service. They were free to try anything and to come up with local solutions to whatever seemed the worst local problems. Labour was in effect saying: wait till the next index of deprivation is compiled in, say, 2005. If it does not show that life in the forty-four most deprived local authority areas has improved, we will have failed.

According to the index the most deprived ward in England was Benchill, encompassing an estate in Wythenshawe, Manchester. Its story was all too typical. Big job losses in the 1970s and 1980s had pushed down income levels; health was poor and so on. It was awash with initiatives. It fell under the Wythenshawe Partnership, a bidder for SRB money: its schools were in one of Labour's education action zones from January 2000; there was a local Sure Start committee. In 1999 the Willow Park housing trust had been set up to receive its 6,600 dwellings from Manchester City Council – the stock in Benchill having previously been improved through the Estates Renewal Challenge Fund. The new housing trust was pledged to invest some £70 million over five years in refurbishing the housing. In collaboration with Manchester College of Arts and Technology a new construction skills training centre was being built. Public and Lottery money poured in to prepare for the 2002 Commonwealth Games; it ought to make some impact locally.

This was community regeneration with a vengeance. The justification for such focus was clear: the figures showed that 25 per cent of crime happened in the poorest 10 per cent of neighbourhoods; some 2,000 identifiable estates were sinks of unemployment and had death rates 30 per cent higher.

But initiatives proliferated. It became difficult even for experts to make sense of the feast of schemes. At best Labour was trying to bring together money spent in such areas in order to refocus it on new skills – human renewal – rather than alleviating the old symptoms of deprivation. New 'local strategic partnerships' are meant to do this – provided, as always, civil servants, the police, councils, voluntary organizations did not just start out together but stayed together. Even counting the array of initiatives was a feat: alongside the various action zones were new partnerships for crime prevention and legal advice. The Treasury weighed in with a social investment fund (from spring 2001). Social security offered an 'income bridge' to help previous benefit claimants become entrepreneurs. The University for Industry (see next chapter) offered access courses for the unemployed; grants were available for a sort of civilian police force or 'neighbourhood wardens'.

A new unit for renewal in the DETR was, from winter 2000, to oversee the whole terrain. But a major problem was joining up so many different interests. Straightforward bribery would be tried: to buy the assent of councils another neighbourhood renewal fund was created, worth £800 million by 2003–4, pushing more money in the direction of eighty-eight councils if they could demonstrate 'partnership'.

Results

It is very hard, as yet, to separate the benign effects of fuller employment from the impact of these specific initiatives. But even a deep-dyed cynic, a veteran of previous failed programmes, could not deny the vigour and commitment of Labour's inner city efforts.

One simple measure of social justice shows that the UK did become a fairer society under Labour. In four short years, the Government managed to have some effect on the share of total income ending up in households at the bottom, after taxes and benefits. By April 2000, after three years, according to Institute for Fiscal Studies calculations, those in the lowest fifth of the population did significantly better. The poorest tenth of people became 8.8 per cent better off in real terms. Meanwhile the richest tenth are 0.5 per cent worse off. By April 2001, the money announced in November 2000 would make this even more pronounced. Add in the extra poor pensioners are due, then with other increased family benefits and the rich paying more National Insurance, we can expect to see a more significant move in this direction. According to the IFS, the good effect on the bottom 10 per cent is almost entirely due to direct Govern-

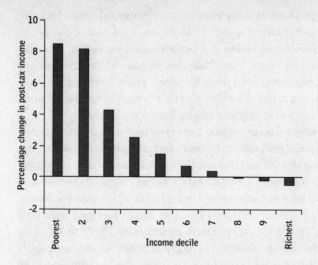

Figure 2: Distributional impact of major Fiscal Reforms announced since July 1997

Source: Institute for Fiscal Studies

ment action on benefits for those in and out of work, the old and children. This was hardly redistribution, in the sense that not much more income was taxed away from the better-off. Instead Labour distributed new money, the proceeds of growth, disproportionately to the poor – giving without taking much away.

A big step was taken towards abolishing poverty for children and pensioners, far more than was promised in May 1997. But poverty is relative – and abolition is improbable if not impossible in a society where the divide between richest and poorest yawns far wider than it did thirty years ago. Could such a social revolution happen without engaging a strong public will for major redistribution?

Yet by spring 2001 all pensioners (except those who could not be found to give the money to) had been lifted out of poverty;

8 million pensioners were significantly better off, including the more affluent. Some 1.2 million children, a quarter of the poorest, had been lifted above the poverty line, on target. Because figures are published years late the impact of policy changes cannot be measured accurately for many years. LSE expert John Hills cautions it will be a while yet – perhaps even 2003 – until even Labour's first changes can be coolly evaluated.

As the Government rightly kept reminding us, poverty is not just a matter of tax credits, benefits and the arithmetic of income distribution, important though they are. It is a human condition leading to exclusion from society's mainstream, so the golden measure will be the fate twenty years hence of the poorest babies born under Labour who pass through Sure Start and improved nurseries, living on regenerated estates, less likely to fall into crime or teenage pregnancy, attending better schools and skills centres. Will they be living more successful, more fulfilling lives than their parents? Will they any longer be poor?

The politics of this vision are not easy. How would Labour enthuse taxpayers without tangible results? Voters need to be persuaded that spending heavily on the poor and on supporting their incomes is not a liability but, like the NHS, a sign of civilized solidarity and – even more than health spending – an investment in the nation's future capacity to produce goods and services. It is all a lot more plausible in an economic upswing with jobs and revenue streams flowing in spate. What if, sooner or later, the economy falters? Labour's resolve would be tested – would the poor and social programmes be a priority in hard times too? Then the tricky political question of redistribution Labour has managed to avoid so far would have to be faced.

Meanwhile, back on the Aylesbury Estate in Peckham, benefits for families are up, pensioners are better off. The estate is inside health, education and employment zones, all offering extra support. The local primary school on the estate has had spectacular results recently. Crime is down, though few realize it and fear is rife. Jean Bartlett, a local resident, chairs the Aylesbury Plus Community Forum, which is struggling to involve the inhabitants in ambitious future plans. In January 2000 they received £56.2 million from the treasury for their New Deal for Communities, but they have not been able to spend it yet. It takes so long, she explains, to get people to agree what to do. Community decision-making with consultations and meetings is not like Tony Blair clicking his fingers inside Downing Street to make things happen. In June 2001 residents vote on whether the council should hand the whole estate over to a housing trust – something happening all over the country. That way they hope to raise another £200 million. Then the tenants will vote on eight options for renewal: 70 per cent support demolishing the whole place and starting all over again in a ten-year rolling plan.

So do the residents feel they have done well under Labour? 'Not yet,' Jean Bartlett says. 'The trouble is that most people think it's all empty promises. They won't believe anything until they see really good changes with their own eyes.' All in all, Labour's frenetic activity represents the best shot Aylesbury and those 1,999 other bad estates have at rescue from the depths.

3

Education Times Three

Education, education, education: Blair said there were indeed three drivers for a policy which boiled down to better exam results – on which, at that crude level, Labour did deliver. Education times one: the labour force had to be sharpened up to serve markets in need of brain not brawn, and in Labour's neo-liberal model of government, schools and 'lifelong learning' *were* things government could do. Labour focused on average attainment in primary and secondary schools, a rough and ready target, but how else to kick-start the improvement that slowly, unspectacularly, Labour did get under way?

Education times two: the Internet arrived in the UK on Blair's watch and he staked a claim, shook Bill Gates's hand and exhorted. But Labour's embrace of IT was shaky, the school computers took time to arrive and indigenous enthusiasm in the Labour Party was shown by the fact that four years after coming to power barely 16 per cent of its MPs at Westminster had their own websites.

Education times three harked back to old ideals, education as emancipation, an antidote to social exclusion, handmaid of social justice. (Education as a liberal art did not get much of a look in.) David Blunkett's life history expressed the powerful conviction that better schooling could lift people out of society's gutters. That meant that the children of those who 'failed' stopped failing and that there was to be, to coin a phrase, a fresh start. In Sheffield, Sunderland and too many other city districts, the school improvement needed to make the aspiration a social fact is now, at best, only at the end of the beginning.

Labour ministers rarely chose to address a swirling debate about education and culture that began in the late 90s. From the

Tories they inherited two strong trends that would have persisted whoever had won in 1997. Better results for sixteen-year-olds in GCSE and for eighteen-year-olds at A level were feeding the expansion of university and college enrolment that had accelerated under the Tories. Ah, said critics, this was evidence of 'dumbing-down' – quantity destroying quality in universities. Labour replied that wider access and high standards were compatible – a view they applied to sport, broadcasting and culture at large. Were Blair and Blunkett Pollyannaish in believing they could have their standards cake and let the masses nibble? As the December 2000 white paper on telecoms regulation showed, they never thought through the cultural consequences of digital television with its multitude of choices. A government concerned with education in its widest sense would have worried about those potent instruments of national instruction, the media. But Labour had doffed its cap to Murdoch and Lord Rothermere before the election and strove might and main not to upset them when in office. 'Culture' abounded, galleries opened and visitors flocked to Tate old and new. But for many the Government's cultural epitaph was Labour's peninsular folly, the Greenwich Dome.

A caning for the teachers

They agreed on bumping up educational attainment but Labour ministers divided over where and how children should be schooled. The dilemmas were cruelly exposed by the choices made *en famille* by the Blairs and Harriet Harman's family. Living both in inner-city black spots, they managed to find distant, selective, high-achieving schools still, just about, in the state sector. But Labour was pledged to abolish all forms of selection, direct or insidious, not quite yet, as it turned out.

The comprehensive remained Labour's ideal – every school such a good school that every parent would choose the school on their doorstep. However, Blair and his advisers were also taken

45

by American 'charter' schools, with specialized curricula, which selected at least some of their pupils. Labour's implicit programme was to attract and keep the middle classes, as growing affluence meant that in each generation more were able to afford private schooling. So comprehensives were to be more rigidly streamed. Who was to run them? Private companies were considered and the role of the churches expanded, a gross anomaly in a secular land. The role of councils was whittled away even if, by autumn 2000, Labour had lifted the threat of abolishing them altogether. On the shape of the secondary schools there was not, in truth, a great difference between Major's and Blair's policies. Yet Labour's grit and determination to improve school performance was palpable; Blunkett had the guts to stake his job on it.

Labour brought the cane down hard on councils and on teachers. Even though the Blairs had long moved from their home in Islington's Richmond Crescent, this was the borough the media identified closest with New Labour. Perhaps it was fitting that Islington became the first local authority to have its education service stripped from it and turned over to a private company. It was failing to deliver those precise, measurable targets for pupil performance that Labour had emblazoned on its list of do-able promises. In a low-key ceremony at the town hall in Upper Street, where Margaret Hodge – become a respectful Blairite minister – had flown the red flag in the mid-80s, Cambridge Education Associates signed an £11.5 million contract that removed Islington's elected councillors from day-to-day control of 'their' schools. For seven years a for-profit firm would supply and inspect schools and pay teachers. Thatcher had blustered; the Tories had dreamt of but could never quite steel themselves to take this step.

As it turned out, Islington's fate was something of a false dawn, potent in the symbolism but no recipe for schools at large. Even Blair could see that killing off councils sat uneasily with aspirations towards community 'empowerment', and the rebirth of local democracy: Islington's fate was visited on few others.

Instead Labour became extraordinarily pragmatic about how

to deliver better schooling. The transfer of single schools to private companies, at King's Manor and France Hill Schools in Surrey, had shock value but did not become the basis of wider policy.

Labour ranks were chock-full of teachers and councillors. Few constituency management committees lacked their quota of NUT members. But who if not these same teachers and councillors should be held responsible for under-achieving pupils? Labour had bought the argument that it was not so much resources as attitudes and organization that explained poor school performance. Teachers had to change their ways or be changed; schools were set tough targets. Labour's conversion was personified in the transformational figure of David Blunkett. Ex-leader of Sheffield City Council, symbol of working-class aspiration, prophet of municipal socialism: here was a figure councillors and teachers could surely trust to maintain the status quo.

Within days of taking office, Blunkett 'named and shamed' eighteen schools. We recall interviewing him in his Commons room in the early 90s, his guide-dog flopped on the floor at his feet, as he struggled to unsay the dogmas without confronting his former comrades in arms. But his conviction that the city children he had grown up with deserved better made him the teachers' potential enemy. By 2001 Blunkett had become one of the longest-serving Education Ministers ever, overtaking Margaret Thatcher's forty-four months, exceeded only by Sir Keith Joseph, in post for over four and a half years. His impact was far greater than either. He abolished assisted places at private schools, established new City Academies, slimmed the national curriculum, brigaded schools in poor areas into Education Action Zones, started Fresh Start and tested and tested again.

That the initiatives did not all go in the same direction was because the script was not entirely Blunkett's to write. Another emblem of the new approach was Chris Woodhead, the arrogant chief inspector of schools inherited from the Tories and, with his departure in November 2000, returning to them. The DFEE played soft cop, hard cop; the game became a farce when Wood-head had to be counter-balanced as adviser with his foe, Tim Brighouse, the teacher-sympathetic Birmingham education director. But Blunkett needed inspectors to tell him where the problem schools were, the places that would have to change dramatically if he was to get anywhere near his public promises to raise attainment. Woodhead deliberately provoked the unions with his cavalier (and unscientific) assessment that 15,000 teachers in England were 'no good'. He kept up a drum-beat of criticism, the claque of right-wing columnists he has now joined applauding; a *bon mot* of September 2000 said university degrees had become too easy and higher education expansion should be cut back. Blair and his influential Oxford-educated Number 10 policy adviser Andrew Adonis lapped it up.

What Blunkett could not do was operate directly on the schools. (Nothing as radical as a National Education Service, like the NHS, crossed Labour minds.) At first he flailed: using the inspectors, changing the way teachers are trained, pushing to link their salaries to their classroom performance. But eventually, prompted by Woodhead's gunfire criticism of elected local edu-cation authorities, Blunkett bit the bullet: if councillors failed they would have to be replaced by central supervision. One new tool was 'special measures' – a regime of close inspection and extra help. It seemed to work. Four out of five schools emerging from special measures in 2000 (after having previously failed an inspection) were deemed successful. Despite the measures, some 396 schools were still deemed to be failing in 2000, representing about 2 per cent of all schools. Inspectors said one school in twenty still had 'serious weaknesses' after Labour had been in power three years.

For all its new powers, the centre did not spend. Between 1997 and 2001 there was no improvement in public resources at anything like the rate that might have been expected from a government which made so much of its education policies. Blun-kett had promised Labour would spend 5 per cent of GDP on education, which, since the economy was growing, would have

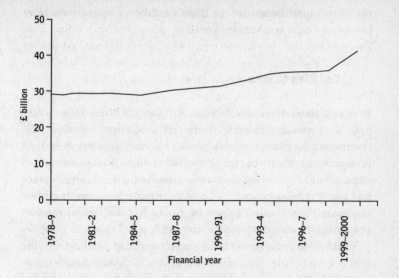

Figure 3: Government spending on education, 1997–8 prices, 1978–9 to 2001–2

Source: Institute for Fiscal Studies

brought a large addition. Even counting spending on vocational training, over four years from 1997 Labour will get only to 4.98 per cent. In the 1998 spending review £19 billion 'extra' was promised. This turned out to be a conflation of money already in the pipeline; but by March 2001 schools will have had a £300 per pupil real increase since Labour came to power.

Perhaps, in the absence of significant cash transfers to schools, Labour's results were all the more remarkable and that may reflect how the DFEE shifted the balance of control. Advocates of local democracy were aghast; parents took a different view.

Labour's education policies were all-age. They began at the beginning, hoping to create a generation of Labour babies whose early success would carry them through to higher attainment later. The great promise to abolish child poverty described in the last chapter depended on Blair's toddlers passing tests from pre-school to A level and beyond.

Toddling to school

Blunkett moved smartly to abolish Tory vouchers for nursery places. Instead, councils were told to put together all-encompassing plans for pre-schoolers, money was found and the pledge to provide places for all four-year-olds quickly redeemed. September 2000 indeed saw a new promise made: a nursery place for every three-year-old. The old struggle between childcare and nursery schooling ended in defeat for the 'social service' approach. It was absurd that the children of working mothers should be looked after without being taught while the only kids able to benefit from the short hours and half-days of most nursery schools with proper teaching were those whose mums were at home. New money was channelled through committees called Early Years and Childcare Partnerships to create 'wrap-around' care, with breakfast, after school and holiday clubs combining with education, usually on primary school sites. Education not social services was put in the lead and Ofsted called in to inspect – not the three Rs but cognitive development and constructive play, aimed at getting all children equipped to start primary school proper.

The first available places were to go to the neediest. There is still a long way to go before every infant from birth to three can claim an affordable childcare or nursery place but that missing link in the Welfare State was at least officially acknowledged as a government obligation. For pre-schoolers Blairite policy was 'modernization' – recognizing the state's role in assisting mothers and doing better by their children. The UK began to look a little like other European countries. For three-year-olds and their parents it got appreciably better.

Reading, 'riting and 'rithmetic

Labour had listened to secondary teachers saying that in the 80s and 90s there was a perceptible decline in the quality of children coming to them from primary schools. Blunkett's response was Napoleonic. He legislated an hour of daily literacy (from September 1998) and then numeracy (from September 1999), waiving the demands of the national curriculum to make space. The new core subject line-up for primaries became English, maths, science, information technology (IT) and religion (RE). Geography, history and music were out and there was less time for physical activity. Though this prompted worries about couch potatoes and future sporting prowess, Labour was single-minded. Grammar was talked up, money spent on ABC primers. By the end of 2000, Labour was two-thirds of the way towards cutting class sizes for 5–7-year-olds to a maximum of thirty children per teacher – a modest enough target. The average class size for older primary children was still 28.3.

Reading improved. In 1997, only 60 per cent of eleven-year-olds reached the official reading standard for the age group. By 1999 some 71 per cent were there, 6 per cent up on the previous year. Improvement was maintained into 2000. The government looked like reaching its aim of 80 per cent by 2002: that is the figure Blunkett staked his job on achieving. But deficiencies lingered. In early 2001 half of eleven-year-old boys could not write at the age standard level. Test results in maths improved, 72 per cent reaching the age standard for eleven-year-olds in 2000.

Reading Blunkett's lips

Primary schools were said to be the first-term priority, but as the standards of children entering secondary school improved, the government turned its attention to 11–14s. Literacy and numeracy hours were added for the first year of secondary school too. At present many of these children have had only a year or two of the strategy in primary school, too late for them to benefit. Literacy levels among fourteen-year-olds have been static: only 63 per cent of boys passed standard tests in 2000 and 72 per cent of girls, both figures slightly down on 1999. Labour would say it is too soon to judge. But some of the omens are dark. Pupil–teacher ratios in secondary schools grew to their worst for fifteen years, at 17.2:1; in 1997 that was 16.4:1. One out of twelve classes in secondaries in England and Wales were taught by a teacher facing more than thirty pupils.

Yet results at GCSE continued to improve. Labour gave itself seven years, pledging that by 2004 the minimum for every school would be 20 per cent of its pupils gaining five A*-C grade GCSEs. The trend was in Labour's favour. The proportion of the 16+ cohort reaching GCSE grades A*-C was 32.8 per cent in 1989, 47.9 per cent in 1999. 'Dumbers-down' sniped: exams were getting easier. But the National Foundation for Education Research confuted this in maths and English, suggesting that the level of difficulty has remained constant over recent years. Extra numbers came forward to take GCSE, which suggested that the amount of examinable learning being done in schools was increasing. Intellectuals might worry about 'credentialism'. Employers might sometimes privately moan about the relevance of GCSE. Nonetheless this examination – created by Tory Sir Keith Joseph – had become generally accepted as proof that a young person had the equipment for work or further study.

Still, Blunkett noted just how many sixteen-year-olds left school without a qualification to their name. If 20 per cent get five reasonable GCSEs, what about the 80 per cent? Young black, Pakistani and Bangladeshi students failed to share in the progress, neither, proportionately, did working-class young people. Some 10 per cent of young people from social class E got at least five GCSEs, compared with 65 per cent from social classes A and B. Some 150,000 16–18-year-olds, 9 per cent of the age bracket, were estimated not to be in education, training or work. These drop-outs became the target of a new campaign to be led (from April 2001) by Connexions, the re-branded youth service.

Labour was clear about standards but much less sure-footed on the form of the secondary schools supposed to deliver them. It did not know, in other words, how to balance the right of parents to choose a school and the right of a school to choose a parent. This is of course the paradoxical underpinning of private education. Private school enrolments climbed slightly from 1997 and schools minister Estelle Morris pronounced Labour their 'friend'. There had been a feeble early attempt to make them contribute something to local state schools, but the idea was never pursued; the threat to remove their charitable status was shed along with other old Labour baggage.

As for the schools attended by the 90+ per cent of secondary-age children, Blunkett had said (at the Labour conference, 4 October 1995), 'Read my lips. No selection by examination or interview.' In office this was redescribed as 'a joke'; what he meant was that there would be no extension of selection. The grammars were an especial problem for Labour, a totem for left, right and middle England. Instead of abolition Blunkett put in place elaborate arrangements to allow local choice on 11+ selection, which meant pro-comprehensive parents in Kent, Buckinghamshire and Ripon would have to battle against the status quo, getting petitions then winning votes, and they failed. The Tories' grant-maintained secondaries – would-be grammars – lost their extras. The new line up was 'community' (council), 'aided' (church) and 'foundation' (ex-GM) – the latter two selective on the basis of subject specialism and religious affiliation. Specialize sounds better than select. What was never spelled out was the relationship of all this to improving performance at the bottom of the ability/parental interest range. There was none: the aim was middle-class confidence.

To that end Labour wanted more state-supported 'independent' schools and Blunkett invented City Academies, very similar to the Tories' City Technology Colleges. Ten are scheduled to open in autumn 2001, on the back of existing but failing schools with admissions policies approved by the DFEE, not the council, which would pass them land and buildings. They made sense as urban regeneration, stemming the flight of middle-income families to the suburbs, but involved a kind of social engineering governments have rarely proved any good at. Labour exhibited its faith that schools could act as vehicles for grand changes in social values. Thus Gordon Brown said he wanted 'to see all schools encourage our young people to consider enterprise as a career', as if schoolteachers had not enough to do without becoming apostles of wealth creation. Brown urged business to 'adopt a school' – by taking students on work experience and teachers on work placements, sending employees into schools to help run enterprise classes, or being 'business governors'. This was consistent with Brown's hope that entrepreneurialism could take root in the inner cities but betrayed credulousness in the public-spiritedness of small and medium-sized companies. Bigger companies such as HSBC bank did put money into the growing number (550 – with plans to increase that to 1,000, a third of all secondaries) of specialist schools. They started to constitute themselves as a sort of élite and registered higher than average passes at GCSE.

For schools at the bottom of the pile, Labour's response was Fresh Start. A small number were to be made over, with new super-heads, fresh paint and an effort to change their ethos. When GCSE results came out in August 2000, it became apparent that the experiment had failed. Islington was again in the spotlight when a catastrophic school, George Orwell, was closed and reopened as Islington Arts and Media School with an idealistic Fresh Start head. He resigned shortly after, victim of unrealistically high hopes. Fresh Start showed the limits of throwing money at a school in crisis. Some succeeded, others should have been closed down altogether.

At the top end of the scale, the number of successes continued to rise at A level (highers in Scotland). In 2000 more passes were recorded, with Grade A passes up 0.3 per cent on 1999. Because the number of university places available rose 2 per cent, critics said this meant dilution of standards, but Blunkett replied robustly that expanded opportunity was welcome progress. However, performance at A level may have got worse under Labour for children from working-class homes, with only 10 per cent from social class E compared with 65 per cent from group A getting into higher education.

The shape of education after sixteen changed; from autumn 2000 sixth-formers and further education students studied Advanced Subsidiary subjects, Labour's effort to meet the long-standing demand (resisted by the universities) to broaden competence and deepen knowledge. Whether university admissions tutors would value them remains to be seen.

Mass higher education

Labour's university formula was more places, fairer access, world-class science but not much extra spending. It was only do-able, said the universities, on the back of a steep hierarchy, 'top up' fees and open élitism and at that Labour demurred.

The UK had entered the era of mass higher education the day the Tories swept away the polytechnics and related colleges, rebadging them as universities. In opposition Labour had given bipartisan support to the appointment of Sir Ron (later Lord) Dearing to head a review.

When he reported in summer 1998, Blunkett turned his recommendations on their head, abolishing the grants for student living costs that for nearly forty years had been encouraging successive generations of middle-class students to live away from home in subsidized accommodation and, to put it bluntly, have a good time on the state. In came loans for all. Students would also have to pay £1,000 a year towards the cost of tuition, from autumn 1999. (This was means-tested and by 2001 only half of students would actually be paying it.)

Loans meant the emergence of a two-tier system, with poorer

students tending to opt for cheaper nearby city universities, mostly former polytechnics, while middle-income students lived away from home, supported by loans they knew they would be able to repay. The ramshackle student loans company Labour inherited, malfunctioning, from the Tories was considerably improved and now has a loans book worth more than £1 billion.

At Labour's October 1997 conference Blair promised half a million extra places in higher education by 2002, a promise subsequently expanded to enrolling 50 per cent of all the 18–30 age cohort in higher education. Some of Dearing's recommendations – higher pay for academics, better grants for poorer students – ran straight into Labour's decision not to increase spending. University enrolment hiccuped in 1998 but was back on track by 2000, with some 34 per cent of 18–19-year-olds entering higher education. Under Blair, a UK student population numbering 1 million became the norm.

Labour, like the Tories, expected universities to take in more students for less money, though in 2001 per capita subsidy was expected to increase for the first time since 1986. Crowded libraries and disgruntled professors seemed to Labour a small price to pay for a marked expansion in educational opportunity. In 1999, 3.6 per cent more students from unskilled backgrounds entered universities compared with the previous year. But universities are still a middle-class preserve. In 1999, successful applicants from the professional, 'intermediate' and skilled non-manual homes made up 64 per cent of the total, partly skilled and unskilled 24 per cent (the social class of the remaining 12 per cent is unknown.)

Dismay at this state of affairs lay behind Gordon Brown's outburst. It was 'an absolute scandal' that Tyneside state school pupil Laura Spence had been denied a place at Magdalen College, Oxford – she won a bursary to study another subject at Harvard. Blunkett said he wanted no class quotas but the universities seemed to get the message. Oxford said it was already succeeding in altering the historical imbalance. For entry in 2000, state school pupils made up 56 per cent of applications and

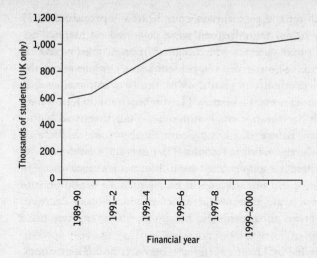

Figure 4: Participation in higher education, 1989–90 to 2000–2001

Source: Institute for Fiscal Studies

53 per cent of those accepted: five years previously 47 per cent of offers of places went to state school students.

Besieged, some universities counter-attacked. The Russell Group of élite institutions said they wanted out. A Tory promise to 'privatize' them and, potentially, free them from social obligations, opened a clear line of difference between the parties.

Universities for industry?

Common-sense said it should be so, but academic research failed to establish a stable causal link between spending on education and productivity. In 1998, American productivity per head was 45 per cent above the UK, which was 11 per cent and 18 per cent respectively below Germany and France. This had to do with innovation and competitiveness, to be sure, but also

57

skills. And yet the picture was complicated – proportionately more Americans than Britons were classified as low-skilled. Gordon Brown went to the Trades Union Congress annual meeting in Glasgow in September 2000 to complain about the UK's poor productivity record – with the clear implication that work practices were to blame. The unions nonetheless repaid him loyally by their staunch support during that week's fuel crisis. What Brown did not talk much about was skills as a key to productivity improvement. That may have been because although the Blair government used 'lifelong learning' often in its rhetoric, it did not succeed in translating the ambition into change on a scale that would affect productivity. Education after school for those who did not go to university remained Cinderella.

A review led by Helena Kennedy, barrister and Blairite peer, made radical recommendations such as taking money from university haves and giving it to further education's have-nots. Instead the Government took a piecemeal approach, seeking to widen access to post-sixteen learning while emphasizing employability. Its focus first of all was on what individuals could do for themselves; grants of £150 were given, experimentally, to young people to allow them to buy courses. Then it shifted attention to deprived communities and the courses available in them, though the resulting Local Learning Partnerships found it hard to stay afloat in the torrent of community initiatives described in the last chapter. On the one hand there was 'youth policy', symbolized by the creation in 2000 of Connexions, a centrally run but locally organized scheme to pick up young drop-outs and relodge them in the mainstream. On the other there was 'further education', supposed to be part of a coordinated national drive to boost productivity at work.

In some ways the ambiguity reflected well on Labour. It was still fired by the ideal of lifelong learning – an old liberal aspiration harking back to the Workers' Education Association – but a booming economy needed more and better-trained employees. The University for Industry (UfI) was meant to help the 7 million people of working age lacking the literacy and numeracy of an average eleven-year-old. It was to reskill Britain: the idea was to get people into 1,000 'learning centres' (libraries, company offices, etc.) to study, mostly online, using materials by a network of colleges – but, the bugbear of training for decades, the involvement of employers, actual and potential, was random. By winter 2000 some 36,000 people were signed up; the ambition is 1 million by 2003.

To keep people in school, virtual or real, they might have to be bribed. Educational maintenance allowances, first mooted when Labour was in power in the late 70s, were introduced in a £100 million pilot scheme offering up to £40 a week to 16–18-year-olds. To study what? The Tories' answer had been 'what employers want' and they set up seventy-two Training and Enterprise Councils (in England, four in Wales, similar animals in Scotland), led by business types, to spend public money on a variety of courses supposedly attuned to local economic needs. They did not work very well and Labour's replacement would be Learning and Skills Councils (LSCs), from April 2001. They do not look dissimilar. Business interests will be in control. A national LSC will coordinate the £6 billion available for education beyond sixteen not in universities – including training at work and sixth-forms. In theory this should connect with the estimated £15–20 billion spent each year by employers themselves on training; but the LSCs may face the same problems as TECs in marrying national deficits in skills with local demands for labour, while also coping with Labour's reluctance to 'burden' business.

Labour pushed changes in the further education and training curriculum. In September 2002, a 'vocational' GCSE is to start; from autumn 2001 a new two-year foundation degree will be offered; teaching for a new 'vocational A level' built on the former General Non-Vocational Qualifications began in autumn 2000. The Government's message, that vocational qualifications had kudos, was marred by the distinct lack of enthusiasm expressed by the Woodhead regime at Ofsted.

Paying pipers

Overall, at least until the July 2000 spending announcement which put £12 billion extra in, the Blair Government tried to effect an educational revolution on the cheap. A serious American academic, Robert William Fogel, looked ahead and said governments should be spending up to 10 per cent of GDP on education – Labour struggled to reach 5 per cent.

Teachers were the key but if – after the pay award in 2000 – a teacher could only earn £23,958 a year from teaching there was something amiss (increments came from 'responsibility outside the classroom'). On paying teachers, on providing schools with information and communications technology, on 'remoralizing' this key profession, Labour's instincts were spot on, but it could not or would not put up the heroic sums of public money needed. Only by Easter 2001 would most teachers see that substantial rise in their salaries needed to signal just how much they matter.

Teachers' salaries were the heart of reform, so much was obvious at the start of the Blair Government. To cut class sizes more teachers – in 1997 it was estimated that 10,000 extra staff would be needed within four years – were called for at a time the labour market was tightening. Demography was pressing too: pupil numbers were rising. Officially the vacancy rate in January 2000 was said by the DFEE to be less than 1 per cent. Other evidence suggested this was Panglossian. A *Times Educational Supplement* survey in September 2000 said there were 4,000 vacancies in England and Wales; according to heads this was an understatement, since they had been forced to employ under-qualified and unqualified staff. Shortages were especially acute in London and in maths and technology; the use of supply teachers grew, 17,200 in 2000 compared with 10,600 fifteen years previously. Incentives were offered to trainees: student teachers now get a £6,000 bursary with £4,000 'golden hellos' for teachers of maths, science and IT. The 'best graduates' receive free

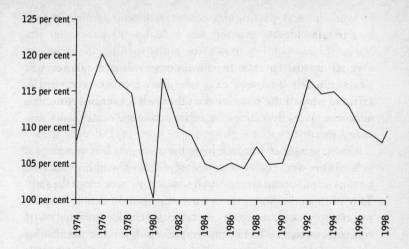

Figure 5: Teachers' earnings as a percentage of non-manual earnings

Source: NASUWT

laptops. Despite them, acceptances for training in secondary teaching were up in the year to September 2000 by only 2 per cent, compared with the 20 per cent deemed necessary to restock the schools.

Back to pay scales. Since the early 90s, teachers' pay had declined by 14 per cent compared to average non-manual earnings, by 11 per cent relative to the police since 1981.

What sort of society paid its police officers more than its teachers? Instead of an unconditional rise for all teachers the 1998 green paper *Teachers: meeting the challenge for change* followed the Thatcherite managerial line of identifying and paying only for individual 'performance'. Teachers' 'output' is multi-dimensional and they have to work closely together; singling out individual merit could be invidious. But the salary review body accepted the principle in February 2000 and when Labour's pay package arrived, it turned out that most teachers (80 per cent) qualified for a threshold increment of £2,000 a year (to be decided by headteachers), putting classroom teachers on a scale rising up to £30,000. Implementation was held up till 2001 after the National Union of Teachers successfully sued the Government over its details. In 2000 the minimum for a new teacher was £15,141; a half of all secondary teachers were on a maximum of £24,000 – top of the scale for the other half (excluding the small numbers taking headships or other leadership roles) was just over £38,000.

Teachers said it was not just the poor pay but conditions. What other profession is expected to work without phones, laptops or private space, rostered to teach 90 per cent of the day? The summer holiday may be a compensation but term-time working pressure, especially in difficult schools with the worst staff shortages, could be intolerable. And yet the number of teachers teaching is at its highest for ten years and, however badly treated and underpaid, teachers secured under Labour some of the trappings of professionalism. In 2000 Labour realized a longstanding aim by creating a General Teaching Council, intended to apply higher standards of professional conduct and performance at no cost; and Labour started dishing out gongs to heads. A National College for School Leadership was set up in Nottingham. It was not to be a staff college on the lines of Bramshill or Sandhurst, which would have meant expensive bricks and mortar and training places. Instead it was to be a virtual college with a skeleton staff, using the Internet to bring heads and academics together.

To their critics Blair and Blunkett were Gradgrinds, focused on homework (new home–school contracts were urged), regimenting schools in tables of performance, every initiative pegged to assessment of performance recognizing one single measure, exam results. Liberal parents complained that their children were losing the more relaxed childhood experience they themselves had had – but education is full of false memory syndrome. Some efforts were made to broaden the secondary curriculum. David Blunkett responded enthusiastically to a report on citizenship education prepared by Professor Bernard Crick, author of the classic *In Defence of Politics*. Noises were made about sport in schools, Lottery money was pledged to community facilities and a ban was put on schools' sales of playing fields. Since France – where there is no school sport worth speaking of – had won the World and European cups while Blair was Prime Minister, the need to pile further pressure on schools was unclear.

Overall, schools expressed their increasing frustration with the Government's interfering and fidgety style: new money always came with particular strings for particular targets that might or might not fit each school's most urgent needs. It was partly in apology for this that Gordon Brown in 2000 suddenly doled out amounts up to £70,000 to every school to do exactly what they liked with, no strings. Schools learnt there were two money streams, one through the council budget – though councils were warned off touching it – and the other directly from Whitehall. Already in 1999 schools had received a 'windfall' grant for repairs and roofs, and then again in November 2000 money came for windows, toilets and capital works, worth some £17,000 for a typical secondary, £5,500 for a primary.

It was only a taster. Serious new money only starts to be spent in April 2001. Scaffolding was already visible as the school capital budget approached £2 billion in 2000 on its way to £3 billion a year in 2003–4, to be compared, Blunkett said proudly, with only £683 million in 1996–7. Surveys started to report parental satisfaction with schooling and approval for Blunkett. One 1999 poll showed parents thought standards had improved over the 90s; not much more than a third registered improvement thanks to Labour, though there was more recognition of improvement in primary schools than in secondaries. More than half parents thought their children's teachers competent; another third said highly competent. The report card says much done – but a mountain still to climb before 'every school is a good school'.

Educating virtually

Blair's policy for the Internet and ICT was the inverse of Teddy Roosevelt's walking softly carrying a big stick: it was more talking loudly with a palmtop. It had three elements. One was general encouragement (except that under Labour Big Brother made sure he had powers to snoop on Internet communications; see Chapter 10); another was measures to stimulate e-commerce, including modernization of the legal code; the last was to build Internet use and ICT into education – preferably without spending much public money.

Unfortunately Government did not set much of an example. Blair's ambition was somewhat fuzzily stated as getting public services all online by 2005. By autumn 2000 about a third of Government services could be said to be online but this often meant no more than running a website. Few were interactive, in the sense of – for example – allowing payment of council tax or road fund tax online. Labour planned a National Grid For Learning (NGfL), but this was not so much a network (like the successful Janet, linking academic institutions) as loose linking of some 6,000 computer centres where the unemployed could go online. All schools were to be connected to the Internet by 2002 – easily realizable since by September 2000 98 per cent of secondaries and 86 per cent of primaries had Internet access. But Labour did redirect Lottery money to pay for teachers' IT training; the state generously offered teachers a 50 per cent grant on the cost of a new laptop or PC. A National e-Learning Foundation was given £1 billion to get children from low-income families online while, with assistance from Bill Gates, the government promised every schoolchild 'access' to a laptop within five years. That would probably involve looking over another child's shoulder: in September 2000 Blair promised a computer per five pupils in secondary schools and one per eight in primary schools by 2004.

The doomed Dome

Replacing the old Department of National Heritage with a new Department of Culture, Media and Sport (DCMS), Blair appointed Chris Smith, who promptly took the unusual step of writing a book. *Creative Britain* wished to celebrate both the arts as traditionally defined and creativity at large – fashion, clubbing but not (see Chapter 8) the drugtaking that peps them up and chills them out. He was mocked for his pains, not just for penny-pinching and philistinism – traditional charges against arts ministers – but for materialism, in treating the arts as an engine of industry, tourism, wealth creation and the export trade in music, film and television. In fact Smith was even more functional in his approach, saying the arts should be a fundamental element in urban regeneration.

Labour inherited from the Tories that great and unusual engine of culture and civilization, the National Lottery, but came close to snarling it up. Smith bemoaned Camelot directors' fat-cat salaries and created a new regulator in the National Lottery Commission (NLC). Such arm's-length bodies can be extraordinarily useful: Smith escaped any blame for delay in reletting the contract to run the Lottery or the subsequent cock-ups, leading to the replacement of the NLC chair Dame Helena Shovelton with Lord Burns. (It was an interesting appointment, since Burns had no reason to love Labour after his ousting from the permanent secretaryship at the Treasury by Gordon Brown.)

Labour redistributed Lottery money from the arts to health, education and urban regeneration, prompting an anguished out-cry from ex-prime-minister John Major about the prostitution of 'his' Lottery. A more serious point was that the Chinese walls between the Lottery and general tax revenues became paper-thin; this was effectively now public spending generated by a peculiar tax on gambling.

Despite Lottery largesse, Labour failed to find the relatively small sums needed to engineer one high-profile policy shift which for many was precisely the type of change many had voted Labour to get. Museum charges were an old, deeply symbolic issue and Smith had wanted to abolish them for the national collections which levied them (the Science and Natural History Museums, for example) and build an instant monument to New Labour. The way to do that would have been to bribe the trustees by upping their grants, but Brown's freeze meant the arts budget was being cut. The 1998–9 allocation was 1 per cent down on the previous year, provoking the formation of a 'Shadow Arts Council' by an indignant arts establishment headed by Sir Peter Hall. Smith lost the battle for a grand gesture. He got some new money in July 1998 and used £100 million to admit first children then pensioners free; in September 2001 charges are to be cut to a standard £1 ticket for all adults and the disabled and benefits claimants will get in free. The Smith era saw 18 per cent more children coming into the national collections. That is New Labour for you: they missed a grand gesture which would have won sackfuls of brownie points but did some good with scant recognition.

Arts ministers confront certain hardy annuals. Labour floated above the opera battles, bemused. Regional arts councils were given more power in an effort to devolve arts spending – part of Labour's inchoate desire for better access. Arts spending in England stood at £195 million in 1997; by 2000/2001 it had risen to £230 million. Councils could bid for a ring-fenced £150 million from the Music Standards Fund to promote local music-making. Labour's old love affair with film resulted (from April 2000) in the diversion of £145 million of Lottery money to a new film council to boost British film. Labour established film director David Puttnam as chair of NESTA, the new National Endowment for Science and the Arts, with a remit to nurture talent on the back of £200 million of Lottery money.

Access meant bums on seats. In 1997 only half the population had ever visited an arts venue. The target was for two-thirds of the people to participate in ten years' time. In 1996/7, 22.8 million attendances were recorded. This rose to 24.8 million in

2000/2001 – 2 million up. The Blair years saw high-profile arts buildings opening in unexpected places – the Walsall Art Gallery, the Lowry Museum, the Salt Mills in Bradford, Tate Modern on Bankside (pity about the bridge). But these were bought by the millions crossing their tickets on a Saturday. Labour could hardly claim credit.

The Greenwich Dome had not been its idea, either. The UK was, by happenstance, turning into an arts-laden country to which the French and Germans flocked in envy and admiration but Labour's fate was to be saddled with a dome. Of course it was Major's doing: his Millennium Commission picked Greenwich in 1996, rejecting a good bid from Birmingham. In the saddle, nothing much built and not a huge amount spent, Labour might have repented. Instead, in June 1997, the cabinet agreed to go ahead with Richard Rogers's design at a cost of £750 million; it would attract 12 million visitors in the single year of its existence. That, the National Audit Office said in its inquest, was the fatal mistake: the targets were 'highly ambitious and inherently risky'. Blair swung behind the cabinet's few enthusiasts, led by Peter Mandelson, grandson of the man who had overseen the 1951 Festival of Britain, Herbert Morrison. He was worried that Labour would seem lacking in panache and ambition if it cancelled a glorious national celebration – Labour the austerity, anti-fun party. Some fun.

It was not till a year later that the die was cast. Mandelson, then Minister without Portfolio in the Cabinet Office, promised the Dome would have a strong spiritual element. Blair believed. In a speech on 24 February 1998 he compared the Dome to St Paul's. Why did he identify himself and Labour quite as intimately, quite as passionately with a project which it was evident then could so easily fall into mediocrity and mismanagement? The resulting deep public anger and mockery was deserved.

The last station on the Jubilee Line extension was opened, just in time, in December 1999, after some £3 billion had been spent. That was the high point. Even though more paying customers trooped to Greenwich than to any other paid-for attraction in the land, projections were wildly out. New Year's Eve was a fiasco. Then the victim count started, as extra Lottery money was pumped in, £60 million in May, £29 million in August, a further £43 million in September and then £47 million on top, as a Tory-supporting business tycoon was brought in to deliver the *coup de grâce*. The Dome had ended up costing the best part of £1 billion, excluding the tube line. For what? Blair's allies, notably Mandelson's successor Charlie Falconer, justified the money as urban regeneration – despite exceeding the total for New Deal for Communities by nearly £200 million. The parallel disaster of the German world fair that opened in Hanover in 2000, its losses projected at £650 million, its visitors only 35 per cent of the original forecast, did little to alleviate the Greenwich gloom.

The Dome was seen throughout the country as a great might-have-been that drained money from good local projects. The lively Greenwich Theatre closed its doors for lack of just £200,000 under the Dome's very shadow. It eclipsed Lottery money successes such as the Eden Project in Cornwall or Dynamic Earth in Edinburgh which at the end of 2000 reported visitor numbers well over target. Labour might not have devised such a thing itself – but ministers lacked the confidence to stop it in those first weeks and it appealed all too well to Blair's messianic streak.

The media

You cannot have much of a 'policy' for education or the arts without also having a policy for the media, which arbitrate so much of our cultural life. Yet Labour tried hard. Blair groupies talked of 'rebranding' Britain and the Government wrung its hands over the Macpherson report – but no one was allowed to cross-refer to the racism and xenophobia of the tabloids. The Blair stance was one of appeasement – accepting the power of Murdoch and the other moguls as a fact of nature, not a deformation of political and cultural life that desperately needed remedy. The only occasion when Murdoch was shown anything resembling a yellow card was when he tried to take over Manchester United FC. (For football, a game in serious need of policy-makers' attention, the best Smith could do was a 'self-regulating' commission meant to ensure Man United and the others did not keep changing their strips every few months, forcing fans to buy expensive replacement replicas.)

The confusion surrounding plans for a new Office of Communications – needed as broadcasting and telecoms converged – reflected political diffidence in confronting the media magnates. We must not exaggerate the importance of print. Broadly, 71 per cent watch television news on a daily basis, compared with 45 per cent who read news in papers and 47 per cent who listen to radio news. Any government concerned with diversity of opinion, let alone the information needs of citizens, should study those figures carefully. Labour cultivated Murdoch because he controlled (depending on estimates) 36–41 per cent of national newspaper circulation. In 1996 the Tories had barred any newspaper company with more than 20 per cent of the market from buying into terrestrial broadcasting – not cable or satellite, where Murdoch had earlier had EU rules bent for him by his friend Margaret Thatcher. Astonishingly, Labour had even tabled an amendment to scrap this 20 per cent limit, at the behest of the Labour-supporting Mirror Group, then lumbering hopelessly into the television business.

In 1997 Labour received support of a kind from the Murdoch press. His reward followed. Labour's revision of competition law in 1998 offered a chance to prevent predatory pricing of the kind practised by Murdoch's *Times* in an effort to kill the *Independent*. Amendments were put up in Parliament to that effect but Labour whipped the bill through. It was a relationship too close, tainting Blair's pure image of himself. The two men talked on the phone, met when the magnate was in London, and ranted, as required, in Murdoch's papers.

Part of Labour's press policy was arrant fear. There was never the remotest possibility that Labour might do the one thing that could make their future electoral prospects brighter – grab the snake by the head and twist it. Labour could have passed a law in the first flush of victory allowing only one national newspaper per proprietor, forcing Murdoch to dispose of his levers of power and break up his television empire. Laws against non-EU media ownership, enacted elsewhere in Europe, would have driven out both Murdoch and the reactionary owner of the *Telegraph* titles, Conrad Black, foreigners with malign influence on British foreign policy. People do not vote on instruction, but the insidious influence on politics of the right-wing bias in the press is too well-attested. The assault on Labour in the next general election when it comes will be deserved to the extent that Labour had neither guts nor gumption in taking on the bully-boys.

For the structure of television, Labour had no general ideas worth the mention, more a set of *ad hoc* responses to rapidly changing circumstances. It cast Channel 4 free from its peculiar funding whereby it was obliged in 1996 to pay the private ITV companies £87 million – whether C4's quality rose as a result was doubtful. Brown entertained thoughts about privatizing the channel but abandoned them – that is now Tory policy.

Labour had rarely challenged the managerial regime imposed at the BBC by John Birt (given a peerage and other emoluments by Labour in order to get him out quickly in early 2000). Greg Dyke, Birt's successor, was more pragmatic, and Labour offered no objection to the BBC's rapid expansion into the private sector as it negotiated with the Discovery Channel and its like to set up digital channels, some of them taking advertising, some only available on subscription on cable and satellite. Like the Tories, Labour encouraged the BBC to try to become a big player in the global media market, cashing in on the international value of its brand name to make money to feed back into better home programming.

Smith, tugged constantly by Number 10, had to decide the BBC's money. Underfunding was made apparent to all viewers as the BBC lost event after event to higher commercial bidders. Without large extra sums, the BBC would be barred from exploiting the opportunities digital television presented – under Blair the UK achieved the highest penetration of digital television in the world, with one in five homes subscribing. Smith turned to Gavyn Davies, a close-in New Labour City economist, who came up with an ingenious proposal for a supplementary digital payment – those with digital services should pay more because they were getting more and could usually afford it. It was BSkyB's Tim Allan, former Labour spin doctor and close friend of Mandelson, who led the protest, and Smith rapidly rejected the plan. It was left unspecified how the Government proposed to stop people watching analogue broadcasting so it then could sell off the frequencies.

The BBC got its money – the licence fee rose to £104, two-thirds of what it had asked for, amounting to £200 million more a year on top of its existing £2.1 billion. Brown added free licences for the over-75s, people without sight half-price. The settlement was to last until 2006, when the BBC's Royal Charter will come up for renewal. Smith criticized the number of repeats and changes in news output to make way for audience-boosting entertainment. He was told to mind his own business. After all what had the state to say about culture in the multi-channel age?

4

The Health of Health

Mavis Skeet did not expect to end her life as a celebrity but, poor woman, she became one of those NHS famous cases that from time to time shake governments to their foundations. The seventy-three-year-old grandmother from Wakefield had her operation for throat cancer cancelled four times in five weeks in late 1999 because of bed shortages. Finally at Leeds General Infirmary doctors said the delays had made her condition inoperable and she was left to die, to the outrage of her daughter, who wrote to the Prime Minister and made a public fuss. Mrs Skeet led the news night after night, to Downing Street's fury.

The anatomy of a panic in the NHS is curious. One story starts off an avalanche. Next came a Hereford man who was shunted round hospitals looking for a bed until he died twenty-four hours later. (In such panics specifics are ignored and it later turned out to be an ambulance driver's mistake unrelated to bed shortages.) There always have been and always will be cases of bad treatment in any health system, people who fall through the net. Mavis Skeet dominated the news because her story resonated with too many other people's experience. The Government was falling behind on its election promise to cut waiting lists by 100,000. The Skeet case was an accident waiting to happen because the NHS always explodes whenever spending has been held down for too long. In the Major years, April 1992 to March 1997, health spending had increased by an average of 2.6 per cent a year in real terms. That was well below the post-war average of 3.4 per cent. Worse, there had been practically no increase at all in 1996–7 – and this was despite the pressure of demography, technology and, inexorably, public expectations. The NHS perennially struggles to meet rising expectations from a richer and more demanding public. It scores low in World Health Organization tables but scores high for efficiency, offering better value with far less waste than other countries which blend private insurance and public provision.

Even Margaret Thatcher had learnt a lesson. In 1987 deaths at a Birmingham children's heart hospital triggered a furore, for the story was a result of exceptionally low spending years, which had led the heads of the mighty medical colleges to march on Downing Street in a formidable delegation. That caused Thatcher to demand reform, which in turn forced some of the highest annual increments in NHS spending in recent times, over 6 per cent in real terms for a couple of years. Now, after Labour had stuck to Tory controls on spending for two years, the resulting cry of alarm had the usual result – a sudden and unexpected leap in spending, 7.4 per cent for 2000 and over 5 per cent a year for the next three years. Tony Blair's shower of money forced the Tories into matching it: they had little choice. So whatever happens in elections in the first half of the first decade of the new century, the NHS will be in the money.

In health, January rather than April is the cruellest month. The new millennium had no sooner opened than an all-too-familiar winter NHS crisis broke. It was not a flu epidemic in the strict sense, but enough old and cold victims succumbed to fill hospital corridors with trolley-loads of patients with no spare beds to put them in. Operations were cancelled to make room, affecting many like Mavis Skeet. A final blow fell when Robert Winston, the country's best-known doctor, offered up a soundbite calling Labour's health policy 'deceitful'. He called the NHS the worst health service in Europe, worse even than poor Poland. Known as a pioneering fertility doctor, Winston had recently become a television personality with his award-winning series *The Human Body* and, what is more, Tony Blair had created him a working Labour peer. After his diagnosis, Labour's health policy lay in ruins. It only made matters worse when heavy pressure from Downing Street forced the honourable Winston into a humiliating retraction that read like the sheep confessing to imaginary crimes in *Animal Farm*. He had Labour bang to rights.

How bad was it? Tight, but not on a respirator. Health spending as a proportion of GDP, dipping under Major, was rising again and the increase in health spending for 1999–2000 was nearly 6 per cent in real terms. But aggregate spending figures do not necessarily tell you much about how it feels on the wards. One hair-raising survey suggested that 20 per cent of lung cancer patients become inoperable while waiting for radiotherapy. But breast cancer deaths had just fallen by 25 per cent, due to better screening and early treatment. Under Labour improvements were steady if undramatic: junior doctors' hours dropped to fifty-six hours a week, still too high but much better than the eighty-plus common during the last decade. Treatments and outcomes go on improving, though few reading the *Daily Mail*'s shrill campaign about 'Britain's Third World Wards' would have thought so during the 1999–2000 winter health panic.

So, like Mrs Thatcher before him in almost identical circumstances, Tony Blair appeared on the sofa of *Breakfast with Frost* early in the New Year 2000. He made an astounding promise. UK health spending would soar to match the European average. It sounded like panic – it was panic – and few believed it at first. It might be, as Labour people claimed afterwards, that Blair had always intended to give the NHS a huge boost, but an outburst from Frost's sofa lacked credibility. Was ever so much money spent to so little effect on public opinion? Equivocation by Alistair Campbell, the press spokesman, to the effect that it was all only an 'aspiration' did not help.

Money

The extent to which the money came as a shock can be guessed from the fact that health secretary Alan Milburn had until only a few weeks before been privately expressing grave concern about NHS funding. He even floated publicly the idea that the NHS could not survive without a 'hypothecated' tax. People would not vote for more income tax but might be persuaded to pay a tax ear-marked for the NHS. He plainly was not expecting a huge new subvention. In any case, spending announcements were supposed to wait until Gordon Brown's review in July 2000, after he had assessed bids. Brown had agreed the money with Tony Blair but was angry that Blair jumped the gun. Other ministers asked what hope there was for education, transport and a hundred other pressing needs if health already had so much of the cake.

It was not until the budget in March that people began to understand just how much had been committed. Aggregate health spending was to rise by 6.1 per cent for the four years beginning April 2000. Take 1 April 1999 as a baseline – the date the first Labour spending review kicked in: health spending would rise over the five years from then to March 2005 by 50 per cent in cash terms, 35 per cent after adjustment for inflation. This was equivalent to a rise in NHS cash spending per household from £1,850 in 1998–9 to £2,800 in 2003–4. This was not an ideal way to plan health yet it conformed all too well to the pattern. From the outset, when Aneurin Bevan's original NHS budget was slashed sharply by Attlee, the NHS has ridden the financial roller-coaster. Still, this time round the health establishment was amazed. Ian Bogle of the British Medical Association tore up his press release as the Chancellor sat down after his budget speech, and rewrote one that began with the most unusual phrase, 'We are delighted.'

It had the salutary effect of silencing the growing Tory calls for privatization in one form or another. Liam Fox, the Tory health spokesman, had toyed at the previous Tory party conference with moving towards a more privately funded system. Other Tories were saying the NHS should only exist for emergencies, everything else privately insured. But William Hague dropped all such talk for the time being (returning to it later) and announced that his party would match whatever Labour spent. After this, too, there was no more loose talk about the NHS no longer being funded from general taxation. The doomsters were silenced and their predictions of the end of a basically free and universal NHS were squashed by the sheer weight of Labour's sum.

While Brown seized the initiative on poverty, Blair had grabbed health. In private he labelled the health establishment a force of conservatism – especially doctors. They were a professional cartel, too eager to protect their fiefdom at patients' expense. Not unlike Margaret Thatcher again, he became absorbed in the entrails of this huge beast, a wholly-owned Government enterprise employing a million people, the biggest single employer in Europe. Blair went through a phase of regaling visitors to Downing Street with 101 shocking facts about the NHS. Did you know, he would say, some surgeons perform only three operations a week while others do thirty identical ones? Did you know that 40 per cent of outpatients referred to consultants turn out not to need to see one at all?

So what did Blair do about it?

Before the election Labour had profited from attacking the Thatcher/Clarke reforms that brought in the 'internal market'. That word market had been a fatal error and it was easy for Labour to stir up fears that Thatcher was bent on privatization. Clarke's scheme was in fact a way of separating health authorities purchasing services from the hospitals and GPs providing them. It created a new transparency; it became easier to calculate costs and purchasers could demand better results.

Labour had pledged to abolish the internal market, although by then it was plainly a system that worked. Minor changes were needed to simplify the excessive paper-chase of bills circulating insanely through the system for virtually every operation, but otherwise NHS staff who had at first resisted it wanted the basic structure to remain. Elections have their own imperatives. Labour had to invent something new to make it look as if they had demolished the market. They picked on the bit of the Tory reforms the public understood, the two tiers of GPs. Some GPs had become fund-holders with extra money to purchase treatment for their patients, who then jumped the queue. Labour promised to introduce a universal system of fund-holding.

Labour grouped GPs in twenty to thirty strong primary care groups, 481 of them around the country. The idea was that they should budget for community services in their district and develop all kinds of specialist clinics to save patients having to traipse to hospitals for routine tests and treatments. They run the community nurses. Eventually they are supposed to become primary care trusts and control the whole NHS budget for their area; health authorities would wither and die. All this was slow to get off the ground. Labour did not change doctors' status. GPs remained private contractors, small businesses not NHS employees. The poorest areas of inner cities, where it is hardest to get GPs to work, have always been badly served by small one-man practices, loath to modernize. Primary Care Groups brought these loners out of the cold but many dragged their heels. Other doctors have not wanted to spend time on administration, away from patients. It is by no means certain that the system will ever be robust enough to take on the burden of all the strategic planning now done by health authorities.

Expectations

Blair realized early on he would have trouble with the NHS. Labour had won the election stoking up expectations that went far beyond its modest formal promises. The manifesto offer was just a 100,000 cut in waiting lists. Nonetheless, the implicit message was that the NHS would flow with beds and nurses the moment Blair entered Number 10.

But of course doctors and nurses have to be trained. So, whatever the telephone-book numbers, spending money both well and fast is not easy in the NHS, where most of the cost is in staff. In any case Labour did not even start spending more till 1999. One option in 1997 was to begin a giant hospital building programme. Some nineteen gleaming new hospitals were given the immediate go-ahead, followed by approval for another eighteen later. Their construction guaranteed that by the next election there would be bright, modern, highly specialized new regional hubs, with smaller older hospitals to act as spokes feeding in their more complex cases. Research showed how intense specialism in regional centres is the answer to improving Britain's poor record on cancer, coronary and other treatments. So how did Labour do it without having any extra to spend? The answer was on the never-never, which is to say by means of the Private Finance Initiative (PFI).

PFI had been invented by the Tories as a way to get private money on the table now, leaving the state to pay instalments later. Under Treasury pressure, health trusts were instructed to sign deals, bringing in private consortia to build and maintain new buildings. The trusts were then committed to a stream of repayments stretching far into the future, mortgaging future generations' health spending for as long as sixty years, by which time these hospitals would be long redundant, still paying money which might have to come out of savings on health care. Critics claimed that new hospitals in Worcester, Durham, Edinburgh and elsewhere cut rather than expanded bed numbers; funds had to be diverted from clinical needs to pay for the schemes. The theory – we will meet up with it again in Chapter 8, with the London Underground – was that the risk of cost overruns would be met by private firms. The history of public sector building projects in health and transport, let alone defence, was bad and many routinely doubled or trebled in cost. But Alyson Pollock of University College London said the risk remained 'substantially with the public sector': the buck would still always stop with the government of the day. She doubted the case and said bluntly that the first PFI hospital to open, the Cumberland Infirmary in Carlisle, had gone ahead on assumptions skewed against the public sector. It was another example of how the Government's – meaning Brown's – prudent obstinacy succeeded in souring the atmosphere around a good news story.

Primary Care Groups and hospital financing were never going

to seize the public imagination so Blair made a habit of leapfrog-ging his health secretary in order to snatch startling new announcements for himself. His political instincts told him people were eyeing the glossy brochures for private medicine and asking why the NHS was not more customer-friendly. People wanted to find that using the NHS was as easy as booking an airline ticket; why were busy people supposed to dance attend-ance on doctors, as if patients' time was so much less valuable? So Blair himself announced the new NHS Direct, with nurses able to give patients quick help and advice over the telephone; soon they may book appointments there and then. It was popular: over 3.5 million calls were taken by the end of 2000. The new service, with an Internet adjunct, may even have cut numbers turning up at Accident and Emergency (A&E) departments or GP surgeries. Twenty-eight per cent of those who used NHS Direct saying they would otherwise have dialled 999 were given advice instead on how to care for themselves, while 17 per cent were guided to more urgent care. Thirty-eight per cent who said they would have gone to their GPs were advised instead on how to treat themselves. Research suggests that 80 per cent of visits to GPs need only a sympathetic ear or an aspirin, not highly qualified treatment. The NHS Direct website received over a million hits a week. Ninety-seven per cent of NHS callers said they were satisfied with the service they received. Blair conjured high-street walk-in clinics as an alternative to GP surgeries: thirty-six opened by the end of 2000. Doctors opposed both innovations, with the somewhat specious complaint that these things undermined long-standing patient/doctor relationships. Following his instincts on the need to keep up NHS appearances, Blair allocated money when more came on stream in 1999 to renovating and improving A&E – the first point of contact many have with hospitals.

Waiting lists

When Labour made its pre-election promise to cut waiting lists the NHS groaned. This was the wrong promise. Waiting time not numbers on lists is what matters: no one cares how many others wait side by side, only how long it takes. Labour added insult to injury with another manifesto promise to pay for the waiting list cut by 'releasing £100m from NHS red tape'. Red tape and abuse of 'bureaucrats' is always dishonest Opposition-speak which promises savings by attacking managers and civil servants, as if they are the problem and not the solution: in Opposition the Tories took up this shabby refrain with equal populist gusto. The battle with waiting lists was harder than Labour expected. Demand for treatment rose, as it always has since 1948. The NHS was treating many more patients more efficiently and yet still the numbers waiting were not shrinking fast enough. The winter crisis of 1999/2000 set things back further.

As soon as the extra money promised in the 1998 review had come in from April 1999, it went to pay off the deficits that many health authorities were accumulating. It went on free flu jabs for the vulnerable to try to head off another flu crisis, more nurses and intensive care beds, which were the cause of so many can-celled operations when they filled up suddenly with flu and pneumonia victims. So, at a price, the waiting list target was met. Early on, struggling to find good news, Labour had indulged in populist quick hits. Bart's Hospital in London had been due for closure, the wrong kind of service in the wrong place. But the hospital had run a powerful campaign and had lofty if ignor-ant City patrons. It was reprieved. Cottage hospitals rightly due for closure were also rescued, as local Labour candidates had all promised to fight for them – regardless of regional plans.

NICE price

One of the complaints during the Tory years had been about the 'post-code lottery' that allocated some patients better drugs and treatments depending on where they lived. Labour promised a truly national service. Its instincts were against more local NHS democracy if that meant less uniformity of treatments. Its preferred model was centralist – for a just, universal service. To that end NICE and CHIMP were created – twin engines supposed to iron out treatment across the country.

NICE, the National Institute for Clinical Effectiveness, was the first explicitly rationing body the NHS has ever known. It set out to examine every treatment and drug to assess whether they worked and offered value for money. It ploughs through the research few doctors have time to read and tells them what works best. It discovered some common operations may be of little use – too many grommets for children's ears and tonsillectomies for example.

Its first test case was an expensive flu drug called Relenza. NICE declared that the drug only reduced flu effects by some hours and was of no proven use in protecting the old and vulnerable. It was too expensive to be worth prescribing. The drug company that made it threatened court action but backed down after an important test of strength. Next came the expensive cancer drug Taxol, which some health authorities prescribed but others did not, to the great alarm of cancer patients. NICE declared it effective and said it must be fairly available to all. That set many minds at rest, proving NICE was not a politicians' instrument for saving money. NICE made rationing open. In the NHS a life saved at colossal price may mean many others lost: from now on such choices will be aired as NICE works its (alas, very slow) way through drugs and procedures, talking openly about cost as well as effectiveness.

CHIMP, the Commission for Health Improvement, was designed as an Ofsted for health, inspecting hospitals, monitoring services and examining results. It was a brave innovation, as its first reports in November 2000 unearthed some hospital horrors that made shocking anti-government headlines. More league tables were compiled each year as better data was collected, refining Tory innovations. As yet there are crude death rates for hospitals but eventually we shall get more sophisticated data, even the operating success of individual consultants.

Blair's guerrilla approach to the NHS led him to set up three separate 'tsars' – for cancer, coronary heart disease and mental health. They were supposed to target poor records in each area and devise ways of galvanizing practitioners into following the best practice in each. All this was up and running before Mavis Skeet set off the great money avalanche. With it a new era began.

National planning

Allowing just four months to prepare it, in spring 2000 Blair announced a new National Plan for the NHS. Despite the Stalinist ring, Blair involved numbers of doctors, nurses and managers in an array of taskforces to draw up spending plans for every part of the service. They included the royal colleges, for the plan stood a better chance if it embraced the professions. So most of it was their plan, or at least one they had acquiesced in. Published in July 2000, the president of the Royal College of Physicians called it a 'once-in-a-lifetime opportunity'. The general secretary of the Royal College of Nursing congratulated the Government on a 'survival plan that puts patients first and tackles the hardest issues facing the health service'. It was singularly non-ideological and non-theoretical. The really big idea was an old one which had been in doubt among alarming numbers of NHS theorists: to prove that the NHS can survive and thrive out of taxpayers' money alone, free to all and used by all. That did not rule the private sector out. A 'concordat' signed by Alan Milburn in October 2000 in fact guaranteed private medicine a share in public funds, as he encouraged health authorities to feel free to buy treatments from private hospitals if the price was right. This was happening anyway in most places and was regarded as an essentially political gesture to stop the Tories claim that Labour's anti-private-practice ideology was stunting potential patient care. It was estimated only some 100,000 would be bought a year, out of the NHS's 6 million operations.

For once this National Plan was designed to spend money, not save it, devoted to outcomes not process, with scores of specific targets to be delivered to patients instead of new management systems. It offered the public a way of seeing, concretely, what the 35 per cent increase over four years might deliver. The plan was a menu: 7,000 extra beds, 7,500 new consultants, 2,000 more GPs, 20,000 more nurses, 1,000 graduate mental health workers, 500 more secure mental beds, 6,500 other health professionals, higher pay, more training, chemists and nurses with prescribing powers, out-of-hours services, good hospital food, clean wards under severe ward 'housekeepers', more and better community care for the old and their carers. On and on it rolled, with price-tags and dates to be achieved by each. The plan's waiting time objectives look very modest, a reminder of how bad some services are.

- Maximum wait for an operation will fall from eighteen months to six months by 2005, and to three months by 2008 (when 75 per cent of operations will be day cases).
- Maximum wait for outpatient appointments to fall to three months by 2005.
- Maximum wait in accident and emergency to fall to four hours by 2004 (average to fall to seventy-five minutes).
- Maximum wait for a GP appointment to fall to forty-eight hours by 2004.

By 2005 all hospital waiting lists will be abolished as everyone is given a definite booked date.

This is what Labour might have offered right from the beginning of its tenure, had the money been there. Now it had become an ambition for a second term and beyond.

Realizing the plan will depend on breaking down medicine's rigid professional demarcations. Nurses and pharmacists would have more say in treatment and prescription of drugs. Barriers between nurses and ancillary staff would be eased as well. Therapists and professionals would get more power and more GPs would become specialists in various fields so fewer patients will be referred to hospital. Drawing up new doctors' contracts – especially with the consultants – proved more difficult. The sticking point was the plan's demand that consultants should be banned from doing any private practice in their first seven years after qualifying. (Only some 6,000 out of the 21,000 consultants do any – obstetrics and orthopaedics mainly.) But far more important, the contract for the first time would specify much more precisely what hours consultants work and what they are expected to do. They would no longer be monarchs of their little hospital teams; they would be managed like other staff, with annual appraisals from their clinical director, and reregistration every five years by the General Medical Council examining these appraisals. Cynics who have observed consultants' ways over the years wonder if they will still browbeat their way through all this. It will depend on the strength of local managers. The need for managers to oversee consultants' work-rate came from evidence such as this: in the 1990s spending on orthopaedic surgeons doubled as more were recruited but the number of operations they did each week fell sharply to an average of just six, while their waiting lists swelled to 250,000. A Bristol University study found that private practice grew whenever doctors moved part of their time into the private sector and created more demand. NHS waiting lists grew conveniently to fuel demand for private operations. Similarly GPs need managing. As private contractors, they keep demanding extra payments for giving new treatments such as flu jabs, as if their contract covered nothing that did not exist in the 1948 days of Vick and Friar's Balsam.

There were plenty of other questions raised about how the National Plan could hit its targets. Take that promise to recruit

	Real terms increases since Major took office in 1992 (percentage)
1992	2
1993	0.2
1994	0.4
1995	0
1996	− 0.4 (i.e. lower than inflation)
1997	1.7
1998	− 0.2
1999	3.1
2000	2.3

Figure 6: Pay for nurses, midwives and health visitors

Source: Royal College of Nursing

an extra 20,000 nurses. Although numbers rose by some 4,000, there were 22,000 vacant nursing posts in 2000, leading to desperate recruiting drives in Thailand, South Africa and the Philippines (and it emerged that some of the 20,000 might be part-time anyway). It was unclear whether the Government was promising another 20,000 nursing posts, or only to fill all the gaping vacancies in the system, but even that would be remarkably hard to do. It is worth rehearsing the nursing crisis as it is just one example of what was happening everywhere in the public sector, where meeting all these targets depended on recruiting and keeping good people in a labour market competing hard for their desirable skills: nurses, teachers, social workers, administrators, lab technicians and managers had to be wooed and paid. As with the rest of these, nurses' pay did rise.

That helped recruitment and retention, as did more flexibility in hours for working mothers. But not enough. There was no longer a large pool of ex-nurses to draw on: 83 per cent of registered nurses were still nursing. An Edinburgh University study in November 2000 found that to procure the 20,000 nurses required by the National Plan, 110,000 more must be recruited over the next four years to cover those projected to retire or leave: the nursing population was ageing fast, with a third of them over forty-five. Where would they come from? Pay in the public sector needed to become a matter not of fairness, but of ability to tempt and compete. Full employment may save heavily on the social security side, but it calls for higher public sector pay in order to recruit not the best but a bare sufficiency of staff. To the Treasury the dead-weight of raising pay for all existing staff in order to attract a few more always feels like money down a black hole, instead of spent on improvement. There was not enough recognition of the need for faster pay rises.

Labour was forced to address another rankling issue – where the NHS ends and social care begins. Old people taken into nursing-homes or receiving care at home paid for it according to their means. The press loved to feature home-owning pensioners who might have to sell up to pay nursing-home costs, instead of endowing their children. The government set up a Royal Commission on Long Term Care which recommended that their treatment should be free, but the Government preferred a minority report which held firm to the idea that those who could afford it should pay. It would have meant paying out a huge sum of NHS money to the better-off elderly simply to ensure they could keep their money to pass it on, rather than regard their life savings as part of paying for their own old age. The National Plan compromised. From October 2001 nursing care will be paid by the NHS, but after that their residential and general care costs must still be covered by their own capital if they have any. It will not satisfy middle-aged offspring who think the state should pay so that they can inherit. But as a sweetener all were given their first three months in a nursing home free, and all over-60s were made eligible for free eye tests.

The NHS plan said patients come first, not the convenience of doctors or managers. Will it happen? It certainly makes a fine manifesto pledge. However, voters will see relatively little change from Labour's first term, though they may now be hearing a lot less grumbling from NHS staff who are better off. They have new machines – 200 CT scanners, fifty MRI scanners, 450 kidney machines, 3,000 automated defibrillators and £250 million spent on new IT technology. (But it turned out only fifty of the CT scanners are new, the others are replacements. Some of the new consultant posts announced had already been planned.) Most A&Es have been comprehensively refurbished. Loyd Grossman was hired to draw up new hospital menus. But until they find the rocket and goat's cheese on their plates, patients will mainly have to take the plan on trust.

The health of the nation

But is the UK any healthier thanks to Labour? The NHS does not deliver health, it merely patches up ill-health. A study by the Chief Medical Officer, Liam Donaldson, confirmed that poverty causes sickness; it is linked with bad diet, smoking, unemployment and depression, all producing more low birthweight babies who in turn start out life more vulnerable. During decades when the NHS had redistributed money to bad-health areas from rich ones, the health gap widened, showing how little real difference the NHS makes: leafy Surrey gets 20 per cent less NHS cash per capita than the national average, Liverpool far more. Even so, healthy Hampstead citizens are operated on more often than the far sicker residents of Tower Hamlets – though even that is a tricky figure, since private practice in Hampstead may urge the rich to undergo needless operations.

Health Secretaries all try to devote more attention and money to prevention, but every Health Secretary is swept away by the angry demands from hospitals for immediate spending. Although extra sums are going towards community health, the proportion divided between acute care, community and prevention has barely shifted. Labour inaugurated Health Action Zones

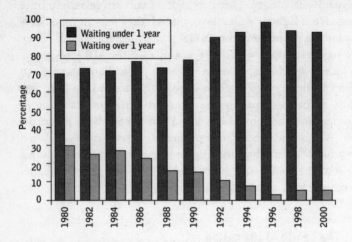

Figure 7: Proportion of total waiting list in England waiting under/over 12 months for admission

Source: The King's Fund

covering 13 million people in the twenty-six most deprived areas, spending an extra £121 million by 2000 on extra drugs and anti-smoking programmes, with GPs able to prescribe subsidies for swimming and exercise, nicotine patches for free and nurseries giving free fruit to young children. Labour took action to improve monitoring of schoolchildren's health, contraception and other health advice for teenagers. Tessa Jowell's *Our Healthier Nation* white paper with its many targets for accident and illness reduction earned Labour the title of 'nanny'.

One of Frank Dobson's first actions as Health Secretary after the election had been to ban sports sponsorship by tobacco companies – leaving Labour with egg all over its face when the major party donor Bernie Ecclestone saw his business, Formula One racing, exempted. Alco-pops were put on trial by Health Ministers – at the same time as the Home Office moved to

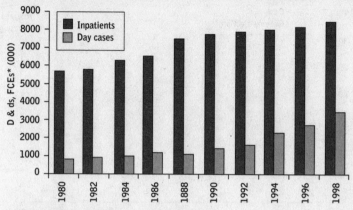

* Deaths and discharges; Finished Consultant Episodes

Figure 8: Hospital activity: Inpatients and day cases: England

Source: The King's Fund

liberalize pub licensing. On the drug alcohol as on the drug cannabis, confusion reigned in high places. What was the public health significance of Home Office measures (set out in the April 2000 white paper, *Time for Reform*) proposing to modernize pub licensing laws? Easier to obtain licences and later opening was all very Cool Britannia but could be bad for health; nor did they fit easily with Blair's intemperate demand that drunken yobs be marched to cashpoints for instant fines.

Labour's enthusiasm for public health was undermined when Tessa Jowell's successor, Yvette Cooper, was appointed a whole ministerial grade lower. But, as with GM crops, this was also a government prepared to back the advance of potentially beneficial knowledge and face down the know-nothings. Labour inherited a situation where scientists were permitted to experiment on embryos up to fourteen days old but only in five categories linked to infertility treatments. A specialist panel of the Human

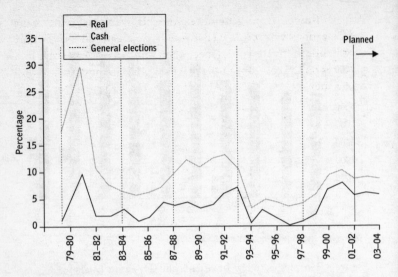

Figure 9: Percentage change in UK NHS net spending: cash and real (deflated by GDP deflator)

Source: The King's Fund

Genetics Advisory Commission and the Human Fertilization and Embryology Authority reported in December 1998 in favour of broadening the categories, for example allowing research using cloning to pursue treatments for inherited diseases. The Government stalled; a second panel led by the Chief Medical Officer looked again. His report, in August 2000, said such work could go ahead – but also promised a free vote in the Commons.

Overall the Government is left with a weak record on achievements so far, only able to promise that the best is yet to come over the second term. It is a very good promise: the money and the determination are there, yet it remains just a plan. Voters will be asked to believe that these tight targets in the National Plan can and will be delivered. Meanwhile, most are agreed that this is the last chance to prove that a modern NHS can still flourish funded from general taxation. If even this 35 per cent increase does not work well enough to create an NHS that commands popular confidence, then the privatizers wait like vultures on the rooftops of the private clinics to move in one way or another.

5

It's the Economy, Clever

Luck and judgement in about equal measure secured the Blair Government's sterling performance. Labour's luck embraced the swift recovery of East Asia and Brazil from recession in 1998 and the continuing mega-strength of the United States, sucking in goods and capital like a vacuum-cleaner. Labour's judgement lay in horse-whispering the right words in the direction of the City and business, which together rode above trend growth, which in turn pumped extra revenues into Gordon Brown's pocket. The right words were *right*. New Labour had to swear repeatedly on the bible of neo-liberalism while Gordon Brown set out to achieve the residual aim of socialism – a more equal society – by stealth.

He certainly covered his tracks. No one seemed to notice how his 1997 changes in pension fund contributions accomplished what one writer in the *Financial Times* called 'one of the greatest raids on corporate cashflow in history'. It and other measures pushed taxes on private companies from 3.5 per cent of GDP in 1998–9 to 3.9 per cent in 2001–2, not a bad feat in a world where globalization was supposed to forbid one-country hits on the private sector.

Perhaps the scar tissue of the recession of the early 90s had never healed, leaving the inhabitants of the UK permanently insecure or, better put, unwilling to give politicians the credit for any prosperity that came their way. Labour's amazing record on jobs and growth did not insulate it from polling chills, and after the American presidential election in November 2000 the old adage about voters favouring the party that delivered the economic goods just no longer seemed applicable.

From 1997 to 2001 the economy boomed. The proportion

of those aged between eighteen and sixty-five in work grew spectacularly. By early 2001 at 75 per cent the employment rate was pushing towards its previous peak under Ted Heath in the early 1970s and was getting nearer the 77 per cent in work in the United States – the more people in work, the more likely the economy to grow. One count, the Labour Force survey, said fewer than 1.5 million people were out of work by year's end 2000; another, the count of those claiming social benefits, put the total by early 2001 at under 1 million. In the year to April 2000, average gross earnings were nearly £22,000 per employee, male, that is – women on average earned 38 per cent less; Labour did not change the gender gap.

True, another arm of the growth machine – output per employee – still looked shrivelled. No miracle cure hove in sight for UK productivity. A telling gap remained between what an average worker produced in the UK relative to other countries, especially those allegedly bloated welfare states of France and Germany – though, typically, Brown chose to point the contrast with the free-enterprise United States.

When it comes to the economy politicians can be more credulous than medieval monks, and Thatcher and Tory Chancellor Nigel Lawson had spied miracles round every corner. As for Brown, his favourite colour was amber. Perhaps caution was just as well when large, old holes in the fabric needed explaining: the UK balance of payments deficit, growing under Labour in response to the upward movement of the economic cycle, regional imbalance, under-investment by both firms and the state, and prevalent human under-performance.

Having purged itself of socialism Labour was left with no overarching economic philosophy. In a 1995 lecture Blair said government's role in the modern economy was limited to keeping inflation low while improving human capital. As for public spending, Labour's rap was straight from the Tory groove: 'how much' mattered less than 'what on'. In a Blair speech in Singapore in 1996 'stakeholding' came to brief life: the economy had to be run for the many not the few in conditions of trust between business and government as unemployment was tackled, small business encouraged and everyone made to feel 'part of the same team'.

Stakeholding then died the death, to be replaced by the equally dreamy Third Way. Pollyanna would have loved its offer of basic minimum rights for individuals at work as Government and industry worked together, enhancing the dynamism of the market not undermining it. Labour's manifesto mixed historical obligation to the unions with modernization. But the key to Labour's tenure was Brown's famous pre-election pledge on income tax: neither the basic nor the top rate of tax would increase.

It was a defining moment: the spectre of defeat in 1992 was laid to rest and a revolution wrought in the way Labour was perceived. But the Big Question now dangles before us. How far, in the electoral circumstances of early 1997, was Brown's heroic gesture necessary? After he made it, polling gurus were telling Millbank that Labour rated 11 per cent more than the Tories on measures of public trust on matters fiscal. Tory recovery was believed to be still possible and the pledge was a prophylactic – Labour practised safe tax. There is a sad syllogism in the making here. Brown's pledge won Labour not just the election but business confidence, but Brown's pledge prevented Labour satisfying the people because it was linked with no spending increases for two years and dissatisfied people may think twice about endorsing Labour again. So Brown may have jeopardized Labour's second term, for among the consequences of his pledge was his bid to pay for spending by indirect taxes (petrol duty for example).

Yet on the pledge hung so many intangibles, market confidence, City expectations, the absence of the capital flight which, literally and figuratively, tipped earlier Labour Governments into pandemonium. In the remaking of Labour it may have been a talisman, but it was also an albatross.

Did pay packets get better?

Things got better for workers and wage-earners, even more so
for the salariat and company directors. You can tell that from
who pays higher-rate income tax – their ranks swelled by at
least 100,000 during 1997–2001, a time when the total numbers
paying tax fell a little. For every £100 of retail spending on the
eve of the 1997 election, consumers had £114 to spend in early
2001; households in total had some £45 billion more to spend.
Each year since the election the economy grew on average by 2.6
per cent. You can compare that with the Tories' 1979–97 average
of 2 per cent, which of course includes economic downturn
as well as upswing. It is a measure of Labour's fortune that
economists could seriously speculate whether such cycles were
a thing of the past. On basic indices, Labour's tenure saw joblessness falling to such an extent that 'full employment' could
become an active goal for the first time in a generation.

But on the crude test of 'It's the economy, stupid', Labour
came incontrovertibly good. How far was it Labour's doing?
The earth was moving across the West and the economy, some
said, was renewing itself at some deep level. Take the way information and communications technology burgeoned. The European IT industry expects to increase employment from 8.6
million in 1999 to 11.3 million by 2003. Half the EU's 222,000
software specialists (1999) were to be found in Germany and the
UK. Given German levels of benefit and work protection, so
often the butt of Blairite criticism, this concentration could not
have much to do with the Third Way or Labour's acceptance of
Thatcher's deregulation of employment. What we can say, at the
very least, is that Gordon Brown and Blair did not ruffle the
golden goose.

Labour took office on a rising curve. The rate at which the
economy could grow without inflation running away rose in the
UK, as it did elsewhere. This was what the Third Way said: it
extolled globalization, which meant competition from alternative

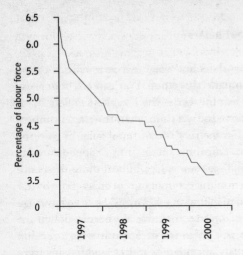

Figure 10: Unemployment rate

Source: HM Treasury

suppliers kept pressure on prices. Productivity was improving, thanks in part to IT and the Internet – even if there remained a telling gap between the UK and competitors. Another reason for improved growth prospects that was specific to the UK was Thatcherite harshness on the work and benefits front. Under the Tories, said Steve Nickell, an Oxford economist appointed by Brown to the Bank of England's monetary policy committee, wage-bargainers had become, as economists put it, more rational in accepting a necessary link between increases and improvements in productivity (though not in the boardrooms). Union decline was a factor. The balance of power in the labour market had swung and Labour was not inclined to reverse it.

Labour watched while the UK's manufacturing base shrank. Manufacturing employment, which had been falling under the Tories, increased in the Major years. Under Labour it fell again, 180,000 jobs down in three years, though this was compensated for by growth in service jobs. Such trends were for the most part beyond the ken of government, and besides, New Labour was not sure it wanted to get involved in opposing market forces. Ask a potter in Stoke or a steelworker in what remained of the UK steel industry in South Wales whether things got better; the honest reply would be: not for those who lost their jobs.

But attitudes had shifted and Labour chose not to counter people's growing belief in the relative unimportance of government, compared to an earlier era, in securing their economic destiny. An example was the way individuals and families were taking more upon themselves in making provision for their future, saving for pensions outside state systems. Pensions did become an issue for Labour – but only three years in, when the disparity between growing national wealth and state pension obligations became glaring. In other respects, such as people's expectation that they would have to make private provision for pensions, the Thatcherite settlement held firm. Labour chose to ask no fundamental questions. We are in the early stages of this shift to individual provision for the distant future and more than one seer has warned how buoyant financial markets have led people to assume saving will be easy. Labour made its contribution by replacing John Major's Tax-exempt Special Savings Accounts (TESSAs) with Individual Savings Accounts (ISAs) and subsequently extending to 2006 the relief they offered on annual savings up to £7,000. Brown's long-term contribution may instead be the way he altered the tax regime on pension funds, bringing in a lot of new revenue without much political fuss, but harming their capacity to pay out in twenty or thirty years' time.

Gordon Brown's mouthful

All things considered, any government in power since 1997 would have enjoyed a benign environment. As for Labour, the party came to office shriven of the ideological sins which revisionists since Neil Kinnock believed made them unelectable. As well as sloughing off old commitments, the Blairites had a theory of what a progressive government should seek to do with and to capitalism.

At the heart of New Labour beliefs was the phrase put into Gordon Brown's mouth by his adviser Ed Balls in 1994. 'Neo-classical endogenous growth theory' accepted there was little the modern state could do to alter economic destiny. It should not even try to intervene to disturb the ownership of capital (a windfall tax excluded) or change commercial or property relations at large. In keeping with the theory, Labour proved reluctant to confront the boardrooms, despite mounting evidence of fat-cats thickening their whiskers with corporate cream. Income Data Services sampled the chief executives of FTSE 100 companies and found their basic salaries improved from £463,000 in 1998–9 to £490,000 a year later; total remuneration packages, as they say, went up from £684,000 to £843,000. Reform of corporate governance – the question of whether shareholders had any real power over executives and their pay – was deferred.

Instead, the job of the state was to foster technological innovation, improve labour force education and skills, enforce tight rules on competition – and preach truth and beauty (Brown, son of the manse, loved to sermonize). The state, in other words, was to be capitalism's better self. Above all the state had to mind its own business. From this flowed the headline commitments made prior to the 1997 election and Brown's golden rules. A government which forbade itself to tax should have no trouble with the other rules for fiscal prudence invented by Brown. There would be no borrowing to finance spending, unless it was long-term investment (calculations to be made over the economic cycle rather than in any given year).

Similarly, over the medium run the state's indebtedness was to be kept stable as a proportion of GDP. Here Brown excelled himself, repaying past borrowing hand over fist and making the UK a European exemplar of prudent housekeeping. Margaret

Thatcher had been fond of that kind of household analogy. If the UK were a mortgaged house worth £200,000, under Brown that mortgage was reduced to £80,000 with a prospect of getting it down further to just over £60,000: most financial advisers would suggest it was time to borrow a bit more.

Labour also promised to stick to the Tories' target for price inflation, 2.5 per cent a year or less. It did – inflation was falling below 1.0 per cent by the end of 2000, on the common or HICP (harmonized indices of consumer prices) measure, well below Euroland's 2.3 per cent. But inflation had been on target for the two years prior to the election. In 2001 the proverbial man from Mars might have looked at the price data and said the downward curve was continuous and it was hard to identify exactly when Labour was elected.

Inflation mattered less anyway. A long-run transformation in UK economic capacity seemed to be under way, leading some commentators to talk about the new disinflationary age. Growth no longer had to be pinched off to secure price stability. The productive potential of the UK economy was growing faster than actual growth. And all this was occurring at a time when the longer-term unemployed were being absorbed back into work, lacking skills and so not much able to improve productivity. Part of the explanation was investment: UK spending on information and communications technology was proportionately the same as in the US.

This was a propitious background to New Labour's experiment in central banking. In Brown's coup of 6 May 1997, the Bank of England was set an inflation target and given control over short-term interest rates in order to achieve it. Decisions were entrusted to a new monetary policy committee (MPC), a majority of its members appointed by the Chancellor. On the money supply, only bankers' decisions would command 'the necessary confidence' – Brown said. This was a clever tactic which succeeded in reassuring the markets that Labour's conversion to Thatcherism was genuine – after all, this was the step at which both she and Nigel Lawson had balked. It was also capitulation to the doctrine that democratically elected politicians are incapable of an entire class of economic decisions. If not interest rates, why should politicians take decisions on tax or (this became Stephen Byers's policy) corporate mergers? Labour left open the question of accountability. The Commons Treasury committee sought to interrogate appointees but its criteria were vague. Perhaps temperament was the key attribute. According to economist Sir Alan Budd, a displaced member, optimists differed in their assessment of inflation prospects by as much as 1 per cent. The Liberal Democrats, confusingly, sought both more independence for the members of the MPC and more politicization of their appointments.

The political bonus from giving the Bank this autonomy was huge – once the imperialist governor Eddie George had been persuaded not to resign over losing supervision of the banks. Labour could claim a new historic identity as the low inflation party. At a stroke, Brown exorcized the ghosts of Montagu Norman, Philip Snowden, Lord Cromer and Denis Healey. But of course he was also tying his own hands. After his July 2000 spending plan and his pre-budget reports in November, where was his guarantee the Bank would not judge his spending 'excessive' and push up interest rates, nullifying the political benefit? It was a point he tried to put to pensioners and hauliers but not an easy one to get over.

The MPC proved to be activist, pushing uphill – rates went to 7.5 per cent in June in the face of unreliable figures showing a surge in wages – then down, as slowdown threatened towards the winter of 1998–9. Was this advanced motoring or lucky learner driving? There is fair agreement that most of its moves were justified, provided you accept that the MPC has a single objective, cutting inflation down to target.

High interest rates of course made the pound attractive relative to other European currencies – eleven members of the European Union were tightly corseting themselves in preparation for the launch of the euro under the terms of the Maastricht Treaty on 1 January 1999.

A Longbridge too far?

The flip-side of euro depreciation, which set in soon after the new currency's launch, was sterling appreciation. A declaration of intent to join at a specified date might have helped but that would have involved, sooner or later, a repeat of the Exchange Rate Mechanism experience. Labour had made much of Tory embarrassment and fought shy of that straitjacket. Sterling rose, causing pain in those sectors of the economy pegged to exporting to Europe, especially manufacturing, its factories often located in Labour heartlands. By contrast the sterling rate against the dollar was fairly stable until, in 1999–2000, it started falling, making exporting to North America marginally easier. The pound slipped down to $1.40, lower than for a long time. Some analysts, indeed, noted sterling's 15 per cent decline against the dollar through 2000 and wondered if that meant it was 'swinging into the euro's orbit' as investors realized the UK economy was not after all particularly like the US, since its long-term growth potential was more like Euroland's.

Ministers offered the manufacturers sympathy and emergency packages. Car-making was a special problem. What was the rationale for supporting car production when environmental policies pointed towards less polluting travel and public transport? Labour had philosophically accepted the imperative of market forces. So, if the board of BMW decided to relocate away from Longbridge, on what grounds might Third Way ministers demur? Productivity at Longbridge was relatively unimpressive; also Rover had lost brand loyalty. The Third Way did offer a glimpse of what should replace metal-bashing industry. Labour wanted to move the UK economy hop, skip and jump to the Internet age; the trouble was a lot of voters depended on manufacturing still. The mooted departure of Ford from Dagenham was a market force too far – arm-twisting and tea at Number 10 ensued. A strong pound cheapened foreign holidays elsewhere in Europe; by cheapening imports it assisted in the fight against inflation. So it took the Chancellor a long time to get around to expressing concern about sterling's appreciation – by some 20 per cent against the euro between January 1999 and autumn 2000, making imports from Euroland correspondingly cheaper. This was a cause of the growth in the UK trade deficit but few seemed to worry about that any more. Those that did worry noted how the UK balance of payments was financed by volatile inflows as the ratio of UK long-term assets to liabilities deteriorated.

How Labour shrunk the state

Labour had no *a priori* thoughts about how big government should be. It was thus by accident rather than the result of deliberate decision that by April 2001 the state should be smaller as a proportion of GDP than in April 1997. Government spending fell from 41.2 per cent in John Major's last year (1996–7) to 37.7 per cent in 1999–2000. In the final year of Brown's planning period, 2003–4, this key ratio was to reach only 40.6 per cent. It had been as high as 44.1 per cent under Major and even under that epitome of moderation, Roy Jenkins, was 41.8 per cent (in 1969–70). New Labour, in other words, did nothing to reposition the UK in the league table showing how big governments are; it remained some way beneath France and Germany but above Japan and the US. Brown said what mattered more than the size of the state was its creation of general conditions for business.

The commitment to spend at Tory levels plus Brown's personal ascendancy in the cabinet gave the Treasury the commanding heights. First, it ordered a 'comprehensive review' of spending – not so dissimilar, it turned out, from the Tories' 'fundamental' reviews. The Treasury made a further bid for control over the minutiae of spending by publishing in 1998 a set of Public Service Agreements (PSAs) with departments and agencies. Many of them were specious, with falsely precise quantities attached. They were also far from fundamental: they

accepted the structure of government as was, failing for example
to question the political rationale of the Ministry of Agriculture.
The broad shares of spending claimed by defence, despite cuts,
and crime remained broadly the same – so much for prioritizing
health and education.

A second, slimmed-down edition of the PSAs was published,
to steer the period 2001–4. Were they really intended to make
government more transparent or were they just a device for
putting the frighteners on the rest of Whitehall? If the former,
said the Committee on Public Accounts, let us monitor them;
the Treasury refused. But Blair's seizure of the health issue
seemed to say the PSAs were irrelevant – health would get the
money because political exigency demanded it, not because of
some abstruse measure of efficiency. Besides, for all the Treasury's supremacy, Whitehall departments were not so easily
cowed. Brown ordered up a National Asset Register, a sort of
Domesday Book of what the state owned. Little was subsequently heard of it. Similarly ambitious plans to rebase Whitehall accounts on resources consumed rather than cash spent –
enacted in 2000 – were scaled back. Existing accounting conventions will continue along with considerable confusion over who
(the National Audit Office, Treasury, Public Accounts Committee, Audit Commission?) is actually responsible for ensuring the
state gets maximum bang for its buck.

But the Treasury had the aggregates firmly in its paws. Within
Tory totals, Brown quickly did some small-scale swopping
around, announcing that from the contingency reserve it was
pulling down £1 billion extra for schools and £1.2 billion for
health, to start in April 1998. House-building by councils was
modestly expanded, paid for from recycled receipts from previous sales under the right to buy. The March 1998 budget
allocated health a further £500 million, schools £250 million
and transport £175 million. This was not 'new' money but the
product of underspending elsewhere.

The July 1998 spending announcement was dangerously over-
sold. First, its money would be spent only from April 1999; its

planning period was 1999–2002. Second, it was basically a health and education review, with 75 per cent of extra spending 1998–9 and 2001–2 going in their direction. It sought to reverse the pattern under the Tories of cutting capital spending. Over the four years from 1997 public investment is supposed to have grown by 12.1 per cent a year in real terms – which meant a huge pick-up since capital spending by the state fell by nearly 5 per cent a year from April 1997 to March 1999. Little wonder that the Government was embarrassed by reports in spring 2000 that the spending was not being delivered – departments and councils had lost the habit.

Then came Brown's apotheosis as spender, the July 2000 announcement, following another review. This one was even less comprehensive, more a collection of bids which, for once, the Treasury was willing to concede – from April 2001 onwards, albeit within the rather conservative framework of keeping total public spending to the 2.5 per cent a year increase 'allowed' by the growth in the economy. One of its most significant elements was the switch to investment. Even pre-empted by the health commitments, it made for a bulging package with net public investment to rise from £8 billion to £20 billion a year, scaffolds up and holes in the roads for years.

PFI v. PPP

Capital spending was also subject to the vagaries of the Private Finance Initiative (PFI), born of the Tories but rechristened by Labour Public-Private Partnerships. According to the theory, computers for the Inland Revenue, a new Treasury building, hospitals and schools would be built and financed by private consortia in return for a string of future payments which would cover both the cost of capital and management charges. It was big money. Net investment by the state in 1999–2000 was supposed to be £6.4 billion, with private money contributing a further £3.8 billion of projects.

Since 1997 contracts have been signed for 150 projects worth over £12 billion, including thirty-five hospitals, 520 schools and four prisons. Crudely put, the state got 'free' capital spending in exchange for pledging current spending in future. A lot of it: PFI-type payments to the private sector would rise from £3.5 billion every year from 2004–5 to 2012–13.

Some of the nation's best accountancy brains were appalled at the open-endedness of the promise, especially because the state could surely afford to borrow in order to invest. In 2001 UK Government debt is 39.4 per cent of GDP, already one of the lowest EU proportions, with a plan to cut it further, to 33 per cent – while Germany's is 59.5, France's 57.1. There were doubts, too, about whether the private sector did it better. A report by the Industrial Society said the PPP insisted on by John Prescott to finance expansion of the London Underground gave poor value (there were safety worries too). PFI deals in the health service were said by expert critics to have cut the number of available beds and diverted money from the clinical front line. For some companies it was a one-way ticket to income. For example, Andersen Consulting supplied a new system for handling National Insurance but – said the National Audit Office – it ran late, paid the wrong amounts to a lot of claimants and cost taxpayers an extra £53 million. Andersen ended up paying just £4.1 million in compensation. Similarly the computers which got the Passport Agency into so much trouble in 1999 were supplied by Siemens Business Services, which ended up paying a paltry fine.

Without PFI, Labour ministers pleaded, these schemes would not have got going. But that is only true if you accept the Brownian premise that Labour could not 'afford' to borrow to invest. And he could.

Gordon gets the money in

The July 2000 spending package was big – £12 billion more for education over the three years to March 2005, 6.1 per cent real growth for health for at least four years, drinks all round so to speak. Yet it was not *that* big. The fundamental balance between public and private scarcely changed, since state spending would increase as a proportion of GDP by less than 1 per cent. Yet it is hard to deny Brown his triumph. Within months of announcing his largesse Brown was forecasting further cuts in public debt – historically it took some beating that a Labour Chancellor could authorize so much extra spending while still reporting a surplus for the state of some £10 billion in 2000–2001. Labour's record of not spending had pushed the public accounts deep into the black, allowing Brown to repay debt and cut interest payments, further reducing spending. Public sector net borrowing improved dramatically, from 3.6 per cent of GDP to a surplus of around 1.3 per cent; it was planned to fall gently back into a small deficit to accommodate the big spending splurge.

Brown got some of his money, initially, from an act of old-fashioned socialist expropriation. The privatized utilities, paying the price of losing public confidence, had to forfeit a windfall tax worth £5 billion. Some £2.2 billion came from electricity, £1.65 billion from water and a further £1.45 billion was extracted (remarkably painlessly) from BAA, Railtrack, BT and British Gas/Centrica. This turned out to be small beer compared with the proceeds of a later windfall. Using a simple but sophisticated formula, the Government auctioned licences for the electromagnetic spectra used by third-generation mobile phones: it raised £22.5 billion, to be fed into the public accounts over a number of years. If Wap and the use of mobile phones for Internet data do not take off, it will constitute an unwonted gift by telecoms companies to the state. A further auction of frequencies at 28GHz was supposed to raise a further £1 billion, though the

Financial year	Net taxes and soc. sec. cont'ns	Total spending by government
1991/2	35.2%	42.2%
1992/3	33.9%	44.2%
1993/4	33.3%	43.9%
1994/5	34.4%	43.2%
1995/6	35.3%	42.9%
1996/7	35.2%	41.2%
1997/8	36.5%	39.6%
1998/9	37.0%	38.5%
1999/2000	36.9%	37.7%
2000/2001	37.3%	39.1%
2001/2002	37.5%	39.7%
2002/2003	37.3%	40.1%
2003/2004	36.9%	40.6%

Figure 11: Tax revenue and spending as percentage of GDP

Source: House of Commons Library

first round of bids raised only £27 million, suggesting that the laying potential of some golden geese can be exaggerated.

Labour had not given up on taxation despite the pledge not to raise income tax. Geoffrey Robinson, Paymaster General until sleaze engulfed him, talked later of a £25 billion 'phased hit' on corporate cashflow. This was fired by changes to the system of advance corporation tax payment, along with £5 billion from abolishing tax credits on dividends. The corporate sector lost real money but, surprisingly, the stock market did not register it.

The Liberal Democrats charged Brown with complicating the tax code, citing the fact that the number of pages in *Tolley's Standard Tax Manual* had increased under Labour by over 30 per cent – and that understated the increase, since the manual's type size had shrunk in the meantime. He certainly made a lot of smallish changes. Many were intended to help small and medium-size firms. He claimed the average corporation tax bill for small companies fell 25 per cent 1997–2001 – only one manifestation of Labour's love affair with small business. Corporation tax rates in fact fell for all companies from 33 per cent to 30 per cent, permitting the claim that UK rates were attractively low by international standards despite changes to pension fund taxation and dividend tax credits. Companies also complained when Brown amended rules to limit the use of 'mixer' companies, often based offshore, to shelter foreign profits from UK tax. Complaints were heard and Labour eased back in the November 2000 pre-budget report. Swings and round-abouts. Buccaneer Brown simultaneously sought to boost venture capital investment by new incentives, especially in the direction of small high-risk and new-tech enterprise.

Tory trends continued – cut direct, raise indirect taxes – so was there a distinct fiscal philosophy behind all this? Total taxes including National Insurance contributions rose a bit then fell a bit then rose. Thanks in part to last-gasp Tory measures the tax take in 1997–8 at 36.5 per cent of GDP was already considerably higher than in any of Major's years in power. When Major became Prime Minister it was just under 34 per cent; when Brown's spending plans reach their fruition in 2004 it would be just under 37 per cent on present plans. It may not sound much – 3 per cent – but it is what has come to distinguish left and right.

Brown muddied his fiscal message by cutting income tax at a time when Labour's failure to deliver on spending promises was becoming politically pressing. From April 2000 the basic rate fell from 23p to 22p – the lowest since the 1930s, Brown said, not the happiest of historical analogies. From April 1999 a new 10p rate was introduced on the first £1,500 of income, cutting the number of lower-rate taxpayers. The share of total income tax liability falling on the top 1 per cent of taxpayers – the seriously rich – remained steady but the share of tax falling on the top 10 per cent rose. (Average incomes of the top 10 per cent are not fat-cat-sized – at around £600 a week.)

Kindly put, Brown was a fiscal activist. His critics called him fidgety, fiddling with details, though that was another way of saying he strove to target impacts precisely. He ended what was left of the nonsensical Married Couples Allowance, made company cars dearer and house purchase a little harder (by cutting mortgage tax relief), penalized motorists and smokers and pushed money towards families in and out of work, pensioners and, marginally, drinkers.

He increased stamp duty on higher-value property transactions but only 5 per cent of house purchasers pay more than 1 per cent – still, Brown's receipts from stamp duties rose by £3 billion. Capital gains tax was lightened to encourage people to hold business assets longer, swelling the wealth of the rich. Companies were encouraged to give employees shares. Lord Grabiner was commissioned to review the black economy and his recommendations led to tighter Inland Revenue procedures and moves towards creating a new offence of fraudulently evading income tax. Much more attention and probably more administrative energy went into his other recommendations on clamping down on benefit fraud. For Labour, like the Tories before them, highlighting benefit fraud was preferable to pursuing tax evaders, though it was much less profitable in man-hours. Brown did exhibit some beneficence. Among his budget packages small gestures were made towards the good society, as when he removed the £250 minimum for Gift Aid tax relief and abolished the maximum for payroll giving to charity.

Labour's Thatcherite religion decreed more privatization as a source of money. Read my lips, Andrew Smith (who became Chief Secretary to the Treasury) had said in 1996, Labour will never sell the air. In office Labour insisted on selling a 46 per cent stake of National Air Traffic System (NATS) and privatizing its management – staff would get 5 per cent and the state keep 49 per cent. John Prescott gladly accepted his call-up papers to fight for this politically unattractive cause opposed by the unions and many MPs. In the background was the £623 million air traffic control centre built by NATS at Swanwick in Hampshire, due to open in January 2002 only six years later than planned, and way over budget. The Commons transport committee wondered why the service could not be run by a not-for-profit trust as in Canada. Others innocently wondered why NATS could not remain under Government control and borrow as necessary. Labour won the legal power to sell but the 2001 election may well see a decision deferred.

Brown the (residual) socialist

Brown strove to keep a progressive political reputation – his briefers portrayed him as the true keeper of the flame of equality. The experts assented. Over the four years the Institute for Fiscal Studies registered a small drop in post-tax income for the best-off tenth of households and a significant gain – 9 per cent – for the poorest tenth: more to come after April 2001. Every little helped, though dour Gordon preferred not to talk about a stealthy increase (from April 2001) in National Insurance for higher earners. At the same time, the redistributionist raised the earnings threshold at which lower-paid people would pay NI.

As for wealth: the trend in the Tory years had been towards more concentration in the upper deciles, i.e. the rich were getting richer. Wealth is hard to measure; pensions for example are in the form of claims to be made in the future. The only current figures are for 1997, when the most wealthy 10 per cent had £63,000 of assets on average versus a notional £100, or more likely nothing, for the bottom 10 per cent. During his reign, Brown did not make it any harder to inherit money. His tinkerings with capital gains may have made accumulation easier for possessors of assets. When the tally is made it could well be that the trends of the early to mid 1990s continued.

Industrial policy? God, forbid

With the November 2000 pre-budget report the Treasury published a document which just about sums up 'Brownism'. Its
watchwords were flexibility and competition. Brown developed
a style of what the Americans call jawboning – hectoring speeches
about enterprise and investment, especially in small businesses
and the inner cities. The state's role, he implied, was to cajole.
But the theory of 'endogenous' growth had to contend with
decline in manufacturing and discontent in the party heartlands.
The compromise was that, unadvertised, Brown and Stephen
Byers primed the pump by means of a growing list of funds,
grants and tax incentives.

The impact of sterling on Longbridge and Sony's Pencoed
plant in South Wales (400 jobs lost) provoked two hoary old
questions. One was about Government's role in fomenting economic change or at least healing its wounds. Was the taskforce set
up when Rover was being sold by BMW meant to bandage the
West Midlands or scout for new prospects? The other question
was why disparities in income and employment persisted
between the regions of England and countries of the United
Kingdom. In these first five years of the new century, the south
of England will grow 3 per cent a year but the north 2.4 per cent.
That is a much smaller disparity than in the past, but a sign of
imbalance still.

Brown and Blair both disliked the idea of rich south/poor
north. It did not fit the new philosophy. The Treasury put out
a paper just before the March 2000 budget talking of a great tide
of employment sweeping the country, leaving only small dry
pebbles of joblessness on the beach – and they would shortly be
washed. The tide analogy was apt. After climbing above 3 million
in the mid-80s and almost reaching the 3 million mark again in
the early 90s, the so-called claimant count of unemployed fell
steadily, pushing down in winter 2000–2001 to breach the magic
number of 1 million. Even the alternative count, based on the

Labour Force survey, showed it falling below 1.5 million, down to 5 per cent of the workforce. But one of the pebbles left behind was black and Bengali men, paid less and more prone to joblessness; another was Liverpool, Sheffield, Wirral, Sefton and other areas, within which pockets of 20 per cent plus unemployment remained. As a report from the Industrial Society said, the 'prevailing focus on welfare to work and supply-side measures are not tackling persistent local jobs gaps. These local areas lack "stickiness"; too much money flows out of the area to build the local employment infrastructure and generate much-needed new jobs'.

This did not fit Brownism, though ministers with problems in their backyards, even Trade Secretary Byers, had to agree. The Chancellor preferred to encourage enterprise and looked west for inspiration, conjuring private investment companies that would stimulate activity in run-down areas. A bulging pack-age was flung at small business: 100 per cent first-year capital allowances for investment in IT equipment; a shift to annual rather than quarterly VAT returns; £60 million to help small firms go online; tax relief for share options in order to keep key staff; a cut in corporation tax to 10 per cent – halving the previous rate and benefiting 270,000 companies. PAYE arrangements were eased, tax credits for research offered. The Inland Revenue was told to be more helpful. A Small Business Service was created in April 2000 offering support programmes worth up to £2,000 for business start-ups.

'We want more entrepreneurial women and ethnic minorities and more small firms in the regions,' Brown said, proffering 'incubators' and support through the Regional Development Agencies (RDAs). The plan for 2001 embraces tax credits on inner-city investments, a 'Social Investment Fund' to back business in the inner cities and a Phoenix venture capital fund for the regions. The RDAs had oversight of economic develop-ment in their areas but why not also, some Labour voices said, the power to stop firms going ahead with redundancies. They might even get involved – whisper it – in 'planning': spotting centres of commercial excellence, helping build up clusters of related businesses.

Another key word was 'flexibility'. Blair preached the message in Europe and it was adopted at the Lisbon summit in 2000. Brown preached it at home, for example when he addressed the Trades Union Congress in Glasgow in September 2000. It meant making it easier to employ, be employed and (logically also) become unemployed as the pattern of trade changed and companies went bust. The UK was, said Blair, the most lightly regulated labour market in the advanced world. This did not stop business complaining or the CBI turning hostile.

Work/life imbalance

Soon after taking office Labour had stoutly opposed French plans for EU-financed job creation. It mocked the French version of New Deal, which created thousands of jobs and introduced the thirty-five-hour working week to try to spread work to the workless by easing overwork for the employed. Labour did sign the Social Chapter of the Maastricht Treaty and, for the first time in a decade, TUC members squeezed through the doors of Number 10 to meet a Prime Minister privately. Labour implemented the European Working Time directive which gave some 3 million employees (various categories of workers were excluded) a maximum forty-eight-hour week with minimum four paid weeks of holiday a year and breaks. However, Britain pressed for, and was the only country to use, a clause allowing workers to 'volunteer' to work more than forty-eight hours. When asked to sign waivers by their employers 4 million workers did. The Parental Leave directive gave parents a right to up to three months off unpaid to spend with children aged under five – but the government knew very few could afford to use it in countries where such time off remained unpaid. The Part Time Work directive improved rights of part-timers, most of them women. Exempted categories were large and these were rights only in the sense that they had to be claimed by individuals or unions bold enough to beard their employers.

Family-friendly talk resulted in little family-friendly policy. Working mothers' lives often remain a feat of heroism, struggling by without a clear right to go part-time or flexi-time and without much affordable childcare. This is the real family policy challenge for a Labour second term.

The imbalance between work and domestic life probably got worse. For many mothers and fathers in employment and many workers at large, things did not appreciably get better in terms of hours or anxieties. 'Flexibility' came to mean workers adapting to employers' needs – at its worst in the notorious 'zero hours' contracts where workers were unpaid to stand by at the whim of managers. The Employment Relations Act (see below) did give employees a new right to reasonable time off to cope with family emergencies. Labour chose to do nothing as dramatic as revise the official figures to include such unpaid 'work' as shopping and childcare. This would have swelled the country's GDP by between 44 per cent and 104 per cent in 1999 if calculated as part of the national accounts – though no other countries include this either. Some concessions were made: from 2002 people looking after young children or elderly parents will see a £1 a week rise in their eventual pension for every year spent caring full-time.

Apart from flexibility, the stanchions of Labour's industrial policy were competitiveness and productivity. This did not mean, as it once had, national plans or alternative economic strategies. The party now stood firmly with the supply-siders: make markets more competitive, workers more productive and jobs and prosperity will follow. The elements of policy were education and, belatedly, reforms to skills training, outlined in Chapter 3, plus strengthening of the competition authorities and, above all, holding the macro-economic ring to create conditions of stability.

The magic additional ingredient was affectionate warmth towards business. The rhetoric was unabashed – Stephen

Byers, Trade Secretary from December 1998, said wealth creation was now more important than wealth distribution. The doors of Number 10 and Number 11 were cast wide open and the band struck up a welcome for the entry of the corporate executives.

The new Government's intention was signalled by the appointment of David Simon, chairman of BP, as Minister for Trade and Competitiveness in Europe. Business people were much sought after for taskforces and adornment. Chris Haskins of Northern Foods (a Labour supporter) headed a Cabinet Office panel on red tape, trying desperately to get the public and politicians to think more clearly about risk and how much we are prepared to pay to minimize it. Bob Ayling became a persona highly grata at Number 10, doing his bit for the Millennium Dome until it and British Airways did for him. Within days of the election Martin Taylor of Barclays was asked to become an unpaid adviser – reviewing work incentives in benefits. That Barclays' corporate strategy of closing retail outlets was detrimental to the government's social exclusion objectives was neither here nor there. Labour, like the Thatcherites, venerated business acumen.

Business did not often return the compliment. Its mouthpieces, the CBI, the Chambers of Commerce, the Federation of Small Businesses and, most raucous and unrepresentative of all, the Institute of Directors, opposed anything and everything that might slightly inconvenience them. They said the minimum wage would lose jobs, but it did not. They protested at the climate change levy, as though the fate of the planet was not a business proposition. When Adair Turner, a former SDP candidate, handed over leadership of the CBI to Digby Jones, Labour had a harder time from the Tory-tainted organs of industry.

Regulation

Brown's emphasis on competition flavoured the way Labour set about modernizing the supervision of gas, water and other utilities. The Tory arm's-length principle would be kept but new emphasis placed on protecting consumers. A Utilities bill appeared in January 2000 covering all the ex-state utilities but by Easter it had lost water and telecoms. The future was to be pragmatic, sector by sector regulation.

Water profits were down, thanks, belatedly, to some active regulating by the about-to-retire regulator Sir Ian Byatt. There was even talk (about which Labour ministers were worryingly silent) of a weird and wonderful 'remutualization' of Yorkshire Water. This basically meant hiving off the profitable bits and leaving householders under a mountain of debt.

The original task given the regulators had changed. Marketeers argued that they had outlived their usefulness: there was now competition in the supply of gas and electricity and telecoms, perhaps soon even for water. In telecoms, Oftel came under fire for not speeding up domestic access to the Internet – or rather for allowing BT to behave like a pachyderm. Labour seemed unable to think in the round about regulation – whether 'personal' regulation worked less fairly than regulation by commission, say, or how the performance of regulators might be compared across different fields, whether regulation might be replaced (in rail for example) by equity participation by the state.

Margaret Beckett produced a white paper in 1998 which affirmed that Labour policy towards industry was strictly hands-off. Self-regulation was preferred. Don Cruikshank was cheered when he criticized retail bankers but legislation to back him up seemed unlikely. Labour's Competition Act replaced the weakened Monopolies and Mergers Commission with a Competition Commission charged with blocking anti-competitive agreements between companies. The Office of Fair Trading acquired new powers and a budget increase. But how far would it judge restrictive and anti-competitive practices on wider social grounds? Not much, seems the answer, for Byers promised to remove himself from decisions on referring mergers to the Competition Commission, except in cases of national security or where OFT advice conflicted with the views of other regulators. Legislation embodying this abdication is unlikely before 2003, provided Labour gets back.

Despite creating a new regulatory body, the Financial Services Authority, Labour made only slow progress in securing redress for people mis-sold policies when the Tories had condoned a wide-boy approach to insurance and savings.

Labour extolled the 'knowledge-driven' economy as the wave of the future. The state generated much of the knowledge, spending large amounts on science and technology through the research councils and the universities. Under Labour the science budget was eventually boosted, even to the extent of giving the helots of the system, postgraduates, a much-needed rise in grant to £9,000 a year. Investment in the science base, thanks to generous additional investment by the Wellcome Trust, expanded by £1 billion. Labour's price was, like the Tories before them, easier passage of science out of the lab into commerce. New funds were set up to back university projects that linked with business. This was safe territory for Labour, going all the way back to Harold Wilson's white heat.

Trickier was how companies ran, made decisions and – the corporate sector's holy of holies – remunerated directors. Labour was bashful, despite soaring boardroom pay. A promised white paper on modernizing company law was long in gestation.

Tidying up, the government delivered legal changes to recognize e-signatures. As for snail mail, Labour eventually decided to retain the Post Office as a state enterprise, a publicly owned plc, committed to universal deliveries and keeping a network of post offices. Here was a classic instance of Labour's social objectives clashing with market forces. Village life and the fight against social exclusion in the cities depend on branch post offices which were threatened by the removal of benefit payments from the post office counters – 40 per cent of their income. It was one of the issues that caused that damaging slow hand-clap for Tony Blair by the ladies of the Women's Institute. Promises were made about some other kind of subsidy, perhaps a Post-Office-based people's bank.

Workers and consumers

Labour was traditionally more a producers' than a consumers' party. It made proposals to restrain gazumping in house purchase and promoted better information for consumers. But the slow speed at which council trading standards offices – a key to improving retail standards – got their Internet act together was indicative of the lack of dynamism in pushing public authorities online. The trouble with saying consumers needed new rights was that it suggested powerfully that they were being ripped off by private business and Labour did not like such contradictions. More in tune with the mood was the launch in April 2000 of a new all-employee share ownership plan, offering tax breaks to encourage companies big and small to offer shares to staff. Similar warm thoughts about the system lay behind the creation of new 'partnership agreements' between staff (unionized or not) and management; only some 265 were made in the twelve months to September 2000. The Government also contributed to a fund to train managers and employee representatives in togetherness. It is hard to say whether this had any effect on productivity, profit or employee happiness.

Trade unions were not entirely spectres at the Blair feast. Since 1980 the proportion of wages set through collective bargaining had fallen from 70 per cent to 35 per cent (in 1998); only 18 per cent of young workers – aged 18–29 – were union members; unions had failed to establish themselves in the new economy. But they remained too big to ignore, with one in three employees unionized (compared with one in ten in allegedly militant France). From a union viewpoint, the score-card had its minuses – Government opposition to an EU directive on information and consultation in the workplace for instance. Pluses included the establishment of the Low Pay Commission. Labour accepted its eventual recommendation of a £3.60 a week minimum wage, with a lower rate for younger employees. It was disappointingly little but a milestone none the less – the accepted figure was nowhere near the 50 per cent of men's median earnings which had been the Labour Party's original position. The minimum wage came into force in April 1999, hardly revolutionary since the US, the heart of capitalism, had a minimum wage decades ago. The Low Pay Commission was kept in business and the minimum increased to £3.70 in October 2000, with a promised rise to £4 an hour in 2001. But by no means all employers played ball. A survey in April 2000 showed 250,000 adults still being paid below the minimum along with 50,000 18–21-year-olds.

Labour's big measure was the Employment Relations Act which extended paid maternity leave to eighteen weeks for all employment – that still left the UK with one of the lowest rates in Europe. The Act reduced from two years to one the minimum qualifying period for an employee to be protected against unfair dismissal. The maximum limits on damages that industrial tribunals could award for unfair dismissal were lifted from £12,000 to £50,000. The limit was removed on awards for unfair dismissals relating to health and safety or to the Public Interest Act 1998 – Labour's useful new charter to encourage whistle-blowers.

A critical promise made by Labour to the unions which had once given it birth as a party was redeemed – they acquired a statutory right to be recognized for the first time. If more than 50 per cent of workplace employees were union members, recognition would be automatic. If, when balloted, 40 per cent or more of employees voted for union representation, unions were in. These were not inconsiderable advances for workers' rights.

Conclusion

Labour gets a gold star for rectifying the UK's finances. The public sector, as the economists put it, had emerged from the 1992 recession unbalanced, spending out of kilter with taxing and borrowing. That was put right by Kenneth Clarke's spending restraint and tax increases followed – seamlessly – by Gordon Brown. But Clarke cynically admitted that the promises made by the Tories before the 1997 election would not have been kept – especially its plans to restrain spending yet further. So Brown probably kept spending tighter than the Tories would have done, though according to past patterns no doubt they would have spent very differently – tax cuts before services. Needing money, he kept taxing too, albeit stealthily.

The Organization for Economic Cooperation and Development (OECD) judged the UK under Blair to possess an 'enviable' record. The UK economy, said this fount of neo-liberal thinking, was less prone to boom and bust than it had been under Thatcher in the 80s. Low inflation was entrenched. The rate of unemployment compatible with stable prices fell.

So Labour realized – temporarily? – Tony Crosland's old dream of floating the public services on an expanding economy. Of course growth is never reliable. Collapse in the Far East in 1997 had threatened a global slowdown. But by Easter 1998 the worst was over and the curves ticked upwards again. Brown's macro-economic stewardship was not magical but, in the circumstances, was sound enough.

Wise owls say Chancellors always misjudge where precisely they sit on the economic cycle. Spending is to rise hugely during the first five years of the century. If total demand is not to rise faster than the trend rate of growth, about 2.5 per cent a year, then private consumption will have to be kept to a growth rate of some 2 per cent a year, less than half the rate it was growing during the two years to April 2001. In layman's terms that means – whisper it – taxation. Still, if the American economy imploded or oil sheiks precipitated recession, the UK economy would be in fair shape to weather the resulting storms. That, at least, is what the captain said: 'Even when tested by events like rising oil prices our resolve will be constant. Instead of returning to stop go we must build from stability to achieve what I believe is now the prize within our grasp – US levels of productivity and thus long-term prosperity for all.'

That was Brown's boast. But how is he going to do it, when UK trend productivity growth was still only 2 per cent a year, its long-term historical average? In a letter to the CBI and TUC in October 2000 Brown said that 'government can sometimes do best by getting out of the way'. That fine statement of neo-liberalism (defeatism?) gives no recipe for securing the change in economic performance Labour, after four years, is still promising.

6

Blair Abroad

There were times when Tony Blair, high-minded champion of human rights, seemed an innocent abroad, with a little ginger Sancho Panza at his side. Yet there were other times when Blair's toughness, a born leader's willingness to use deadly force, belied his inexperience – and there was Robin Cook at Yasser Arafat's side, a courageous would-be mediator as Israeli shells fell in Gaza in October 2000.

If foreign affairs in the Blair era had a theme, it was how far human rights could be asserted in a post-Cold-War world. With bipolarity gone and the United States hegemonic, fissures opened for death and dispute within nations and regions – Fiji, Sierra Leone, the Balkans, Kashmir and of course, again, the Middle East. How was the rhetoric of rights to be wielded within such bodies as the World Trade Organization and the International Monetary Fund, now openly challenged in Seattle, then in Prague, for their systemic biases? Look around at contemporary examples of regional conflict, abuse of rights, poverty and inequality and you may be tempted to say, with the apostles of Realpolitik, 'twas ever thus, Labour made no difference. To even hint that things have got better is to provoke hubris.

Yet it is fair to say that on Labour's watch the world did take a few stumbling steps towards greater mutual responsibility for human rights and human welfare: the presence of Blair in Number 10 and Robin Cook at the Foreign Office did help the process along. Perhaps the very facility with which Labour resorted to the language of rights was itself progress. The speech delivered by Tony Blair in Chicago in the middle of the Kosovo bombing evoked high principles. But the reality of negotiation and Whitehall strife between competing departments made much of that talk look hollow.

So does Labour's conduct of foreign affairs turn out to be any more principled than what went before? Visits to China in pursuit of trade went on, Tiananmen Square forgotten; Britain remained as ambivalent as ever in the conflict between India and Pakistan over Kashmir. Yet Gordon Brown's leadership on the question of forgiving the external debt of the very poor countries did precipitate a round of debt reduction. Blair galvanized European diplomacy during the Balkans crisis and Cook proved himself by stimulating intervention by the Australians in East Timor. Labour went to war in Kosovo (and Iraq) in pursuit of moral goals; but it stood and watched in Chechnya. Labour upped the ante with ethical talk, but when all was said and done there remained scores of Labour MPs with defence installations in their constituencies who knew what the military-industrial status quo was good for.

As throughout this book, the fairest grounds for judging Blair and colleagues have to be their expressed intentions. Did they better integrate foreign policy with trade and defence objectives? Yes. Did they make the UK a player, mobilizing the UK's striking (and strikingly anachronistic) position within Nato, the EU, the Security Council, the nuclear club, and the Commonwealth, that ex-colonial sin-bin? That is harder to judge. The UK punched above its objective weight, but then it had for years – that is its post-war party trick. What we need to assess in this chapter is, first, whether a distinctly British spoor can be detected in foreign affairs and, second, whether it leads however falteringly in the direction of the good.

As with Europe, Tony Blair and Robin Cook did not wage a *popular* foreign policy – they failed at critical points to convey their intent, shying away when sniped at by an isolationist or Atlanticist press. An intellectually cogent review of defence obligations was soon undermined by the temptations of power, deploying force that could not be sustained and going ahead with a weapon (the Eurofighter) for the sake of industrial and diplomatic objectives running contrary to the adopted strategy. Labour talked, in one of the first open debates about the UK's foreign profile ever, of 'rebranding' the country as modern and 'cool' – Gordon Ramsay, Vivienne Westwood and all. But why then keep ageing Trident submarines? Why should the UK accommodate the destabilizing American National Missile Defense system without so much as a peep?

In their pre-election master-class Peter Mandelson and Roger Liddle had couched foreign policy in terms of maximizing the UK's advantage in possessing the English language, trading on the reputation of the BBC, the RSC and the universities. A report from the Demos think-tank published four months after the election in 1997 talked of a new identity for the UK overseas – fewer Beefeaters, more high tech and Hoxton clubs. Heathrow and Dover were to be overhauled to offer a 'stunning welcome' to travellers (except illegal immigrants or asylum-seekers). The Foreign Office itself, bastion of secret diplomacy, talked of bringing international policy to people through the use of open forums and the latest ICT; it even stumped up £12 million for the electronic delivery of information and services overseas, including (none so far operating) Internet-based information kiosks in strategic locations around the globe.

A new spirit blew in the BBC's Bush House – at last Tory cuts in World Service funding were repaired and, from April 2001 on, real spending would rise. We always were the party of internationalism, Labour said, hence under us the UK will be well placed to benefit from this 'global age'. But first the past had to be dealt with and Blair had no compunction about apologizing. A royal visit to India in 1998 saw the Queen expressing regret (to Prince Philip's evident chagrin) in Amritsar at the site of a 1919 massacre by colonial troops. Blair did the same over the mid-nineteenth-century Irish famine. The Elgin marbles would, however, stay in Bloomsbury.

An ethical foreign policy

Ethical foreign policy, as it was immediately dubbed, was launched on 17 July 1997 with a media spectacular at the Foreign Office. The walls resounded with language that harked way back to Ramsay MacDonald and the Labour Party's early years – though it also echoed declarations by President Jimmy Carter and indeed Tory Foreign Secretary Douglas Hurd, who in 1992 had established the first human rights policy unit within the Foreign Office. The Government committed itself to support human rights worldwide. All nations belonged to the same moral community, which imposed on the UK an obligation to seek to secure for others rights enjoyed at home. Indeed, to be consistent, the Government was moving quickly to incorporate the European Convention on Human Rights in what became the Human Rights Act 1998. Robin Cook set out twelve steps that would 'put Britain at the front of the drive to raise standards of human rights'. (This never was a government to let hyperbole get in the way of exaggerating its story.) He proposed to condemn regimes which grotesquely violated their citizens' rights and support sanctions against them. Weapons would not be supplied from the UK to be used for internal repression and the UK would support a permanent international criminal court.

No sooner uttered than compromised. The Americans, potent allies, tried to veto the international court. A licence for the export of six armoured Land Rovers to Indonesia was refused but the sale, worth £300 million, of Hawk jets and other kit went ahead. The former, it was said, could be used for domestic repression by the Suharto government but not the latter. It was a specious distinction. A subsequent decision to ban Indonesian arms exports in October (worth £1 million) did not improve matters since it was followed by approval for surveillance and communications equipment. After all, at the end of 1996 the UK had been the world's second largest arms exporter, with annual exports worth £5.1 billion (that is some 25 per cent of the global export market); at home the industry employed 415,000 people of whom some 90,000 probably depended on exports for their livelihood. Labour banned the export of any form of anti-personnel landmine – those fetching pictures of the Princess of Wales – and equipment that might be used for torture. 'Thanks to Labour no British soldier on operations will ever lay a single anti-personnel landmine again.'

The problem was consistency. The UK armaments industry did not suddenly collapse. The Scott report, about which Labour in Opposition had made so much noise, had commented on the sketchy nature of legislative control of arms exports; in power Labour promiscuously used 'gagging orders' (public interest immunity certificates) to conceal the involvement of the intelligence services in the supply of arms to Iraq under the Tories. Arms control legislation was mooted, but did not appear in the final Queen's speech. Labour did produce two annual reports on strategic export controls, claiming they made the UK the most transparent country in Europe on arms-licensing decisions. Having endorsed the Nuclear Non-Proliferation Treaty (something of a dead duck given nuclear enthusiasm in south Asia), Labour said it was complying fully with biological and chemical weapons conventions; a government paper set out a £270 million action plan for investment in research and medical countermeasures.

Cook's 17 July statement singled out human rights abuses in Iraq and Nigeria but did not mention Tibet, China, or the role of Indian security forces in Kashmir or an Indian constitution which made advocacy of the province's secession a criminal offence. Realpolitik trumped Blairite idealism. The Chinese received Hong Kong, without any concessions on UK citizenship beyond what the Tories had agreed. How much consistency should we fairly expect in public policy? Yet Labour must be credited with raising consciousness over human rights.

Dangerous, some might say, if it also raised expectations of specific action by the UK Government: that implicit promise was soon to be tested. Rights were in the air. During a chance visit to London by Augusto Pinochet, a Spanish magistrate's warrant was executed by the Metropolitan Police with, we must assume, the tacit approval of the Home Office. The consequences were lengthy court proceedings, the humbling of the judicial committee of the House of Lords and Home Secretary Jack Straw's embarrassment, none of which could be foreseen.

Straw's eventual decision to send Pinochet back to Chile rather than to face a possible trial in Spain looked like a cop-out, but by then a kind of justice had been done: proud Pinochet had been declared a suitable case for litigation in the courts of the civilized world and real or feigned old-age incapacity was his only defence. Perhaps civil society and legal procedure in Chile also benefited; after his return the courts there found that in principle he had no immunity. The courts, here, were found wanting. With a lofty inadvertence, Lord Hoffman sat to hear the initial case against Pinochet. But Amnesty International was joined in the suit and Hoffman, probably to his credit, had a prior connection with the charity. The case had to be reheard with a different band of judges. One disgraceful anomaly, hang-over of a colonial past, meant members of the judicial committee of the House of Lords continued to approve death sentences in former colonies in their role as Privy Council appeal judges.

While the Pinochet case progressed, however, the human rights of the growing number of asylum-seekers arriving in the UK, often as a result of regional instability in Africa, south-east Europe and Asia, were held to belong to a different discourse. Chapter 8 assesses the Blair record here. Imperfection in one quarter does not mean a government is not capable of heroic effort in another, and this is probably how we should judge Blair in the Balkans.

'I intervene therefore I am'

In the aftermath of the Kosovo war Dominique Moisi, the French foreign affairs writer, amended Descartes: these days, he said, it should be 'I intervene therefore I am.' This comes close to Blair's position as the Kosovo crisis unfolded. To intervene, despite cost and political danger, was an expression of political identity. Polling guru Philip Gould called the military campaign against Serbia 'the great crisis' but it went unremarked at the time as a grand test, perhaps showing how quickly Blair had acquired confidence in office.

The writer Timothy Garton Ash called Kosovo the last European war of the twentieth century and Nato's first. It was a chapter of mistakes. Nato and the European Union misjudged both Slobodan Milosevic and the mettle of the Serbian people. (It was not until they forced Milosevic's departure after the 2000 presidential election that it became apparent that their experience of Nato bombing did stiffen their resolve to be rid of him.) The Kosovo campaign was a military failure; the allies' tactics were deficient and they lacked a post-war strategy. But Kosovo was also a triumph for the human rights doctrine enunciated by Labour and for Blair himself. He proved himself as a war leader, using the Whitehall machinery with aplomb. As Professor Peter Hennessy noted, no previous post-war premier, barring colonial emergencies, had fought two wars (the Gulf and Kosovo) inside six months. Like prime ministers before him, Blair by-passed MPs. He had sought specific approval in the Commons for the use of military force against Iraq should the occasion arise but did not refresh the mandate. There was cabinet discussion prior to operations in Kosovo (more debate about Kosovo than the budget, one member quipped) and Blair offered regular updates. But Parliament and public opinion were never enthused and pollster Gould noted how remarkably quickly these events faded from public and political imagination.

To recap: Belgrade had imposed direct rule on the constituent Yugoslav province of Kosovo in 1989, provoking an Albanian insurgency. Remnant Yugoslavia (Serbia in effect), apparently emboldened after the settlement of Bosnia, undertook a campaign against the Kosovo Liberation Army (KLA) in 1998, producing refugees, death and mayhem. It nullified the effort by international bodies to monitor and protect inside Kosovo. In

June 1998 Cook issued a 'last warning' to temporizing Milosevic, though the Americans were lead negotiators and a deal was struck in October. The massacre of Albanian country-people at Racak in January 1999 precipitated a series of events embracing last-minute talks at Rambouillet in France in February which failed. So the bombing of Serbian targets began on 24 March.

The UK Government played a significant part in ensuring the military action took place and in holding together the coalition of Nato and EU members. Argument has since raged over whether Nato bombing caused massive flows of refugees or whether the expulsion of the indigenous population of large tracts of Kosovo by Serbian forces began before Nato pulled the trigger. Garton Ash's judgement will probably stand the test of time: after the expulsion of the UN 'verification mission' and (confirmed by German intelligence) large-scale movement of Serbian forces, 'a humanitarian disaster was already there'. Numbers of victims have since been scaled back. The International Criminal Tribunal estimated in August 2000 that the total number of Albanians killed by the Serbs in Kosovo was 3,000, not the 10,000 announced by Nato.

In its manifesto Labour had promised to help establish a permanent international criminal court under the UN. Interim tribunals were established to examine war crimes in Yugoslavia and Rwanda. The UK paid for a new court building in The Hague and British forces played no inconsiderable role in arresting suspected war criminals in Bosnia. The UK took a lead at the Rome conference in July 1998 which adopted a statute for a permanent court and became one of the eighty-one countries which signed up; the court is some way off still, depending on ratification of the statute by sixty states.

In its early-twentieth-century incarnation as an idealist social-ist party Labour had always wanted to believe in international action, institutionalized in the League of Nations then the United Nations. Left-wing critics stirred by the Kosovo war made much of the lack of UN sanction for the action. Blair and Cook did indeed seek legal expedients to get round the absence of a

Security Council resolution, which is why officially it was never a 'war'. The UN could never act against Chinese or Russian interests – they had vetoes on the security council – and they were deemed to be at stake in the Balkans. In a trade-off between acting for the good and observing UN procedure, practicality won – for the good.

In hindsight the conduct of the war was little short of a farce. Targets had to be agreed between Nato ambassadors and were probably telegraphed to the Serbs in advance. The American imperative of avoiding casualties dictated high-level bombing with limited effect. The assault on the Chinese embassy in Belgrade gave an impression of incompetence. Post-battle analysis confirmed that only a tiny number of Serbian tanks were hit.

But looked at another way – and Blair bears much credit for this – the very fact that this unprecedentedly plural coalition held together was remarkable. Blairite rhetoric played a part in stiffening resolve. In Germany the Social Democrats and the pacifist Greens stayed the course. In Rome daily demonstrations against the use of Italian bases for bombing Serbia shook but did not break a fragile administration. This was a stretching test of European unity but, as the conflict wore on, the coalition if anything got stronger.

Nato held its fiftieth anniversary summit in Washington amid footage of military impotence. By late April 1999, as long urged by Blair, ground forces at last became a practical threat. President Clinton's achievement was to get the Russians to put pressure on Milosevic, proving that all along a convincing threat could have stayed his hand: he was, as events a year later proved, a rational calculator who would move when he had to. A Commons defence committee study commended Blair's role but pointed out military shortcomings, the cluster bombs of limited value and the paucity of UK aircraft (they were busy bombing Saddam, said the MOD).

Kosovo resolved nothing for keeps, either in the Balkans or in terms of the principled bases of intervention. Dictators and strongmen will rise again. Garton Ash concluded that the West is structurally incapable of threatening them in advance. 'Western liberal societies that care more about stopping gross violations of human rights in other countries also have the most difficulty in willing the means best suited to achieve that end. This is our post-Kosovo dilemma.' Yet the charge probably sits more lightly on the Blair Government than other European governments. For a prime minister who had spent his leisure hours as a student managing a rock band rather than parading with the OTC, Blair handled military emergencies with calm authority. When faced with difficult calls – such as the rescue of soldiers kidnapped by rebels in Sierra Leone – he seems not to have hesitated.

That West African nation was another test. If the UK could not help restore peace in Sierra Leone with its 4 million people, international development secretary Clare Short said, what hope was there for Congo or Sudan? The former British colony, independent since 1961, had been founded in 1787 as a refuge for freed slaves. It was the largest per capita recipient of UK aid in Africa and British military assistance remained significant. International sanctions had been applied against it from October 1997 after a military coup; these included a UN-sponsored arms embargo. But deposed president Kabbah won promises of Commonwealth support and in 1998 hired a London security company, Sandline International, to provide arms and mercenaries to fight Revolutionary United Front (RUF) rebels. The contract contravened the embargo but was privately encouraged by the British High Commission in Freetown. After a Customs investigation of Sandline a political row broke and a parliamentary inquiry followed, the results prematurely leaked to Cook. The official investigation into Sandline by Sir Thomas Legg, a former civil servant, exonerated ministers. It was an example of policy-making of the kind Labour wanted to leave behind: good intentions but illegal methods and lots of official deniability.

In February 1998 a West African force restored the Kabbah government, leading to a peace accord. But in April 2000 RUF rebels, keepers of the lucrative diamond-producing territory, captured UN peacekeeping troops. The Blair Government mobilized a force of paratroops and Marines, secured Freetown airport and helped capture the RUF leader Foday Sankoh. Was the commitment temporary or permanent? UN resolutions banning the sale of so-called blood diamonds and permitting the international trial of Sankoh did not secure order. A 250-strong British contingent remained to train Sierra Leone Government forces. But in August 2000 the RUF held eleven of them hostage. Blair approved a successful rescue operation and more troops were committed, the long-run prognosis for such military assistance as unclear as ever. Securing the peace would take long enough; rebuilding a state and a civil society – not jobs at which soldiers are skilled – would take longer.

This was another example of disinterested good done by the Blair Government, but with as much stealth as they could. Instead of proclaiming their good intentions, or even their success, they fudged and mumbled when under sustained attack by the right-wing press for intervening in a place with no financial or power interest for Britain.

Defence

Sierra Leone was a textbook example of inter-service 'rapid reaction'. 'In future,' said the script, 'littoral operations and force projection, for which maritime forces are well suited, will be our primary focus. These tasks, which range from the evacuation of citizens from an overseas crisis to major war-fighting operations as part of a joint force, will be highly demanding.' The script was Labour's *Strategic Defence Review*, published in July 1998. It was meant to supply an answer to the question: what for, what military objectives was the UK pursuing in the post-Cold-War world? Questions abounded, such as why did the UK invest so much in an above-par presence on the European mainland and an 'independent' nuclear capacity?

Labour's 1997 manifesto promised to keep the Trident nuclear system (while pushing for multilateral reductions in nuclear weaponry) and a strong defence industry (while pushing for diversification to civilian uses). The review did not, no surprise, produce any fundamental reasons for all this but as such exercises go it was a lot better than recent precedents.

While the review was still cooking, the RAF decommissioned the last of its atomic bombs deliverable by aircraft, making the Trident submarine force the sole carrier of the British 'deterrent'. The review authorized four Trident-carrying boats but reduced their stock of warheads by a third, from 300 to 200. A blow for open government was struck when the review disclosed the size of UK stockpiles of the plutonium and uranium needed to prime them. What was less obvious was where the submarine missiles were to be targeted, now that the Soviet Union was not supposed to be at the rainbow's end of their trajectory. Where, too, did the expensive Eurofighter fit in all this, beyond giving work to UK industry (at £1 million a job) and keeping European allies sweet?

And what if British forces started fighting and had to dig in while at the same time there were calls for intervention in another, distant place – a disaster, evacuation from Zimbabwe, further breakdown in a potential site of conflict? HMS *Ocean* (the helicopter-carrier cruising off Freetown) could not be in two places at once. It could not even carry the scores of fighters the RAF had ordered; nor can the next generation of carriers now on the draughtsman's block. That probably would mean buying sea-transportable American aircraft. Labour, like its predecessors, was still unwilling to cut its defence coat according to the cloth available to a second-rank power. The review's analysis of risks (ethnic and religious conflict, environmental pressure) was sound enough. What was less clear was the case for the exceptional size of UK defence spending, relative to the rest of Europe, except France.

The armed forces' 'missions' boiled down to peace support and humanitarian operations, regional conflicts inside and outside the Nato area and the amorphous 'support to wider British interests'. Two new aircraft carriers were needed 'to deploy more rapidly to trouble spots around the globe'. A new Joint Rapid Reaction Force clearly fitted the new dispensation with promises of greater mobility, better transport and back-up. This new emphasis on logistics was welcome, since the Tories, short-term in outlook for all their pretensions to be the pro-defence party, had raided this area for cost savings.

Beyond the Army's continuing presence in Northern Ireland, resources would permit contributing to an operation of Gulf War size plus a simultaneous but smaller deployment to some other crisis. It was 'tough-minded', in the cynical sense that pre-election aspirations towards defence diversification were forgotten; emphasis was instead put on technology transfer from defence projects to civilian industry and closer cooperation with the private sector across the board, including new 'smart' procurement.

In its own terms, the review was a success. No admirals walked the plank, no air chief marshals blitzed Downing Street in protest, despite a planned reduction in the proportion of GDP devoted to defence from 2.7 per cent in 1998–9 to 2.4 per cent in 2001–2 (it got money back in the 2000 spending plan). Officers were later to voice concerns that the fighting forces were losing their cutting edge by having so much humanitarian work to do. But the same type of officer kept remarkably silent (compared to what happened in the United States) when Labour lifted the ban on homosexuals serving with the armed forces, using a September 1999 ruling by the European Court of Human Rights as its pretext.

Keeping the Americans sweet

However, Labour still did not answer the key question: why was UK defence spending still so high, comparatively speaking? No other EU country, bar France, spent anything like as much. One answer, never spelled out, was that big defence impressed the Americans enough to keep them interested in defending Europe.

Especially the UK's nuclear missiles: Labour ministers held to the mysterious doctrine that they were somehow an insurance – not against nuclear strikes on London by agents unknown but against American isolationism. Blair, friend of Bill, was going to do nothing to upset the special relationship. This included, where necessary, silent complicity in American folly.

Until Bill Clinton deferred questions of deployment while continuing with tests, the Americans had proposed a new missile system which would have required new installations on UK territory. In the post-Cold-War world, American defence planners feared for 'rogues' with nuclear capability. The response was a $60 billion son-of-Star-Wars, the Strategic Defense Initiative proposed by Ronald Reagan in 1983. National Missile Defense was a system of ballistic missiles designed either to hit incoming missiles or disrupt and destroy them by nearby mid-air explosions. American alarm had been triggered by the surprise launch of a North Korean missile over Japan in 1998: the North Koreans evidently had a three-stage solid fuel rocket with the potential to reach the United States. The Iranians had a missile with a 1,300-kilometre reach; the Indians had warheads and rockets, too. Saddam's Iraq could develop a long-range capacity if sanctions were lifted.

But the question hanging over any new American missile deployment was whether it could counter the ballistic arsenals still held by Russia and growing in China. That called into question the 1972 Anti Ballistic Missile Treaty, which prohibited the Russians and Americans from building nationwide defences against each other's long-range missiles. The failure of American tests in the South Pacific in July 2000 deferred the hard questions till after the presidential election. The question for Blair – as for any UK Prime Minister – was whether they are just bystanders or whether they should actively collaborate in American projects designed with the interests of the UK far from anyone's mind. The protests over Cruise missiles at Greenham Common would be nothing compared to the protests against any British deployment of a missile system that seriously jeopardizes global stability.

Special relationships

Blair's personal relations with Bill Clinton were excellent, but to what effect? Blair did not seek to move the UK away from its traditional deference to American interests. Not a squeak was heard after American strikes against alleged terrorist bases in Sudan and Afghanistan beyond unequivocal approbation by Blair.

So too over Iraq. Labour wore the Tories' clothes without blushing. The UK refused to define Iraq as a purely regional question, in which case the emphasis would need to shift to healing the sore of Palestinian–Israeli relations. Nor was it a world problem, for in that case the non-participation of the world in garrisoning the Gulf was a scandal. The war to get Iraq out of Kuwait having been won by the 'United Nations' – the United States with small support from allies – became a US–UK effort to maintain pressure on Saddam's regime. The UN Special Commission (UNSCOM) set up in 1991 by the UN Security Council to monitor the elimination of Iraq's weapons of mass destruction was being subverted. Saddam played cat and mouse during 1998. The French, Russians and China applauded. Despite Kofi Annan, the UN Secretary-General, UNSCOM was pushed out in October 1998. After clear threats, bombing by the US–UK Gulf forces followed in operation Desert Fox. This was, said Cook, entirely in accord with UN Security Council resolution 1284, which provided for suspension of sanctions if Iraqi arms could be monitored.

Nothing changed on the ground in Baghdad, where weapons development probably goes on; the Iraqis showed no sign of accepting UNSCOM's successor, the UN Monitoring, Verification and Inspection Commission. The petrol crisis of autumn 2000 gave the Iraqis, sitting on top of a large chunk of the world's proven oil reserves, greater leverage still. The religious leaders and humanitarians urging the lifting of sanctions may be joined by motorists.

To paint Blair and Cook as lackeys of the United States would be unfair. Over East Timor, the physical limits of UK power were evident but diplomatic effort independent of the Americans bore some fruit, with an Australian-led peacekeeping operation securing the liberation of this fragment of a disintegrating Indonesia. Cook, who survived the media scandal surrounding his adultery and divorce, was able to offer something, even in those theatres where British military involvement was entirely out of the question, such as Israel. During the UK presidency, Cook had gone to Israel wearing an EU hat only to offend the Israelis by appearing to criticize Israel's encroachment on the West Bank lands. The EU, sadly, was all but invisible when Palestine blew up in 2000; Cook's offer of good offices simply exposed the limits of that kind of bilateralism.

Lengthy diplomacy secured the trial in the Netherlands under Scottish legal jurisdiction of two Libyans accused of planting the bomb which destroyed the Pan Am plane over Lockerbie in 1989. As a second-rank power the UK had to tread a fine line between impotence and braggadocio. UK honest broking and good offices were sometimes compromised by the colonial past, sometimes welcome. Where Blair took a lead – for example in his wooing of Vladimir Putin, who replaced Boris Yeltsin as Russian President in May 2000 – human rights policy was left far behind. Such calculated gambles are intended, of course, to secure national interests but they may also contribute to stability.

Two large questions hung over Blairite international activity. One was the balance between Europe and America. The other was the British contribution to rethinking the architecture of the post-Cold-War world. Was Europe to become united enough to act as a counterbalancing political bloc?

On the eve of the United Nations millennium summit in New York in September 2000, Tony Blair put his name to an article along with the Dutch and German premiers claiming an emerging consensus around Third Way beliefs. The circle of 'winners' in the new economy should be widened, civil society strengthened; it argued for an international social compact promoting debt relief for poor countries and global pollution control. It promised the emergence of Europe as the most dynamic, knowledge-based economy in the world by 2010, thanks to (neo-liberal) reforms in capital, product and labour markets. Allowing for press secretary hyperbole, it was a noteworthy intervention, as much for what it did not say as for what it did. Did Blair believe Europe should become a bloc to challenge the US? Sometimes yes, sometimes no. Was this just an example of his rather jejune faith in universal 'modernization', exhibited during his visit to China in October 1998 when he appeared to embrace Chinese Prime Minister Zhu Rongji as a kind of oriental Third Wayer?

Trade and aid

What implications did the Blair vision have for world trade and financial order – was he after a kind of socialized neo-liberalism? By late 2000, defenders of the neo-liberal status quo such as the Organization for Economic Cooperation and Development (OECD) were feeling beleaguered. Protests at the World Trade Organization (WTO) summit in Seattle in December the previous year and at the joint annual meeting of the World Bank and International Monetary Fund (IMF) in Prague unsettled a world order. Labour had few big thoughts to offer on the transition – if that was what it was. At the 1997 Commonwealth Heads of Government Meeting (CHOGM), the UK put much emphasis on free trade and open markets but also, implicitly, on active government. Labour had been fairly passive over the proposed Multilateral Accord on Investment, an American-inspired effort to break down barriers to corporate investment worldwide – it broke down in October 1998. On the WTO, the UK after Seattle still wanted a multilateral trade round – coordinated tariff reductions – as the basis for global economic growth but it also wanted the WTO to be 'more transparent' and appreciative of the rights of developing countries.

It is easy to mock this kind of official speak. Labour should, however, be credited with seeing how intertwined foreign and trade policy had become. In May 1999, British Trade International was set up to 'join up' services provided to business by both the Foreign Office and the DTI.

Clare Short, following the Prime Minister, more than once hailed globalization as, on balance, a force for good; she would have no truck with green activists who condemn development for others while themselves wearing Nike trainers and carrying mobile phones to organize protests over the Internet. Globalization, she wrote in the *New Statesman* in May 2000, is not necessarily benign; the poor may be marginalized. But it provided an opportunity to millions to move out of poverty: with the right policies, for example massive investment in education and openness to inward investment, growth was possible, as the east Asian 'tigers' had shown. So, if trade and investment and transnational corporations were parts of the solution, the UK was in no mood to press for fundamental changes in the organizations responsible for international financial and economic management. Indeed Short's public criticisms were directed against the UN and its agencies. The UK would use its donations to reward performance and penalize failure. UK support of the UN Development Programme would increase to £35 million a year from 2001 and support of UNICEF to £15 million a year over three years. But UNESCO would get no more until it took primary education in developing countries more seriously.

Before development could take place there had to be peace and order. Money would be available for improving UN peace-keeping performance. The Government, with Liberal Democrat support, launched a proposal for a UN military staff college; Cook said the UK would be a good home, given national expertise in peacekeeping. Active intervention in order to establish then uphold the peace, said Cook, had superseded the UN's former more passive truce-monitoring activities. It needed the force to act with determination. In parallel but without success the UK backed reform of the Security Council, to include Japan and Germany and more developing countries.

Clare Short was an *enfant terrible* of the Blair administration but her reputation should not obscure some considerable achievements in development assistance. The creation of her Department for International Development (DfID) led to the first white paper in the field since the Wilson Government in 1975 (*Eliminating World Poverty*, November 1997). Short was right, if undiplomatic, in her insistence that European Union aid went to poor people, not intermediaries. Thanks to her and Gordon Brown the UK took a forward position over cancelling debt owed to Western governments by poor countries. Labour first cancelled all Overseas Development Assistance loans, then abolished debt to the UK Government owed by all countries that applied through the Highly Indebted Poor Countries (HIPC) Trust Fund, including debt owed to the Export Credit Guarantee Department. The total package was worth some £5 billion – but cancellation had the proviso that money saved was to be used for social priorities. The government of Zimbabwe considered its social priority to be the expropriation of white-owned commercial farms. Labour's insistence that compensation for land reform would be paid only if it benefited the poorest in Zimbabwe rather than Robert Mugabe's cronies was strengthened by Mugabe's thuggish tactics during the 2000 parliamentary election.

Labour promised – all the main parties did – eventually to attain the UN target for aid of 0.7 per cent of GDP. In the Tories' last year in power the Overseas Development Administration, by then back inside the Foreign Office, commanded 0.26 per cent of GDP. Short's programme accepted the 1992 Rio targets on reducing poverty, mortality and gender disparity in education. But the white paper was short on financial commitments; it kept the provision that UK aid meant purchases from the UK. The 1998 Comprehensive Spending Review increased DfID's budget, but only from 0.26 per cent to 0.3 per cent of GDP. In 1999, therefore, the UK was well down the aid league, below France (0.38 per cent) and the Netherlands (0.79 per cent). The world's bastion of neo-liberalism, the USA, contributed just 0.10 per cent.

In Labour's self-estimation, four years of Blair had seen the UK repositioned at the crux of alliances and international politics. An exaggeration of course, but it contained a truth recognized by impartial observers: under Blair and Cook the UK had been refashioned as 'a more multilaterally minded, ethically motivated international player' with a much more constructive view of relations with the poor countries of the south. Blair certainly had the vision. A fully-fledged doctrine had been set out by the Prime Minister in the middle of the Kosovo war in his Chicago speech. Globalization was not only an economic but also a security and human rights phenomenon; the institutions of the international community were sometimes too weak, so intervention on the side of good – unilateral if necessary – was not only justified in principle but a moral imperative for a decent nation. There could be no ethical foreign policy without that resolve. What did not follow, however, was the education of the British public in what the vision entailed, for defence spending, for European integration or for the potential costs of future intervention.

7

Europe

Had Tony Blair truly wanted to make the UK a leader in Europe, there was no better time. A month after Labour's victory, the French socialists took power, leaving the right fractured for years to come. Despite big differences (Premier Lionel Jospin had Communists and Greens in his coalition), Paris and London spoke the same language – literally so, when in March 1998 Tony Blair addressed the French National Assembly in creditable French, a feat few of his twentieth-century predecessors could have managed. Six months after that the long reign of Helmut Kohl ended as Social Democrat Gerhard Schröder became Chancellor of Germany, again sharing power with the Greens. When left-of-centre leaders gathered at Malmö in Sweden a month after Labour's great victory, the scene looked set for close cooperation across Europe: the left held power also in Italy, Portugal, the Netherlands and of course in Scandinavia.

The band of brothers got used to hearing parson Blair preach, as if Labour alone had the true gospel: the Continentals were as impressed by his confidence as they were dismayed by the vacuity of Third Way prescriptions. In practice policy in the different countries converged. If by 2000 the fiscal policies being pursued by Gordon Brown in the UK, Hans Eichel in Germany and Laurent Fabius in France looked strikingly similar, that was because economic growth was buoying revenues and, in their different ways, the European countries were all coming to terms with demography and the restructuring of welfare states. The Blairites claimed the 2000 Lisbon summit (European Council meeting) as a great triumph for Tony Blair's vision of open markets and dot.com jobs. They cited Romano Prodi, President of the European Commission: 'Few are any longer in denial,' wrote Prodi that summer, 'over the need for tough structural reform, deregulation, flexible labour markets and the modernization of pension systems.' In fact, since the indices of productivity in both Germany and France remained strikingly better than the UK's, Blair's triumphalism was misplaced. The Germans and the French *were* adapting – but their approach (for example in privatizing state-run businesses) was pragmatic and never lost sight of employee interests. The idea that British was best was belied by the macro-economic indices. Besides, the only way the EU was going to be led was by the successful selling, in Paris, Berlin, Rome and Madrid, of some convincing story about Europe itself. The British, self-excluded from monetary union, were never going to be convincing raconteurs.

But all that was over there. At home, Labour's European policy was broken-backed. The Government's refusal to conduct a positive campaign in favour of the euro let public opinion drift in a sceptical direction, making a referendum campaign, if it ever gets fought, all the harder to win. At the end of 2000, ICM recorded 18 per cent yes votes against 64 per cent no.

Before the election New Labour had always come at the subject gingerly. A united Europe of states, not a united state of Europe, had made its rhetoric sound not so different from the Tories. A referendum on the euro was Labour's only concrete election promise on Europe; the other commitment, 'reform of the EU', could and did cover a multitude of sins.

A tone had been set in the pre-election opus by Peter Mandelson and Roger Liddle, who took on the European portfolio in the Number 10 think-tank: both too timid and too boastful, it promised Labour would be constructive without being a 'soft touch' for Euro-enthusiasts' (implication – barmy) schemes. Labour would cut waste and fraud, reform the Common Agricultural Policy and – this one was critical – strengthen the legitimacy of the EU in the eyes of the people of Europe. Blair opposed a 'federal superstate' (it was not clear who, apart from German Foreign Minister Fischer, was actually in favour of that). The lady had not vanished . . . curious echoes of Thatcher's Bruges speech of 1988 could be heard in Blair's Warsaw oration in October 2000. His 'union of nations' phrase had first surfaced in a John Major white paper.

The expedient euro

Tony Blair was to try and try again to engage with the EU without resolving the question of UK membership of the single currency: it made his European policy well-nigh impossible. Labour came to power with a policy on the single currency that was electorally expedient. It had promised a referendum, less as a matter of principle than a device to accentuate Tory disarray. For, barring mavericks, Blair faced no party dissent; his problem if anything was with enthusiasts such as John Monks of the TUC who wanted in now.

With hindsight, that post-election afterglow summer of 1997 might have been used for a quick declaration in favour of joining followed by a referendum. Say it had gone Blair's way, convergence with the Euroland economies would have required the Treasury to be brutal, perhaps taking direct control of mortgage lending. But Blair did have the muscle then, the trust and the unstoppable forward impetus to part (in the phrase of our colleague Michael White) the waters of Euroscepticism like a latter-day Moses. The decision might have derailed other schemes; would the newly independent Bank of England have played ball? Although this was, in Gordon Brown's words, the most important political decision of a generation, the Government was reluctant to risk a huge slice of its precious political capital.

But delay may prove permanent. For as the Tories revived, Labour's fear of failing to be re-elected created an internal mantra – the voters must not be distracted by Europe when domestic social achievements are our trump electoral card. That meant, as policy hardened during 2000, putting off any likely referendum; even I, Blair said in October, would vote no on admission today.

The euro had rapidly become a subject hedged round with evasion. The Government's first major statement, itself delayed, was from Brown in October 1997. The UK was making no specific commitment to join but there was no constitutional barrier, he said, using a phrase that would come to haunt him. In principle a successful single currency would benefit the UK. That was it. The sparsity of the rhetoric implied that the political task of convincing sceptical inhabitants of the UK could be wished away. The only considerations, Brown seemed to say, were utilitarian. He announced five economic 'tests', four of them so general (to do with investment, impact on the City and employment) that a clever government could pick and mix them at will. Only the first was specific: the UK and the Euroland economies had to converge sustainably. Which was in fact what happened. As sterling appreciated against the euro, Euroland interest rates rose, coming within hailing distance of the still remarkably high UK rates. But, Brown said, there was no way his tests could be met by 1 January 1999, the target date for establishing the euro. The first Blair term would be used instead 'to prepare'.

It did not happen. The people were not prepared, quite the contrary. If entry had been Blair's clear intent, Labour surely needed to make a continuous and convincing public case. Labour would have had to set its face against the howling gales of anti-Europeanism swirling through the pages owned and written by Tories, little Englanders and North Americans (Murdoch and Conrad Black) with peculiar fantasies about the size of the Atlantic. Refused membership of Euro-X, the committee of finance ministers that was to oversee the single currency, the UK had no stake in the contested appointment of Wim Duisenberg as Europe's first and peculiarly clumsy central banker. It was not that the Blair Government was inert. Just after the single currency was born on 1 January 1999, a 'national changeover plan' was announced but it was to be a technical, not a political exercise. The political issues, Tony Blair blandly said, had been resolved.

Meanwhile non-membership began to cause pains in Labour heartlands. Sterling's strength against the euro was not the only factor in BMW's retreat from its involvement in Rover, threatening Longbridge, but the episode was a painful reminder of interdependence and the logic that said a single market needs a single currency. When Tony Blair talked convincingly of closing the gaps in the single market, pushing for cross-border finance and energy supply, the omission of money from his rhetoric became embarrassingly awkward. Yet the marked depreciation of the euro after its birth was as much a political as an economic fact. Thatcher had never even tried to educate the public who voted for her in the basics of her liberal economic creed; they were wedded to atavistic ideas about 'strong' currencies (good) and 'weak' (bad). Brown was silent, allowing the temporary strength of sterling against the euro to be cited by antagonists, even as it ate away at the country's industrial base.

The commercial facts of life were unassailable: Euroland took 48 per cent of UK exports and a further 4 per cent went to Sweden, Denmark and Greece, while only 16 per cent went to the USA. Economists argued over how much investment, how many jobs depended on EU membership, but the portents seemed to point in the direction of that inexorable ever-closer union: one symbol was the proposed merger of the Stock Exchange with the Frankfurt bourse and if not that then takeover by Swedes or merger with Paris and Madrid. If single capital markets were fine, why fear single money? The antis could never quite acknowledge the ambiguity of their position: they said you need your own currency if you want to control your own interest rate to deal with country-specific shocks. But in a world of footloose capital this means a floating exchange rate. Floating rates are themselves a source of instability and a deterrent to long-term investment.

Under Duisenberg, the European Central Bank (ECB) was easy to fault, less open than the Bank of England but no more ambiguous or unaccountable than other central banks in the way it balanced inflation and employment. Credit to the ECB or not,

Euroland economies picked up, creating new jobs and pushing down unemployment growth rates: the paradox of the euro's fall was the health of the real economy in France and Germany. The euro fell victim to the herd mentality of the markets but its low rate was also caused by the marked imbalance in capital movements across the Atlantic. European companies have been buying into the United States despite the dollar's strength but there has been no corresponding movement into Europe, despite the euro's weakness. Wise owls kept saying a correction would come.

In its absence advocates of UK entry hesitated. Stories appeared (for example in early spring 2000), prompted by briefing from Robin Cook talking about fightback, about taking on the Eurosceptic press. Stephen Byers said inward investors were telling him of a need for a clear commitment to join and a lower exchange rate. Tony Blair himself appeared at the launch of a Britain in Europe campaign, shoulder to shoulder with Michael Heseltine and Charles Kennedy. But little then happened, except further depreciation of the euro and the Danish referendum – far less meaningful than a UK vote since the Danish currency was already in a fixed relationship with the euro. On a key test of leadership, Blair made no attempt to change the public mood: he talked grandly of leading in Europe, but it was of little use while at home he followed popular opinion where he should have led.

The heart of Europe

Labour's manifesto had identified completing the single market, enlargement, reform of the Common Agricultural Policy and signing up to the Social Chapter as priorities. The single market remains incomplete, though the UK has pushed steadily for the inclusion of financial services. French intransigence over beef, made all the less acceptable because of periodic scares about French beef, did not help to make the case at home. Agricultural policy still needs major surgery, as one of the stumbling blocks to the admission of Poland. But it is fair to say Labour broadly delivered on its promise to engage the UK more intimately in European discussions – within the limits imposed by vacillation on the euro. By autumn 2000 Tony Blair had worked out a philosophy of Europe with a degree of intellectual force, one directly opposed to the federalizing vision of the Germans. What Blair would not say was what the UK would do if the German version – tighter integration of a small core of 'old' member states – won out.

And so its own position, too, came to look pretty sceptical. The Social Chapter, yes, but not the Schengen agreement on passport-less borders. The Treasury stoutly resisted proposals to harmonize tax on savings: harmonization, said Brown, should be driven by market forces, not Brussels bureaucrats. The plan for a withholding tax on non-resident savings was dropped in favour of better exchange of information between tax authorities – but the merits of the case was drowned in us-and-them rhetoric. Tony Blair himself fuelled it. A notorious column under his byline in the *Sun* in October 1997 had made much of 'no surrender', flatly contradicting Cook's promise to 'keep on making the case'. Disputes such as those over beef and tax were inevitable. Cook said, 'It is time to get those disagreements in perspective and stop reacting as if every step towards closer cooperation between member states of the European Union is the same as a step towards a superstate,' yet Blair took fright whenever the Eurosceptic press bellowed.

In a big speech in Ghent in spring 2000, Blair said the UK's hesitation over Europe had been its 'greatest miscalculation' since 1945. Yet that implied he should resolve the euro question by some bold stroke. It was not forthcoming. The public used the opportunity of the 1999 European Parliament elections – the small numbers that bothered to vote, that is – to express their equivocation. Labour rested its case on the choice between a government which knew how to handle dealings with the EU and isolationist Tories; in the event the latter won a remarkable number of seats. Labour had sleep-walked into the contest, displaying either its confidence or its arrogance by failing even to bother to produce a UK manifesto, relying instead on the necessarily general fifteen-country manifesto of the Party of European Socialists – an ambiguous association for the emphatically non-socialist Blair Government.

When Peter Mandelson visited Bonn in early March 1998, he expressed his master's anxiety about the 'democratic deficit' in European institutions but also his scheme for 'leapfrogging' the UK's more integrationist-minded partners by presenting the case for reform. It was not that European leaders were unaware of the growing problem of popular sentiment – at the Pörtschach summit in Austria in October they had pledged to 'bring the EU closer to its citizens'. Labour's positive attitude towards Europe meant that Tony Blair's set-piece contributions to the ongoing debate about Europe's shape were listened to. The UK was no longer alone. Blair could write newspaper articles jointly with Swedish Prime Minister Goran Persson and trade on a good relationship, personal and diplomatic, with the conservative Spanish Government headed by José-María Aznar. The speech Blair made in Warsaw in October 2000, billed as the UK response to German Foreign Minister Joshcka Fischer's thinking aloud about a federal future, did excite attention in the capitals of the EU. When in October 2000 the French central banker Jean-Claude Trichet declared UK membership 'unanimously and warmly welcome in the euro area' he did not just mean as an economic counterweight.

Shortly after taking office Blair had gone to the Amsterdam summit, where he rode a bicycle for the cameras. The treaty resulting from that summit sailed through Parliament – without, again, much effort made to explain or sell it to an uncomprehending public. The treaty strengthened the powers of the European Parliament, which flexed its muscles a couple of years later to secure the dismissal of the commission led by Jacques Santer. At Amsterdam the UK had resisted the extension of EU involvement in security questions by its absorbing the Western

European Union, the hybrid post-war defence network. The signals then changed and Blair, educated by the Kosovo conflict, became the most urgent advocate of the EU's acquiring a military role.

Choosing its timbre

The UK presidency, from January to July 1998, was a success. But Labour had a problem in finding the right timbre of voice to talk about Europe; it needed desperately to educate a British public that ought to know, for example, that the EU budget constituted barely 1.1 per cent of EU GDP while public spending in the EU totalled 46 per cent of GDP – some threat to national patterns. Clare Short launched a valid critique of the way development aid was handled. But such criticisms of EU performance, valid though they might be in specifics, only added to the surrounding sceptical noise. The same dilemma was posed by reform of the Commission. Neil Kinnock played a blinder as the guarantor of probity after the scandal surrounding Edith Cresson (she with the strong views about the failings of English manhood), but mud sticks. Europe got its own back on the mud front: the Commission found in July 2000 that only forty-six of 541 British beaches complied with minimum pollution standards. Was this what the Blair Government wanted from the EU? It did not want a European Charter of Fundamental Rights, which came forward for confirmation at the Nice summit in December 2000 – despite the Blair Government's enthusiasm, described in the last chapter, for human rights all round. It was as if Blair envisioned some Third Way between the enthusiasm for closer union displayed by the Germans and the antagonism, rapidly becoming isolationism, shown by the Tories and the bulk of the national press.

The media were undoubtedly biased, and even the BBC was dragged by newspaper impetus into running stories critical of European institutions. A good example: when the *Mail on*

Sunday started another Euro-myth about the imminent scrapping of the royal emblem on British passports by Brussels, the BBC led its news with this nonsense. But elsewhere in Europe, too, Europe got a bad press. Most EU matters got minimal media coverage, and that was usually slanted. History shows that consistently negative coverage erodes support for particular leaders (Neil Kinnock's fate), governments and policies. Likewise a persistently Eurosceptic press damaged early public confidence in the euro – not just in the UK but across the EU.

Vision in Warsaw

Caught between the rock and the hard place, Blair sought to refine a specifically British take on events and was helped by the growing awareness across Europe that things could not go on as they were if the EU was to be enlarged to take in Hungary, Slovenia, the Czech Republic, Poland and the long list of other aspirants. The thinking coloured the speech Blair made in Warsaw in October 2000. Blair's recipe was less Brussels and more ad hoc agreement between the nations, harking back eerily to Margaret Thatcher, even to Charles de Gaulle. On the other hand, he proposed a second European parliamentary chamber or senate composed of representatives of national legislatures as a means of cementing Europe into national consciousness. But there should be no extension of majority voting in the European Council to embrace taxation, border control or defence.

It was not that Blair was unenthusiastic about military cooperation. The UK and France spent more than other members of the EU on defence by a wide margin; nothing would happen without their agreement. EU countries spent 65 per cent of what the US spent on defence but, because it was disconnected, ended up with less than 10 per cent of US capability. The defence commitments of EU members remained a bone of contention: the suggestion was that all should commit 2 per cent of GDP to fulfil common defence objectives. The British calculation was that the UK defence manufacturing firms ought to benefit from such an increase – but, among many other things, it would depend on domestic political considerations in Italy and Germany, both eagerly trying to cut public spending.

Military cooperation

A new chapter in UK–French military cooperation opened in December 1998 with the signing of the St Malo declaration. It was hard, admittedly, to see any benefits from it as Europe struggled to mount a coherent diplomatic let alone military response on Kosovo. But a new plank was put in place by the transfer of Javier Solana from the general secretaryship of Nato to head the EU's security operation; the UK supplied George Robertson as his successor. An EU rapid reaction force was agreed at the European Council in Helsinki in December 1999. The Americans agreed and Nato would have prior approval of its missions. An EU force of up to 60,000 was to be deployable from 2003 to tackle crises when Nato as a whole was not engaged, its task mainly humanitarian and rescue missions, peacekeeping or peace enforcement.

Whatever Europe's shape was to become, these tentative steps towards building capacity in Europe to protect and project, intervene and defend represented an achievement. Yet how much more might the UK have done in determining that shape if it were indeed a full member of the EU instead of semi-detached. The UK's position within the EU is as undecided – at home as well as viewed from Brussels – as it was in May 1997, perhaps more so.

8

Massaging Middle England

Close to the heart of New Labour lay a concordat with Middle England. But the Blairites were not naturally attuned to the habits of Mondeo Man and they used the *Daily Mail* as a weathervane for his instincts and prejudices. So the rabble-rouser founded by Alfred Lord Northcliffe, who had set out to give his readers a 'daily hate', became a good guide to Labour policy. Under its influence Labour got into the habit of denigrating 'liberals'; the new theory was that Labour had lost in the past because gay and black rights, women's equality and a love of freedom had taken priority over the 'family'. Above all, because of crime. The pollsters said Labour had been thought soft – its 1992 manifesto had devoted only a tiny section to it.

Crime was where Blair came in. As shadow Home Secretary he had set his seal on the new philosophy with his brilliant slogan, 'Tough on crime, tough on the causes of crime.' The phrase encapsulated a bargain, not in itself ignoble but hard to carry through. Poverty was the cause of crime; it would be rooted out. But no apologies or excuses for criminal behaviour would be entertained. In this twin-track approach Labour would devote itself to the poor with egalitarian fervour. (So it did, behind closed doors.) But lawbreakers put themselves beyond sympathy so prisons and tough new sentencing laws awaited them.

While other ministers set about the causes of crime, Jack Straw was made custodian of toughness. He became guarantor of the pact with Middle England, the guard-dog whose baying would drown any bid by the law-and-order hounds of the press to charge the Government with softness on crime or asylum-seekers. It was a role destined to make him hated within his own party and he took to it with gusto, ad libbing about Hampstead and 'liberals' whenever he got the chance. He often went down well in the heartlands, on the housing estates of his Blackburn constituency. It was from there he drew inspiration for such policies as child curfews and curbs on noisy neighbours.

His attitude was prefigured in Opposition. Straw had clung limpet-like to Michael Howard at the Home Office in the latter years of the Major Government. Where Opposition spokespeople traditionally set out alternatives, Straw imitated. However far Howard went, Straw was there at his shoulder; time and again the Tories tried to throw him off; but whenever Howard struggled to put clear blue water between them, he found his shadow swimming after him, stroke for stroke.

Howard adopted a policy that had already failed in the United States – 'Three strikes and you're out' for burglars. (When a man was automatically jailed for stealing a slice of pizza, the slogan had fallen into disrepute.) Howard knew he would not be there to implement it when he squeezed the law through Parliament just before the election. It was meant to be an elephant trap. Home Office researchers were appalled at the recklessness of it, estimating that over the years it could add another 25,000 prisoners to the 60,000 already crammed inside. Howard said at the time he had finally trounced Straw – surely he could not sign up. Straw did.

Straw's Rottweiler act worked brilliantly. The Tories could hardly point to the formidably illiberal front put up by Blair, Straw and Blunkett and convince voters they were soft on crime, vandals, drugs, punishment, truancy, authority or discipline. 'Rights and responsibilities,' they chanted over and over and it made them invulnerable.

The tough straw man

Soaring numbers drove prison governors to despair, their jails too crowded to offer any kind of rehabilitation to inmates. Chief Inspector of Prisons Judge Stephen Tumim was scathing, especially about the lack of prisoner education. Wait and see, Straw had suggested in Opposition, though not on the record.

In office he pursued a twin-track policy which on the one hand seemed almost to rejoice at the swollen numbers inside but on the other tried hard to stop young offenders being jailed. He worked hard at stemming the flow with programmes aimed squarely at juveniles, catching them straight after a first offence – to try to head them off a life of crime. The tools were education, training, therapeutic groups, anger management courses; research had shown many young people could be diverted. Straw invested heavily in drug treatment, creating a new class of court order designed to push addicts away from prison into treatment. He tried to speed up the legal process: one of the famous five pledges had been to halve the amount of time between arrest and sentencing for juveniles so they were not left to drift and commit more offences while waiting. It turned out to be the most difficult pledge to meet, not necessarily Straw's fault, for power over the courts rested with the Lord Chancellor, Derry Irvine.

These preventative policies were a breath of fresh air in a Home Office that for long and foetid years had been run by Tories who took no interest, ignored research and punished for punishment's sake. Straw wanted evaluation and it went two ways. Two liberal experiments were found not to work: group therapy for men violent towards women, and go-kart and motor mechanic courses for joy-riders, which just made them better at it. Both were dropped. Straw got scant credit for his empiricism and constructive policies – but that was because he rarely chose to talk openly about keeping people out of court and out of jail. His public pronouncements accentuated the punitive. He relished his macho image. No more liberal winks and nods to liberal-minded interviewers: on and off the record Straw staunchly defended the rising prison numbers under his regime – more prison and more treatment, tough and tender, pity for causes, punishment for miscreants.

Year	Average population
1996	55281
1997	61114
1998	65298
1999	64771
2000	65008

Figure 12: Average population in custody in England and Wales

Source: The Home Office

Counting crime

Jack Straw wisely avoided triumphalism when the crime figures went in the right direction: it is doubtful whether Home Secretaries ever have much direct influence on them. Michael Howard was much mocked for trying to claim credit for a fall in crime on his watch thanks to locking more people up. Of course incarceration has some effect on crime but the Home Office's own research said it was minimal. What affected the level of crime were prevailing forces in society – jobs and the state of the economy above all. Social and economic policies carried out far from the Home Office were likely to have more impact than anything the Home Secretary could do. But lead times are long and causation indirect. Take the Labour Government's ambitious Sure Start programme for pre-schoolers. If it were to work as well as Head Start in the United States, it would be fifteen years before its promise of a better life for deprived babies and nursery age children showed up in reduced youth crime. Even if a Labour Home Secretary might not reap the rewards, Straw was a man for the long haul, and a strong Sure Start advocate.

Crime figures are tricky. Official figures blip in response to

what police officers do as much as the actual behaviour of criminals. A blitz on drugs in Sun Hill division can make it look as if
drugs consumption has suddenly soared. A council campaign to
get women to report domestic violence or rape sends the recorded
figures soaring. For this reason the British Crime Survey (BCS)
is by far the best guide; it samples 19,000 people every two years
and asks them about their personal experience of crime, picking
up a swathe of unrecorded crime. (From 2000 Labour paid to
have it done annually.)

Straw inherited a four-year-old downward trend in crime, as
measured both by the BCS and by police records. For 1999 the
latter showed a 3 per cent rise, less than had been predicted. The
BCS found a fall of 10 per cent in its October 2000 report, on
top of a 15 per cent fall in the previous two years. The broad
picture is that ever since 1918 crime has risen by an average 5
per cent a year, with a sharp rise from the recession years of the
early 1980s through to the mid-1990s.

UK rates have traditionally been high compared with other
European countries and remain so. But during the late 1990s
across thirty-five western nations including the USA crime fell.
No one is exactly sure why. When the Home Office sparred with
the Treasury over money it was asked to prove its schemes were
responsible for winning the 'war on crime'. Its civil servants
impudently replied that they would do so provided the Treasury
could prove economic prosperity was all its own doing and not just
part of an international trend. Asked to account for the fall, Paul
Wiles of the Home Office research department suggested crime
was 'simply becoming a less fashionable pursuit for high-risk age
groups'. But he added that this was just another way of saying
that the 1 million increase in jobs in four years had given young
men something else to do and somewhere else to get money.

Well aware of all that, Straw did not boast about the BCS
figures (though he could not help beaming at the press conference
announcing them). They covered the two years since Labour
took office and were all the more astonishing for being better

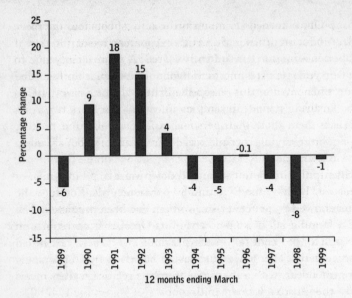

Figure 13: All notifiable offences: underlying trend from the previous year

Source: The Home Office

than predicted. In autumn 1999 Straw's own researchers forecast that burglary was set to rise by 30 per cent over the next year, which panicked Downing Street. Instead it fell by 21 per cent. The projection had been based on the usual suspects: the number of young men in crime-prone age groups was rising; rising wealth meant there was more to steal; more goods were insured. Instead car thefts dropped by 15 per cent and thefts from cars by 16 per cent.

Even overall violent offences had fallen by 4 per cent in the BCS figures. Within that total 'stranger' violence rose, mainly drunk young men assaulting each other, as the real price of alcohol dropped as spending money grew. Belatedly in 2000, the

Home Office turned its attention to this substance, far more crime-inducing than soft drugs. Apparently soaring street robberies – up 14 per cent in two years – were mainly due to sixteen-year-olds stealing mobile phones from each other. The same phenomenon was mapped in the police figures; parents were insuring their children's mobiles and therefore reporting thefts.

A quarter of violent crime was domestic. Scotland Yard commissioned research that showed there were 600 domestic violence incidents an hour; the 570,000 reported were only a fraction of the total. Four-fifths of victims were women attacked by male partners, 8 per cent men by women; children witnessed half these beatings. Yet somehow the extent of this never filtered through to the Family Committee established by Straw. It talked sentimentally about marriage as a 'corner-stone' and single parenthood as less than ideal – though escaping violence was often the cause of women ending up bringing up their children alone. A Family Research Institute was set up. Straw was divorced, one brother was the liberalish chair of Relate, the marriage guidance agency, another was prosecuted for sex offences, but he set aside family experience.

Despite the great noise the Countryside Alliance made about cuts in rural police, the BCS showed yet again how country-dwellers were at less risk of crime. William Hague seized upon the case of Tony Martin, where it was claimed a rural crime wave excused the farmer's shooting of a boy burglar. The Tories said crime was rising and rural crime rising dramatically – both assertions entirely false. But Labour's fate was that opinion polls showed the public believed Tory lies. In 2000 a third of people thought crime had risen since 1997. Unreasonable fear distorted fair political judgement.

In a fit of anxiety about slightly slipping poll ratings, Blair suddenly announced that policemen would be empowered to seize drunken yobs who threw traffic cones into the street, frog-marching them to cash-machines for on-the-spot £100 fines.

Using the odd surroundings of a religious conference at Tübingen in Germany, he sneered that of course the 'libertarian left' would not like it. It did not. But neither did the boys in blue. This was the kind of law-and-order on-the-hoof policy the police had endured for years under the Tories. Chief constables descended on Downing Street to tell Blair he was wrong. His proposal was rapidly redescribed as a 'metaphor' and dropped.

It was a bad omen. Blair did it again to the despair of prison governors in a speech shortly afterwards, claiming there were 4,000 prison 'vacancies' into which offending yobs could be dumped. This would mean yet more overcrowding, doubling prisoners up into tiny cells built for one, locked in most of the day. That suggestion also rapidly disappeared into the ether within days.

Yet, quietly, on another track there was Straw spending considerable sums on preventing crime. Simple measures: he looked like hitting his target of a 30 per cent reduction in car crime in four years by introducing better locks and security. He hit his target of a 5 per cent reduction in burglary in poor high-risk households by spending £400 million on 'target-hardening' – locks and protection on the worst council estates. Yet still, in public, he preferred to take the other tack, talking prison and punishment. Nor did he boast about the remarkable success of the electronic tagging scheme, despite such high-profile customers as Jonathan Aitken. Thanks to the tag he got out of jail early; tags offered an economical alternative to prison.

Bang 'em up

Prison numbers had been rising. Michael Howard inherited 40,000 prisoners and increased their number by 50 per cent, leaving the UK with by far the highest proportion of its population in prison in Europe, 70 per cent of them inside for offences not involving violence, sex or drug-trafficking. Howard's 60,000 rose to over 66,000 under Straw. He said the numbers did not concern him and the judges always take their cue from the Home Secretary. Since 1997 no extra criminals have been caught and charged but the courts handed out more and longer sentences. The proportion of those found guilty getting custodial sentences rose by around 9 per cent.

At the election Straw had promised to reduce the 11,000 people kept in prison on remand awaiting trial. Instead the number rose – a real injustice and a needless addition to overcrowding, since only half of remand prisoners eventually got custodial sentences.

Conditions in prisons did steadily improve, thanks in part to the building programme begun by the Tories. Slopping-out ended and every cell now has a lavatory and sink. But 12,000 prisoners were still doubled up in cells built for one. This was despite the new prisons, to which Labour added four, with another three due to be opened in 2001 at a total extra cost in capital and running costs of £1.084 billion over five years, rather more than the Dome to rather less outcry about waste.

The amount of time prisoners spent out of their cells in what is euphemistically called purposeful activity improved slightly. Since most crime is committed by a handful of people, getting hold of them while in prison is, in principle, a great opportunity to treat, train and educate them intensively to try to reduce reoffending. But due to lack of staff and facilities, in 2000 the Prison Service failed to hit its very modest target for giving all prisoners twenty-four hours a week of work, education or treatment. Much praised anti-reoffending courses were given to only one in twenty-one prisoners: the target for 2002 is still only a meagre one in ten. One of the key predictors of criminality is illiteracy. Two-thirds of all prisoners are so illiterate and innumerate that they are ineligible for 96 per cent of available jobs; 70 per cent of young offenders could not complete a job application form. But as prisons filled up, Straw looked unlikely to get even the 15 per cent reduction in inmate illiteracy that he sought. Random drug-testing grew along with drug treatment programmes. Drug-free wings were created but drugs are still rife and many start taking them inside.

Until 1994 Labour had opposed all prison privatization, but nothing was said in the 1997 manifesto and by 1998 Labour was inviting bids for new private prisons and renewing contracts on others. Private prisons became a permanent part of the system.

One of Straw's great successes was electronic tagging (known officially as Home Detention Orders). At any one time 2,000 short-term prisoners – those sentenced to less than four years – were released early. Straw had aimed to let 4,000 prisoners out on these orders at a time, but the prison governors who make decisions on release were too nervous to let so many out early, thanks to the law and order climate Straw had himself done so much to foment. On average 60 per cent of short-term prisoners reoffend, many of them in their first weeks out. But remarkably only 1.9 per cent of those let out on tags reoffended and only 5 per cent broke their curfews. It has yet to be seen whether those disorganized lives made orderly by means of tagging remain crime-free once cut loose from their electronic anklets. Tagging is certainly cheaper then prison.

What works was supposed to guide Labour policies. Instead, missing his usual rigour, Gordon Brown allowed Jack Straw unwarranted sums for his huge prison budget, wasting money in expensive pursuit of populism. No attempt was made to lessen the public's appetite for punishment.

Police

Populism again. People feel safe when they see a uniform, even though patrolling officers do nothing measurable to prevent crime or catch criminals. Home Office research found a police officer on foot patrol only came close to a crime in progress once every eight years – and then might not notice it. Still the cry goes up for more bobbies on the beat. Jack Straw made the mistake in his party conference speech in 1999 of seeming to suggest that police numbers would rise by 5,000 under his regime, when in fact they had fallen. The Opposition was quick to pounce. So the Spending Review promised 4,000 more police by 2003, although each of them costs £46,000 a year to run. Here was another example of crowd-pleasing flying in the face of empirical evidence from the Police Foundation, from the Audit Commission and from the Home Office itself. Measuring what the police do is not easy, since results from different forces with the same underlying crime levels vary enormously. But changing the way officers operate is politically fraught. Neighbourhood patrols and civilians can do some police work more cheaply but are resisted by police unions. The best that Straw could claim was that resources were better accounted for.

Probation

Straw was contemptuous of 'community' sentencing. He liked to tell of finding a book on probation theory called *Radical Non-Intervention* on one officer's shelf. He was having no more non-intervention and set out to transform the service from a liberal befriender of those convicted of offences into a vigorous strong arm of the law. He toyed with renaming them Community Punishment Officers, to emphasize that a probation order was not a soft option but a punishment.

He had good reasons. If he was ever to move towards less imprisonment and more non-custodial sentences, then he had to persuade the public that punishment outside jail worked better to prevent reoffending. He had to prove that offenders could not fail to attend without severe penalty. Researchers followed 10,000 people given probation: there were 2,000 hardcore offenders who consistently failed to turn up for appointments. While half were sent back to the courts, no disciplinary action was ever taken against the other half. Sometimes six appointments were missed before an officer caught up with the offender. Straw said putting more of them into prison for breaching probation was a price worth paying for turning probation into a credible sentence. But the result might be between 2,000 and 15,000 extra people a year in prison.

Straw looked around for other instruments and hit on one that provoked great anger on his own benches in the Commons. The Child Support, Pensions and Social Security Act (2000) included a clause that would withdraw all benefits for six months automatically from offenders failing to comply with their community orders, to deter the 30,000 who defaulted for a second time. The strongest objection was that this might simply make them more inclined to return to crime, having no other means of support. Critics said it was an abuse of the criminal justice system and of the Human Rights Act, since it was a punishment that could only fall upon those on benefits, not on those in work, such as the many defaulters who are well-off motoring offenders. The criticism had some effect: the act was implemented only in pilot schemes to judge its impact.

The Probation Service was now back in favour. It got an extra 1,500 officers and 3,000 other staff – a rise of nearly a third. New pathfinder programmes did intensive work mainly in groups with offenders on violence, addiction and poor social skills – they were shown to have led to dramatic falls in reoffending rates, as high as 15 per cent. With the findings so hopeful, a target was set to treat 60,000 offenders a year on these schemes by 2004. This tough-and-tender pincer movement on offenders is expected to cut the 56 per cent rate of reoffending by criminals by 5 per cent – even this modest target not easy to meet.

Crime in the community

Both Straw and Blair repeatedly pointed to the nuisance caused by small numbers of troublesome families to neighbours on housing estates. Straw cited his own childhood in Essex on an estate where one family had tormented everyone else. (Naturally the press found the family, who protested vigorously and said the Straws were 'stuck-up'.) Other Labour MPs with problem estates knew the volume of complaints they received about disruptive and violent neighbours. To those who called him authoritarian and bullying, Straw replied, 'Hampstead people', who did not themselves live next door to terrorizing bullies.

But selling it proved difficult. The number of families evicted from estates rose, mostly dumped into private accommodation where private landlords began to complain. Most of the new devices for dealing with these anti-social problems were contained in the 1998 Crime and Disorder Act. Repeated police cautions were replaced with a final warning, young offenders were to be 'fast-tracked', reparation orders would make good harm done by offenders, wayward children would be subjected to curfew. The age of criminal responsibility was reduced to ten and police given new powers to deal with truants (whose numbers continued to rise). Child protection orders allowed police to pick up young children found roaming at night.

But there was a marked reluctance to use the panoply of new powers. By July 2000, no police force had made an application for such a child protection order. Only two applications were made for new child safety orders. Straw moved to increase the age at which children could be subjected to curfew to fifteen. The centrepiece was to have been Anti-Social Behaviour Orders, under which courts could command the parents of out-of-control and constantly offending children to attend sessions to be *trained*. But by November 2000, only 132 of these had been given out. In many areas anecdotal evidence suggested they were applied exclusively to single mothers of boys. In one area every mother on an order had herself been abused as a child and was the victim of domestic violence, the boy often having watched his mother being beaten. Many mothers welcomed help with parenting, desperate for assistance of any kind. But the fear is that some of the mothers who lead chaotic lives and break their orders will eventually become liable to jail, only making matters worse.

Such measures helped attach to Labour the label 'nanny state'. With them and health prevention projects New Labour was easily caricatured as bossy and interfering by Tories who had rarely ventured near the estates Labour MPs represented. Whereas old Labour might have regarded bad families as themselves victims, New Labour was more inclined to regard the first victims as their next-door neighbours. The criminal route has proved a resounding failure: it is yet to be seen whether the New Deal for Communities on the worst estates can do better with carrots not sticks.

Youth justice

Jack Straw's National Youth Justice Board is likely to be his landmark contribution to reducing crime in the long term, since young boys commit such a high proportion of crimes – teenagers do 40 per cent of burglaries and 28 per cent of violence. When Straw arrived, young offenders were being shovelled through the courts time and again, sometimes with cautions, sometimes locked up, but with no single authority responsible for them and their families. They might have a social worker, a probation officer, the police, a teacher and a GP, all concerned with the family but uncoordinated, none of them knowing what was happening with any of the other agencies. Time and again young offenders slipped through the net until eventually they were old enough to fetch up in prison. The press loved the tales of Rat Boy and other out-of-control child monsters who committed hundreds of crimes yet seemed to escape punishment.

All these agencies were brought together in 155 local Youth Offending Teams (YOTs), pooling their money and efforts by edict of the national board, working together to create programmes of education and training, reparation schemes, parenting classes, bail supervision and drug treatment. If an offender received a custodial sentence, the YOT would arrange a seamless action plan both for their time inside and for when they were back in the community, to get them coherent education and treatment. By the time YOTs rolled out nationally there were already hundreds of schemes, closely scrutinized by the national board. Replacing the old police caution was a new final warning which delivered young offenders to the local YOT on first offence: the idea was to catch them young before an entrenched pattern of crime set in.

But along with this humane and constructive community programme went new detention and training orders, designed to lock away persistent young offenders. In the four months after they came in, the Howard League for Penal Reform reported with concern that the number of young offenders imprisoned shot up by 10 per cent. Many were crammed into over-crowded institutions which destroyed much hope of constructive education or treatment. There was an acute shortage of 500 places in the south-east, meaning many had to be locked up more than 100 miles from home, too far for families to visit.

This was Straw being tough and tender. While plainly the wildest and most desperate cases were bound to end up locked away, for most of the young, treatment in the community might teach people how to live ordinary non-criminal lives. Prison only taught them to become better criminals. Over the years, with close monitoring of outcomes and follow-ups by the YOTs, it should be possible to prove conclusively what works, ending once and for all some of the treatment v. punishment disputes that have raged for decades.

Labour's formal election pledge had been to halve the period of time between arrest and sentencing, so that offenders could be taken into the YOTs as soon as possible: often young boys commit several more crimes while waiting for trial for their first offence. It looked as if that ambitious target was the only one of the five pledges that would not be met: in 1997 it took an average 142-day wait, by October 2000 it had been cut to ninety days, an improvement but not the seventy-one days promised.

In his 2000 party conference speech Straw announced that

starting in April 2001, the 2,500 most persistent tearaways would be put under twenty-four-hour surveillance – outside jail. The fifty most hardcore repeat young offenders who had committed four or more offences recently in each city would spend six months under curfew, some with tags, others with voice-recognition telephones at home, obliged to call in several times a day to prove where they were. They would have to attend special education and other courses at least five hours a day, with no chance of bunking off. Since 25 per cent of youth crime is committed by 3 per cent of offenders, keeping these repeat offenders out of trouble ought to bring the figures down while also putting some structure into chaotic lives. It was widely welcomed as a far better option than locking them up. But its explanation by Straw was designed to satisfy the appetite for revenge – tagging sounds tough. Nothing was said about how education and therapy work better.

Football

For all the Blairites' ostentatious sporting of their team allegiances, they did not have much luck with the game on or off the field. After English yobs displayed their national culture in the bars of Charleroi (and the England team crashed out of European contention), 'something had to be done'. This was the Football (Disorder) Act, which came into being in August 2000. As ever with law and order legislation reacting to immediate events, it passed with minimum scrutiny. Until then only those actually convicted of a football-related offence could be banned from home grounds for up to three years (474 people had been so excluded). Some 115 international banning orders were in place. Under the new law banning orders could be issued against people not convicted of anything. If the courts were persuaded someone had been involved in violence or disorder anywhere, they would be banned, forced to hand in their passports during specified periods, near to matches. Home Office ministers could be heard praying the England team would do too badly to play in key games abroad.

Asylum-seekers

Throughout Europe people were on the move, some seeking a better life, some refugees from tyranny. In Italy, Albanians crossing the Adriatic and migrants from Africa and the Far East became a major issue likely to determine the result of that country's 2001 general election. In Spain there were riots over the presence of Moroccan farm-workers – without whom crops would not be harvested. Under Labour the UK continued to accept just under the EU average; ten other EU countries received more per head of population than the UK. Here the usual race-tinged anxieties were stirred by the right wing, in the press and the Tory Party.

The strictly defined question of UK obligations under inter-national convention was constantly bound together with the wider question of immigration and in turn with race and identity. On Labour's watch there was a swirling debate about *Britishness* (see pages 172–3) and about the supply of qualified manpower, especially for IT and nurses. But black or Asian software engineers were one thing, gypsies or Muslim escapees from Balkan conflict quite another. Labour was scared by what poll-sters such as Philip Gould told it about public sentiment – reactionary and afraid. Too often Labour pandered to that mood and helped stoke the flames of prejudice by promising to be tougher. The Tories outdid Labour, stirring up hatred, using begging gypsies as the exemplar of all refugees, without ever quite daring to advocate the banning of refugees.

The liberal left whinged. They seemed to want to let all comers in freely but did not quite go that far. Wiser critics said faster adjudication and fair income support for those waiting should be Labour's goal. Asylum leapt up the agenda when in 1999 a hijacked Afghani plane arrived at Stansted and many on board immediately applied for refugee status. This was too tempting for the right and it was a test of New Labour's decency – one many subsequently felt they failed.

Before the election Labour said the system was grinding to a halt. The backlog rose to 60,000 cases awaiting adjudication; on the one hand genuine political refugees, on the other economic migrants, emotively labelled as 'bogus' or later by Jack Straw as 'abusive'. By March 2000 it had got much worse, with the backlog rising to 103,000. The slow processing of cases sprang from a bungled computerization brought in by Ann Widdecombe when she was Immigration Minister. Jack Straw had been slow to grasp the problem.

In March 2000 the Home Office introduced tough new rules for asylum-seekers to try to deter economic migrants or refugees from choosing Britain. Straw copied a new German system, denying cash benefits to applicants, giving them instead food vouchers of just £35 a week each, banned from taking any kind of job. The vouchers were worth only 70 per cent of normal income support for people who often arrived with nothing but the clothes they wore. They were given £1 a day in cash, sometimes not enough for a bus fare to the supermarkets where their vouchers could be redeemed. The administration of vouchers was expensive, with a whole new DSS department and 300 extra staff just to run it. Asylum-seekers were dispersed around the country to spread the burden on housing, health and education evenly among local authorities: if they moved away, they lost their vouchers. If they sought a judicial review of their case, they lost all benefits. But councils were given no extra money and many resisted it strongly. Dover was the pressure point, where overt and growing racist violence stoked by a virulent local newspaper made the dispersal policy necessary: the south coast and London boroughs were under great pressure.

Meanness was not much of a deterrent, it seemed. Six months later in July 2000 the number of applicants was still rising, to reach 6,435 for the month of September 2000. It still took thirteen months on average to process a case, leaving people poverty-stricken in desolate dumping-grounds. Some 10,000 had been waiting for five years for adjudication. The number ultimately accepted as genuine refugees fluctuated; during the Kosovo crisis it rose to 70 per cent, but the underlying average is somewhere around 35 per cent.

From April 2000 the Government tightened the screw: every refugee newly arrived and transported to some Yorkshire sink estate had to fill in a twenty-page application form for asylum in English, without access to a lawyer, within fourteen days. If they failed this obstacle course they were deemed 'non-compliant' and automatically refused asylum. They had seven days to appeal on another form in English. The Home Office at one point claimed that only 5 per cent of applicants are granted asylum status, a nonsense to pacify a hostile press. No official asylum figures quoted by Home Office ministers could be taken at face value. Until forced to own up by a Commons committee in November 2000, the Government kept quiet about the unknown hundreds of thousands of failed asylum-seekers who had simply disappeared before they could be found and deported.

The Refugee Council said it was on the whole broadly satisfied with the fairness of the final decisions on appeal, but gross delay, sub-poverty benefits and petty harassment caused the worst injustice. At the end of 2000, the four countries from which most applicants for asylum came were Iraq, Somalia, Afghanistan and Iran, among the worst and most war-torn in the world.

A Mori poll in October 2000 showed 80 per cent of voters thought the UK a soft touch. Two-thirds thought 'there are too many immigrants in Britain', although asylum applications dropped 9 per cent between summer 1999 and summer 2000: the public also grossly over-estimated asylum-seekers' benefits. Faced with such fears, the Government caved in. Straw promised his new system would be 'firm, fair and fast'. It was none of these. There was little sign of hitting his target to ensure every case was processed within six months. Nor was there much effort by the Government to explain publicly why the UN Convention on Refugees was both necessary and humane.

Race

The wave of racist sentiment unleashed by the asylum question hurt a government determined that whatever other liberal causes it neglected it would always be tough on racism. One of Labour's first acts was to set up the inquiry so long resisted by the Tories into the 1993 racist murder of Stephen Lawrence and the failure of the police to prosecute his murderers. The resulting Macpherson report accused the Metropolitan Police of institutional racism, causing turmoil in the force and soul-searching among organizations of all kinds. It led to the Race Relations Amendment Act 2000, which extended the coverage of the Commission for Racial Equality (CRE) to the police, prisons, local authorities and the NHS. It would no longer be up to individuals to take a case: the onus would be on the institutions to demonstrate a fair racial policy.

There had been little in the manifesto to suggest much strength of resolve on race, but the Macpherson report changed the climate of opinion. One result was a perverse one: the reporting of racial crime tripled. The CRE doubted there had been more racial attacks, but after Macpherson there was growing confidence among ethnic groups that the police would take action if they reported them. Targets were set for the recruitment and retention of ethnic minority police officers, with new police disciplinary procedures, a new code of practice proscribing racist language and a three-year programme of race-awareness training for the police – much resented in the force.

Race also fired the growing uncertainty about what it meant to be British or English. Due partly to devolution, this identity crisis was also an outpouring of grief from a Tory establishment which had been dispossessed of 'its' England. Tony Blair made a stab at defining nationhood, his Cool Britannia the most regrettable and regretted effort – all Islington, not Ilford, let alone Immingham. In October 2000 the Runnymede Trust said history needed revising, rashly suggesting that the word 'British' had racial connotations. The resulting furore showed again the edgy, anxious state of the right under Labour, sometimes pointing out the small size of the UK's ethnic minority, some 7 per cent, sometimes talking of 'swamping'. Runnymede's pleasing finding that the UK had the best race relations in Europe was hardly reported.

Drugs

Labour was no less confused than its predecessors: all 'drugs' were harmful, except of course those supplying the Treasury with ready revenue. One third of the population (49 per cent of the young) had taken illegal drugs, mostly cannabis. Drugtaking was a fact of life and most ministers accepted it; many had liberal but unexpressed views. In public orthodoxy ruled. When first Clare Short and then Mo Mowlam made quite harmless remarks about the need for more debate on cannabis they were both forced to recant humiliatingly.

Once again, the Government's wish to base policy on evidence clashed with its fear of Middle England, which it turned out to misread. The determination to charge even small-time cannabis users as criminals – 78,000 cases a year of possession for personal use – continued to distort the national drugs budget: 62 per cent was spent on prosecution for drugs offences against only 13 per cent on treatment.

The UK evidently had a drugs problem. Some 2,100 people died each year. A third of all property crime was committed by addicts feeding a £10,000–£20,000-a-year hard drug habit. While in 2000 there were 30,545 addicts registered locally, the Home Office estimated there are between 100,000 and 200,000 problem users. In 1998 Tony Blair appointed Keith Hellawell, former Chief Constable of West Yorkshire, as drug tsar to pull together the disparate elements of drug policy in 'joined-up government': like other such initiatives it struggled to make headway inside Whitehall and new Drug Action Teams on the ground had an unclear chain of command. Hellawell promised to meet a target of halving heroin and cocaine use by under-25s by 2008, cutting it by a quarter by 2005. (This target included the same figure for cuts in the use of all illegal drugs, soft as well as hard, by the under-25s, which would be nothing short of miraculous.) One target promised to reduce repeat offending among drug-users by 50 per cent by 2008, 25 per cent by 2005. Few thought these could be reached at the present rate of spending, but Hellawell stoutly asserted he was on course. The first drop for many years in drug use by schoolchildren was reported in 2000.

The Government did promise to spend more on drug treatment programmes – £234 million in 2000 rising to £377 million for 2002/3. It introduced drug treatment orders to allow courts to divert addicts away from prison if they were willing to have treatment. In pilots for this scheme, one-third of addicts broke their orders and had to be summoned back to court, but a two-thirds success rate with one of the most difficult groups was regarded as high.

But there were ever-growing waiting lists, many as long as six months: some addicts went into prison only to find themselves still low on the waiting list when they came out. Every six months 30,000 more users tried to get treatment so there was no lack of demand. Every £1 spent on treatment saved £3 in crime, but the Government failed in its promise to shift the emphasis of drug policy sharply enough away from the courts to treatment. The tone was still the 'war on drugs', which had failed all over the world. In 2000–2001, although a total of £695 million was spent on combating drugs, only £234 million went on treatment to cut off demand at source. A further £353 million was spent far less effectively to stifle the availability of drugs on the streets.

In 2000, a commission set up by the independent Police Foundation recommended that the penalty for Class A drug-trafficking should be raised from fifteen to twenty years. But it was their modest proposal for decriminalizing cannabis that swept the headlines. The report said cannabis should be demoted to a class C drug since it was less dangerous than alcohol or tobacco. Before it was published the Government condemned its findings and said there would be no review of the cannabis laws. They were caught somewhat off-guard when the *Times*, *Telegraph* and *Mail* all praised the report and called for reconsideration. It was even odder when by accident the Conservative Party opened up debate after Ann Widdecombe promised a £100 instant fine for all cannabis users. Horrified at how out-of-touch their party seemed, seven Tory front-benchers simultaneously confessed to puffing while at university. They knew the consensus had shifted. An ICM poll in October 2000 found that only 20 per cent think personal use of cannabis should remain a criminal offence and they were mainly the over-65s. Some 43 per cent went a step further and said its use should be legalized completely. Yet still that year 78,000 people were prosecuted for cannabis possession, and 4,500 fetched up in prison for cannabis offences, over 400 just for possession.

Pollsters said the crude 'Just Say No' message of successive governments was one reason for the alienation of young people from politics – but the Government was adamant. Decriminalization was probably made all the more difficult for Jack Straw to deal with after his schoolboy son was lured by a newspaper *agent provocateur* into buying her a small quantity of cannabis. At least Straw was never known in private to have expressed any other view than his firm public stance: he may be one of the very few in the Government who sincerely believed in the policy.

Gay rights

Labour's record was good. It sought to equalize the age of consent for gay and heterosexual people at sixteen, while its Sexual Offences Amendment Bill also made 'abuse of trust' an offence for predatory teachers or care-workers seducing those under eighteen. But ferocious opposition from the right-wing press and the House of Lords delayed the measure. A second stalled reform was the repealing of Section 28 of a Tory local government act – labelled slightly differently in Scotland – which outlawed the 'promotion' of homosexual lifestyles by teachers or other council employees. No one had been prosecuted but its existence was an affront. In Scotland a religious transport entrepreneur convened an unofficial referendum but the Labour–Liberal Democrat coalition held firm and implemented change there. An extraordinarily rabid campaign in England led by Mrs Thatcher's only woman cabinet minister, Baroness Young, and (inevitably) the *Daily Mail* was more successful. It has never been quite clear whether the failure to get this reform passed through the Lords was a semi-deliberate ploy or a mistake: most think it was a simple technical error. Because the Government introduced the bill into the House of Lords first, it was imposs-ible to invoke the Parliament Act and force it through and so it fell. There were promises to reintroduce it in a second term.

Labour's third reform allowed openly gay men and women to serve in the armed forces. The pretext was a finding in the European Court of Human Rights in favour of a group of men and women who had been sacked once their homosexuality was revealed, without any accusation of sexual impropriety. It had always been, and remained, illegal for any form of sexual activity to take place between any serving men and women, gay or straight.

The courts

Following a scandal about the Crown Prosecution Service's fail-ure to prosecute police corruption cases and perceived chaos and delay in an under-funded service, Director of Public Pros-ecutions Dame Barbara Mills resigned in 1998. The service was restructured into forty-two regional offices, coterminous with police districts. With an added £30 million, the CPS took over prosecutions from the moment a defendant was charged and a team of lawyers, police and case workers jointly prepared cases, hoping they would be faster and better prepared for earlier court hearings.

A determination to secure justice quicker is the kindest explanation for Labour's controversial bid to abolish the right to trial by jury for a large category of defendants. When Straw announced in May 1999 that he would end the right for some 18,000 defendants, uproar ensued in two houses of Parliament stuffed with lawyers. The measure was meant to save public money, but only of the order of £100 million, and even this figure seemed to have been plucked out of the air. Straw had a point: of the 5 million cases heard in magistrates' courts, only 100,000 get moved up for jury trial in the crown courts. Straw, backed by commissions and reviews, said too many defendants opted for crown court as a delaying tactic, 70 per cent of them switching to a guilty plea at the door of the court, wasting a huge amount of police, lawyer and witness time. In Scotland the prosecution decided where all cases should be heard, with no choice by the defendant. In England Straw proposed the magistrates should decide.

Criminal justice cost some £9 billion a year; the savings through abolition of the jury trial option were paltry. The Lord Chief Justice, high court judges and magistrates were all in favour – but lawyers and the civil liberties lobby were passionately opposed. (Lawyers stood to lose work under the proposals – a magistrates' case cost on average £2,500, a crown court case cost £13,500, much of it paid to barristers.) It was, they claimed, a breach of Magna Carta itself. But Straw replied that the right to choose a jury trial had only existed since 1885. It was not that crown courts favoured defendants, for they were three times more likely to get prison sentences than in magistrates' courts and sentences were on average two and half times longer. Keeping the cases in magistrates' courts would mean less, not more, prison. Here were reforms with some justification but, in the wider scheme of things, was it worth the aggravation?

Conclusion

Straw's critics were rarely willing to acknowledge the way every Home Secretary has to balance the rights of offenders and victims, authority and liberty. He got little credit, for example, for the necessary and popular manifesto commitment to ban private possession of handguns, effected by the Firearms Act in 1998. Some 180,000 weapons were immediately handed in by the public. Similarly, it was Straw who was in the middle of public anger fanned by the tabloids over paedophiles. The murder of eight-year-old Sarah Payne stirred the country more than other murders, partly because there was such a long, agonizing wait between the child's abduction and discovery of her body. Her murderer was not found, but that did not stop the press identifying the perpetrator as a 'paedophile' and agitating for a British version of 'Megan's Law', which forced American police to inform communities when a paedophile was known to be living in their midst. The *News of the World* published the names and photographs of scores of paedophiles, despite strong pleas from the police that it was counter-productive – forcing them to move away, out of police supervision. Vigilante attacks and community protest followed, including the daubing of a paediatrician's home – the mob could not tell the difference. Straw behaved with aplomb, refusing to bend to public demands for mass removal of convicted or alleged paedophiles. Instead he promised a reasonable law to prevent released paedophiles being sent back to the districts where they had abused children in the past.

The office of Home Secretary will always be a thankless task. Even Roy Jenkins, now regarded as the great reformer, was vehemently attacked at the time by his own party for introducing the Prevention of Terrorism Act, suspending habeas corpus for terrorist suspects. It was Labour that introduced tough new immigration laws in the wave of the immigration panic that greeted the expulsion of Ugandan Asians by Idi Amin. Politically Straw played a blinder in keeping the Tories at bay. Try as they might, neither Ann Widdecombe nor William Hague found any chink in Jack Straw's armour, no soft spots. Straw seemed to revel in this lack of significant difference between Labour and Tory policy, without seeming to ask himself what was the point of a Labour Government, beyond more efficient administration. Some politicians might have welcomed a chance to hand back to the courts the curious powers of the Home Secretary to decide the fate of high-profile prisoners, but Straw chose to keep a grip on the Bulger killers, until the European court of Human Rights intervened, and on Myra Hindley, who may also make a human rights challenge to such arbitrary political power.

Labour failed to challenge old fears, prejudices and unreasons on law and order, as on taxation and public spending. They were happier following than leading public opinion. Jack Straw had a chance to carve out a Third Way, an ideological space somewhere between a hyper-liberal view of crime as a social disease and the right's view that all crime is purely a matter of individual sin. There was a chance to allay exaggerated public fear of crime – but too often Blair and Straw preferred to exploit it for political effect. Their final Queen's Speech contained almost nothing but tough-sounding fraud and crime bills.

For their second term, Labour has laid down no foundations for a change in public opinion, no reasoned explanation of what really works. Those same old inflammatory topics – asylum, drugs, punishment and prison – will burn as fiercely next time, for lack of robust and honest political leadership.

9

The Greening of Britain?

Never mind things, did the chances of humankind's survival get any better under Blair? Measured against the prospects for the planet as global warming accelerates, the Blair Government barely twitched the dial. But assessed against other countries' contributions and the public's hypocrisy over burning fuel and turning on light-switches, Labour might deserve a prize in the every-little-helps stakes. It made the UK a world leader in cutting carbon emissions and grasped the nettle of taxing industry to cut energy consumption. Motorists were pillaged with the fuel price escalator, until they rebelled, though fulfilling the manifesto promise to cut VAT on domestic fuel to 5 per cent was hardly conducive to encouraging homeowners to consume less. Economic growth was good, it cut unemployment. But growth also meant pressure on green fields and extra emissions of greenhouse gases, at least from transport. The picture, shall we say, was dappled.

The manifesto made some keen green promises on tax and the promotion of green technology. Labour understood 'sustainability', the big idea born at the Rio Summit. Labour's biggest promise – and the area they probably achieved least – was to 'join up' environmental concerns. A single department was created under John Prescott, marrying the environment and transport briefs. DETR did produce, in 1999, a Sustainable Development Strategy but it was little more than a list of indicators ranging from measures of 'social investment' (transport, hospitals) to numbers of houses judged unfit to live in and the quality of river water. When it came to the rural and urban white papers, as ever growth – in jobs and prosperity – was uppermost: if it could be accommodated on 'brownfield' sites or in the midst of previously developed villages, well and good. But in the language of priorities, growth and prosperity trumped environment every time.

Warming the world

Labour strove to reconcile business interests with the welfare of the planet: a series of uncomfortable compromises followed. John Prescott followed the precedent set by Tory predecessor John Gummer by cutting a dash at foreign conferences. At Kyoto in Japan in 1997 Prescott affirmed the UK's target of reducing by 12.5 per cent the greenhouse gases emitted in 1990, to be achieved by 2012. He did even better and upped the ante by promising a 20 per cent cut in carbon dioxide emissions by 2010. Of course it would not be enough – environment minister Michael Meacher admitted it would take world cuts in carbon emissions five or six times those agreed at Kyoto to cope with climate change. Such cuts were, needless to say, not forthcoming at the follow-up conference at the Hague in late 2000, by which time the science had moved on: the idea that large forest plantation would create 'sinks' for CO_2 was disputed – although some oil companies had begun to try trading their right to pollute by planting rainforest in recompense.

Labour's bid to cut carbon emissions was not going to involve a serious attempt at substituting non-fossil fuels in producing energy. The official target is for 10 per cent of UK electricity to be generated from renewable sources by 2010. But small support was offered and wind-farms have not sprouted along the coast. Solar cells are not much in evidence – yet a test roof on a terraced house in Richmond proved itself by pumping surplus electricity into the grid: panels are expensive and the solar industry could never get off the ground without Government subsidy at first. BP moved its solar manufacturing from Britain to elsewhere in Europe where public money was available to kick-start renewables. Tidal power consists of a few tiny experiments off the west coast of Scotland. Other countries, such as Denmark, decided state investment might reap commercial reward, which it did, and it became the world's windmill exporter. But state intervention seemed to offend the Blair Government's economic doctrines and it spoke volumes when, in a big environment speech in October 2000, Blair's promise to finance research on renewable sources of energy turned out to be founded on £50 million not from the state but from the National-Lottery-supported New Opportunities Fund.

Nor did Labour turn to that other great source of non-fossil fuel, nuclear reaction. Nuclear was out of sight, out of mind. The programme of decommissioning reactors had been made urgent once privatization had exposed the true cost of nuclear electricity: three Magnox stations closed in the 1990s, eight more are to shut down during the next two decades. In its enthusiasm for privatization Labour scheduled British Nuclear Fuels Ltd (BNFL) for sell-off by 2002, provided health and safety were sound. It was a big proviso for, among other scares, a shipment of reprocessed fuel to Japan was found to have a suspect safety record, damaging BNFL's export potential. Deep storage of waste had been abandoned in 1997, leaving the lucky inheritor of BNFL, if ever there is one, to find a safe place to store plutonium for centuries.

Lacking alternatives, Labour sought to discourage use of fossil-fuel energy and here was one of the Blair Government's most substantial achievements. Having commissioned businessman Lord Marshall, who reported favourably, Gordon Brown announced a climate change (fossil fuel) levy in his March 1999 budget to come on stream in April 2001. It will surcharge companies for their energy consumption and, on good estimates, could cut atmospheric carbon by hundreds of thousands of tonnes. Unlike its use of the fuel escalator as a general revenue raiser, the Treasury could not be accused of using the levy as a cover. Proceeds (which fell in estimate from £1.75 billion to £1 billion a year after concessions to business) will return to companies through cuts in National Insurance payments and subsidies to greater energy efficiency. Industry protested that this hit manufacturers harder than services, because they employed more plant than people so would get less of a rebate. Besides, they were already smarting from the high value of sterling. The Commons Trade and Industry committee agreed the tax was a blunt instrument. Unlike the parallel German energy tax introduced in April 1999, Labour's plan did not make allowances for energy with different carbon content. A heavy round of negotiation followed during which rebates of up to 80 per cent were agreed for energy-intensive industries if they met pollution control targets.

It was nonetheless an achievement, which shone as a green beacon all the more brightly after Michael Portillo pledged to sweep it away if he ever became Chancellor. But why, asked business, were households not also taxed on energy? Labour had fought the election on a promise to cut VAT on fuel used for home heating and in July 1997 Gordon Brown did precisely that, from 8 per cent to 5 per cent, the lowest level permitted under EU rules. True, he also cut VAT on insulation from 17.5 per cent to 5 per cent in the July 1998 budget; new help to lag roofs and seal windows was aimed at poorer households. The message from the Blair Government was not always consistent. Restrictions were lifted on new gas-fired power stations from October 2000, part of the new competitive regime in the supply of gas and electricity: of course those companies' interests lay in maximizing rather than minimizing fuel consumption and gas was not renewable. Labour also sought transitional aid for what was left of the UK's deep-mined coal industry, old sentiment tugging against new green imperatives.

Yet Labour can claim a bit more 'sustainability' here and there. Leakage from water pipes was cut 25 per cent, though that was a longer-term trend inherited from the Tories. Likewise UK coastal waters became somewhat less filthy: by 2005 all coastal sewage works serving towns with over 2,000 people will have at least 'secondary' sewage treatment, according to a Labour promise. Meanwhile household water bills (in England and

Wales) fell by an average of £30 in April 2000 thanks to tougher regulation. Water chiefs squealed – and they had a point in claiming that the cost of consuming water could not be cut at the same time as improving infrastructure, not in a privatized industry anyway. In March 2000 Green Gordon announced a new tax on aggregates – gravel for building – payable from April 2002, part of the proceeds to go into a Sustainability Fund to pay for research on alternatives such as recycling and environmentally friendly quarrying. Labour had increased tax on landfill introduced by the Tories from £7 to £11 a tonne, hoping to reduce that form of waste disposal, more common in the UK than elsewhere in Europe. But the green lobbies were none too keen on a ready alternative, incineration. Labour moved to introduce new restraints on plants, suspected by some of pumping dioxins into the atmosphere. But volumes of waste that the public could not or would not recycle were growing. That growth, increasing energy consumption, expanding traffic were all a cause of climate deterioration, no amount of talk about sustainability could stop.

Pumping gas

While the climate change levy put all the money collected back into saving the environment, the fuel duty escalator had been invented by the Tories and ruthlessly used by Labour as a machine for pumping money into the Treasury. There were environmental benefits: one estimate said petrol duty increases between 1996 and 1999 would save between 1 and 2.5 million tonnes of carbon emissions by 2010, a significant contribution.

Between May 1997 and autumn 2000 the pump price rose 42 per cent, of which twenty-two percentage points were due to tax, worth some £6.1 billion to Gordon Brown, the rest to OPEC. In his March 2000 budget Brown finally caught the rumblings of motorists and hauliers, abandoning the Tory-devised automatic above-inflation increases in fuel duty. It was promised that any future above-inflation rises were to go into a dedicated pot for public transport and roads. This was proclaimed a belated victory for Prescott's long-delayed transport plan – every 1 per cent real increase in fuel duty yielded over £200 million a year – but it came too late to stave off big political trouble.

If petrol tax had been linked from the start (or at least since 1997) to public transport, the motorist might have been persuadable – though it would always have been politically difficult to tax poorer drivers who had no alternative way of getting about. The real cost of motoring was said to have fallen by 30 per cent since 1964, car purchase prices included, but motoring was a significant chunk of some family budgets and, once you add in the psychological and cultural significance of the car, here you had the makings of a formidable political lobby. The September 2000 blockade of terminals by William Hague's 'fine upstanding citizens', the public indignantly in support, brought Labour low and led to alarmed speculation about governability, the end of deference to democratic rule and so forth. Brown's response in November was expensive semi-capitulation – tax concessions to hauliers, a gesture in the direction of making less polluting fuel for ordinary motorists cheaper – that ducked the big questions about sustainability Labour had once sought to pose.

Other fiscal devices of a faintly green hue were deployed. Vehicle excise duty was manipulated to favour lorries and buses with cleaner engines and less powerful cars; from 2002 company car tax allowances will be linked to carbon output, big cars bad, small cars good. Where the political logic broke down was Labour's ambivalence along the critical axis of transport policy, public v. private.

On one end of the seesaw sat Mondeo Man along with the industry which built his vehicles at Longbridge, the epicentre of Midlands electoral marginalism. Even the Prime Minister jumped when, to his annoyance, his passage from Heathrow was impeded by a new bus-only lane. On the other end of the see-saw sat poorer people, many of them carless women who relied on unfashionable buses to lead a half-decent life. They were supported by the urbanists. Personified by Richard Rogers, experts offered lots of ways in which our cities could be made as liveable as Amsterdam, Barcelona or Bologna. Labour ministers stood anxiously in between.

Some Labour promises seemed unequivocal. 'I will have failed,' John Prescott wrote in June 1997, 'if in five years' time there are not many more people using public transport and far fewer journeys by car. It's a tall order, but I urge you to hold me to it.' But trends in rail and tube use were up, up and away even as he said it; even bus journeys were growing. As for less car travel . . . that would only have been because the pumps were dry or the roads congested (in fact car travel continued its upwards move).

Labour's transport mantra was 'integration'. Prescott did not deliver, though eventually, if fully implemented, his ten-year plan announced in summer 2000 might. There had been talk of Transport Direct, a single source of phone or online information about all ways of getting about. It never happened, partly because Labour could not get its head around the need to bring the state back into transport. Fragmented companies just would not do it. Local authorities were to make plans embracing motion of all kinds, from walking to trams. But the invisible writing added: councils will be the scapegoat on difficult issues such as congestion charges and parking restrictions. Even the manifesto promises had been tinged with defeatism. On rail Labour would only 'improve the situation as we find it not as we wish it to be'.

Road and rail

It could not even deliver that minimal manifesto commitment. Labour accepted rail privatization as a *fait accompli* because it seemed to make no sense to spend billions on compensating shareholders in order to renationalize before even starting on transport improvement spending. Deeper down, Blair (Brown and Prescott too) had acquired an elemental faith in the effectiveness of private companies and the state's management incapacities. Yet the 'railway renaissance' it devoutly hoped for depended upon some new alignment of profit-seeking and public purpose. Gerald Corbett of Railtrack proved to be a fragile instrument for it. It was not necessarily easier if the state did run railways – track maintenance problems were delaying famously punctual German trains in November 2000 as losses exceeded expectations and planned privatization was deferred. Prescott's political ineptitude did not help, for he lost his place in the queue for parliamentary action in 1997 and his flagship legislation was delayed for nearly four years. That well-photographed 200-yard drive at Labour's 1998 conference stuck him with the two-Jags label.

The Tories had struck deals for a number of roads to be built under the private finance initiative (PFI), and the shadow tolls paid to the companies that designed and built them were taking an increasing share of road spending. A 1998 white paper, *A New Deal for Transport*, promised extensively, but signals were mixed. On roads, the emphasis shifted from new building to making existing roads better but that later changed again. Motorway tolls were mooted in the 1998 white paper but then abandoned.

People had been abandoning rail till the mid-1990s when, paradoxically, privatization and fragmentation hit just as passenger numbers started to grow. Between 1995 and the end of the century, the number of journeys increased by nearly 30 per cent, from 760 million to 947 million; rail was now carrying more people than at any time since 1945 and there were some 1,700 more trains operating daily in 2000 compared with five years previously.

No mystery there: in a small country with congested roads and rising incomes you get about by the best available means. John Major had sold off a prime national asset disgracefully cheap and safety was compromised in the split between track and twenty-five train operators. Railtrack – it was learnt after the Hatfield crash in October 2000 – openly boasted of driving down costs of maintenance.

Prescott blustered. Until 2000 he had no money, though the problem staring every passenger in the face was capacity. The regulatory model was supposed to let the state get shot of problem industries into the private sector but then retain the power to boss them around: it did not work. The privatized companies were simply not investing enough nor providing a good enough service. If the Government berated Railtrack and the train operators then the public – who quickly perceived them as no improvement on British Rail – questioned why they were not to be taken into public ownership. Investment had risen to £1.7 billion a year since 1997 but much more was needed to expand capacity, push up speed and guarantee safety. The Government inherited 7–15-year-long franchises and a mysterious system by which public subsidies seemed to transfer direct into the pockets of franchisees' shareholders. The Association of Train Operating Companies blamed failure on success in attracting more passengers and there was something to this, for a record number of trains was carrying a record number of people. Connex South Central commuters celebrated when the French-owned company became the first to lose their franchise, but what were the guarantees its replacement would be any better?

The Government stayed with the regulatory model but did little to simplify a dreadful complication summed up in an organization chart produced by the DETR. The Office of the Rail Regulator (ORR) gives operating licences to train operators but their franchises are decided by the Strategic Rail Authority (Prescott's new invention); the ORR decides Railtrack's finances but the Health and Safety Executive looks after safety. Then there are Passenger Transport Executives with train responsibilities in seven metropolitan areas, rolling stock companies, rail passenger committees and of course the DETR itself.

The Government appointed a tough guy to the ORR while the expert chair of the SRA, Sir Alistair Morton, was only part-time. The SRA remit was truncated: why could it not take an equity stake in Railtrack since it proposed to pump so much money into the private firm? It took muscular public intervention to secure the fast link to the Channel Tunnel: was not that the way forward across the network? Prescott's promised omnibus transport bill was delayed as Blair told critics transport was 'one for the second term'. Ladbroke Grove then Hatfield a year later pointed up his political error.

Rail safety became the issue. Before Lord Cullen's inquiry into the Paddington disaster was over, four people died in the derailment outside Hatfield, due apparently to one weak rail among scores already reported but not mended. Line closures and slow and non-existent trains added to the sense of a government not just lacking power but unwilling to command the public interest in safe and speedy travel. The fundamental confusion was financial. During the first five years of the century, the ORR is allowing Railtrack to spend nearly £15 billion, some £8.8 billion to come from train operators (i.e. passengers and the taxpayer via grants to train companies), some from its other business and £4.7 billion from Government grants. Amazingly, on top of that Railtrack would be allowed £2.6 billion 'rate of return' – profit. When the regulator announced that, Railtrack's shares rose 58½p in value – no wonder, when the state is so generous.

In the spending plans for 2001–4 announced in July 2000, rail spending was to increase in real terms by 125 per cent (compared to 18 per cent on trunk roads and motorways). Some £26 billion of the £60 billion the railways were supposed to invest in the first decade of the new century would be public money, with no shares in return to show for it. The rest would be paid by passengers in fares or private borrowing, backed by further fare increases. Similarly in London, without tax money it would have to be travellers who paid for expansion, regardless of the form of finance.

For the Tube, the Government was fixated on its PPP scheme: private firms would lease the lines while the Greater London Authority owned stations and signals. It smelt horribly like the same fragmentation and lack of accountability on the overground railway. Dislike of the scheme helped propel Labour renegade Ken Livingstone to the mayor's job. A theological debate ensued over how the money for capacity expansion was to be raised, through municipal bonds (Livingstone) or the PPP (Prescott). The crux questions were different – what was going to be the balance between subsidy from taxes and income from passengers? What management scheme would maximize safety and efficiency? In the meantime, after lengthy delays and mighty over-spend, the publicly built Jubilee Line was extended – a perfect example of public sector incompetence at big building projects, claimed the Blairites. The Docklands Light Railway, built privately, which had come in on time and on budget (though a far less difficult engineering task), was the perfect example, said the Blairites, of why they were opting for more public–private partnership. But the London public looked at the British Rail privatization fiasco and shuddered at the thought of the tube following in its tracks.

Horse-drawn speeds

Conscious of Mondeo Man's car passion, ministers rarely pointed out in public how many times safer it still was to travel by train than by car: it hardly seemed the thing to say in the wake of train crashes anyway. Labour is now promising an independent safety agency covering all transport which presumably will point up the comparison. For roads Labour promised new safety targets for the future: a 40 per cent reduction in road death and serious injury by 2010 and a 50 per cent reduction for children. But in 1998 road deaths were lower than at any time since records began in 1926. Politically controversial reductions in car speed, a precondition for cutting child and pedestrian deaths, were to be left to local discretion – meaning don't blame us.

Of course the safest way to travel by road is slow and, inadvertently, this was where we were heading. When Labour took power, traffic in central London moved at 10 m.p.h. on average, little better than a horse-drawn cart. Projected twenty years forward, every major road into the capital would be congested every day. Even on the most favourable assumptions, road traffic volumes in the UK at large will increase by 17 per cent by 2010. The answer was either to increase the cost of urban motoring or to improve public transport, or both. Number 10 took fright and instead of a general policy for city life, congestion charging was a hot potato passed on to councils. They could not be trusted to run schools or social services but they could take the flak on roads.

An independent study of congestion charging in London showed that a £5-a-day charge for cars in central London would cut traffic by about 10 per cent and raise about £250 million a year which, in principle, could be used to improve bus and train services. Experiments were run, for example in Leicester. Charging was a plank in the Livingstone campaign but in office he too appeared to get cold feet: charging was not acceptable until there was better transport, but there can be no better transport until the money comes in from charging.

That about sums up Labour and urban mobility: some local action, some good ideas but no overall sense of direction and scant willingness to offend motorists. Labour encouraged councils, as part of newly integrated transport plans, to 'calm' traffic. A start was made in the promotion of partnerships between councils and the bus services they once owned, offering better traffic management (bus lanes for example) and better schedules. Labour, mealy-mouthed, talked of 'quality contracts' between councils and bus companies but they had to await the delayed passage of the Transport Act. A quick glance round city streets will confirm or deny one promise – that the average age of buses would be cut to eight years by 2001. Improvements were made, notably in new tram and light rail systems. The July 2000 spending plan envisaged twenty-five new lines and double the number of tram passengers within ten years. Croydon tramway – the first in London for almost fifty years – was a successful public–private consortium established under the Tories. Schemes are under way in Nottingham and Sunderland; Bristol and Portsmouth want to follow. Private finance schemes can produce infrastructure but reliance on them may explain the half-heartedness that characterized Labour's transport planning. Public money could not be found, either, for cycling. Labour said it wanted to see 10,000 miles of cycleways by 2005, but two-thirds of these would be tiny tracks on dangerous existing roads where car congestion was building – and much of the construction would depend on the charity Sustrans and money from the Lottery.

Farming the public finances

Before Blair, Labour had been as much the farmers' sugar-daddy as the Tories: it was the Attlee Government that began extensive price support. But Labour's gut instinct was caught by John Prescott's remark about the 'contorted' faces of countryside protesters. The farming lobby was as cunning as the foxes they hunted: they cloaked their pro-hunting passions in a package of sentimental tropes about the country 'way of life', blurring the lines between the real agricultural recession and the carnal pleasures of the rich sportspeople. In opposition Labour had made hay with BSE (bovine spongiform encephalopathy was the cattle disease that produced a variant form of the fatal neurological condition Creutzfeldt-Jakob disease in humans). BSE was an aspect of the sleaze they were elected to clean up – greedy farmers fed cattle remains to herbivores for cheap protein. Blair – in the spirit of Harold Wilson's great faith in science as modernization – wanted to identify his government with the advance of knowledge, symbolized by the laboratory manipulation of plant and animal genetic structure. Fatally ambivalent as ever, he wanted the farmers, the fox-hunters and Monsanto in his big tent too, along with the greens and consumers.

So Blair sought to avoid urban v. rural, us and them divisions. The long-awaited urban white paper was published in

November 2000 just before a rural paper, implying that need was as great in one quarter as another when of course vastly more people lived in the towns and cities and vastly more of them were disadvantaged; no rural ward suffered the concentrated deprivation common in Manchester or Merseyside.

So it was striking how much obeisance the Government made to farmers, a group which were marginal demographically as well as economically. Their only real importance was in their stewardship of the land: they manage 75 per cent of the area of the UK. Even in the most intensely agricultural communities, only 4 per cent of the workforce was still engaged in farm work. The Phillips inquiry into BSE demonstrated just how much in thrall to the farmers the Ministry of Agriculture, Fisheries and Food (MAFF) was, and Blair had no wish to break that mould. In early April 2000, rather like Chris Tarrant on *Who Wants to be a Millionaire?*, he was seen to tear up one cheque and replace it with an even bigger one before handing it to the leader of the National Farmers' Union (NFU).

Blair's generosity was puzzling. The economic doctrines of competitiveness, flexibility and above all capacity to change apparently did not apply to farmers. Blair had been blindsided by that clever and determined lobbying group, the Countryside Alliance. Formed to protect fox-hunting, it had managed to persuade politicians and press that it stood for a mystical soul of the nation, a 'way of life' deserving public money and legal protection. Urbanites were passive as the myth was propagated. Labour had made gains in rural areas in the 1997 election and could not quite steel itself to say that the fate of the countryside did not depend on insulating fox-hunting farmers against market forces.

Farming was suffering a deep recession. Trade had shifted: for example impoverished Russia no longer bought British sheepskins and ever-precarious hill-farming collapsed. The big retailers squeezed suppliers. Labour pressed for faster reform of the Common Agricultural Policy. Meanwhile it delivered most of the money to all the wrong farmers – the very rich arable farmers who grubbed up ditches and produced grain mountains. Too little went to the impoverished tenant farmers of the hillsides whose dry-stone walling, hedging and ditching preserved the kind of countryside that the majority of the population – town-dwellers – wanted to use for their recreation. Farmers wanted to be producers, despite gross European over-production, and they complained that they did not want to become the nation's park-keepers. But tourism was for many their only destiny.

BSE

Agricultural incomes for cattle-farmers had also been jeopardized by farming's spectacular own goal, BSE, a compound of farmyard greed, scientific ignorance and administrative cowardice and ineptitude. The Phillips report in October 2000 tentatively fingered guilty men in Whitehall and the Tory Party but was reluctant to address deeper questions about food quality and price. So were Labour and the Food Standards Agency, set up in April 2000 with an independent chair and a £160 million a year budget for 2,000 staff recruited mostly from the ranks of MAFF.

Labour's first contribution to this sorry tale was in December 1997 when Jack Cunningham banned the sale of beef on the bone for two years; it was the right decision taken expeditiously. Typically it led to an outburst from the farmers and the right, as if BSE had never happened. It became a bizarre emblem for right-wing commentators of the imaginary 'nanny' state, as if BSE were a joke. Even Prince Charles made a point of eating illegal beef on the bone in front of the cameras. Since then the supply of beef tissue for human consumption was said to be as near safe as scientific evidence could say. But the UK still did not routinely test for BSE in cattle slaughtered for meat and did not, as some other countries, destroy all the animals in herds where a case of BSE had been identified. The long gestation of the disease meant it was during Labour's tenure the human death toll started to grow, as people showed symptoms of nvCJD contracted, it seems, from eating contaminated beef as long as fifteen years previously. British cattle are still contracting BSE. Anxieties were stretched by the suggestion that symptomless animals may be carriers. To the Government's credit it did not quibble over compensation for victims and their carers.

BSE played some part in accelerating Euroscepticism when in December 1999 the French refused to heed a European Commission judgement on the safety of UK-produced beef. Silly gesture politics by the heir to the throne and Nick Brown, Cunningham's successor as Agriculture Minister, did not help, as the latter declared he would not eat anything French and brandished £5 million for a Buy British campaign. Only an Agriculture Minister would have been permitted to behave so crassly. A lethal blend of food panic, hyper-patriotism and Euro-scepticaemia seem to have infected brains even around Blair's cabinet table.

Yet as to what should be grown on farms, rationality and humanity prevailed. Subsidies were offered to organic farmers and 'agri-environment' schemes. The £140 million over the years to 2005 for organics was not enough for the queue of farmers who needed help converting fields to cover the fallow years this required. £500 million was given for improved 'stewardship' of the countryside. Subject to EU approval, Brown put £152 million over a longer-run diversification plan for farms. Labour deserves some credit for its role in promoting a new EU directive on the welfare of farm animals, which came into force on 1 January 2000, to set minimum standards for the housing and feeding not just of hens, pigs and calves but all farm fauna.

The Government took the robust view that genetically modi-fied (GM) crops had to be tried out before they could be condemned. Only field-scale trials would produce the evidence, though ministers had to think again about distances between GM fields and neighbouring flora. Blair's watchword was 'informed and balanced debate' – not easy in a press-fostered panic over 'Frankenstein' foods and the green Lord Melchett tearing up crops for the television cameras with his bare hands. The Government established an Agriculture and Environment Biotechnology Commission to provide advice and in September 1999 extended compulsory labelling of GM products to catering. No GM crops were to be cultivated commercially till 2003 and then only if some kind of scientific consensus had been reached. This was cool politics in a hothouse of emotions, for which Blair deserves commendation.

Uncool was Labour's response to the first march by the Countryside Alliance in 1997. A Countryside Agency was created and it was even headed by a landowner. Lacking any clear idea how much in total was spent on rural districts (or urban for that matter), the Government rushed to throw in *ad hoc* hush-money – £170 million extra for buses and rural transport, safeguards for village shops and post offices through 50 per cent rate relief, an end to the policy of closing small schools, NHS Direct saving people from visits to the doctor and extra subsidy for rural housing.

Hunting and roaming

On hunting, the Government at first prevaricated, doing itself no favours. A private member's bill to ban hunting with hounds was scuppered. The ensuing promise to legislate 'as soon as we possibly can' was slow in realization. Lord Burns, the Treasury mandarin sacked by Gordon Brown for his Tory attachments, was asked to review claims of lost jobs if hunting dogs were no longer allowed to tear their prey apart. He was not persuaded. Yet again Blair chose to air his convictions unexpectedly on a television show: after all the hedging, he now declared his intention to ban hunting. A vote on four options was offered in the Queen's speech in December 2000.

More progress was made on a statutory right to roam, a cause close to the heart of the old left of the party since the Kinder Scout mass trespass in the 1930s. It was one of the issues that had the Countryside Alliance up in arms – townies tramping on their private green acres – but on this the Government rightly faced them down.

The Countryside Act would open up 4 million acres of countryside, though developed and agricultural land is excluded, other than that used for extensive grazing. Local forums are to be set up to discuss access. Labour established new national parks with their strong planning regimes covering the New Forest and parts of the South Downs, and the 'countryside' itself extended: 30,000 hectares, three times the size of Bristol, was newly classified as Green Belt where development was tightly controlled. Admirable: but where then were people to find homes? Labour's response was only marginally less of a prevarication than the constitutionally pro-Nimby Tories had been.

Cities

For townies were growing in number. Projections based on 1998 said England would have some 4.3 million more households in 2021. This implied some 50,000 extra homes coming on stream each year in the south-east of England – but the Government had chickened out of making such a projection ahead of the election. About a third of the new homes would need to be 'affordable', built by councils or social landlords. If they were not built, overcrowding and involuntary sharing would grow – not necessarily a catastrophe, but carrying consequences for lifestyles and amenity. Meanwhile the big cities of the north were losing numbers, though mainly to northern regions rather than the south. London, too, was losing people, but total population there is going to rise thanks to international migration. Where once Labour ministers would have relished regional plans and dreamed of new towns to cope with such patterns of change, the Blairites merely shivered.

Mindful of its new political presence in the shires of the south-east, Prescott strove to palliate the Nimbys, choosing figures for house-building to put to councils that were lower than those produced by his own department. Instead of the Tory scheme of 'predict and provide', Labour's formula was provide, plan and monitor. The difference was not clear: central government still had one way or another to persuade or force the south and east to make room. Labour's alternative was 'brownfield', the re-use of derelict land developed in the past for housing or industry, together with renewal of existing housing. In principle a large chunk of likely growth in households and commerce over the next few decades could be accommodated by such recycling. The official target was to build 60 per cent of new housing on previously developed land. A new database of brownfield sites was commissioned, with the hope that it might eventually be extended to include all empty properties. But brown fields were expensive to reclaim and Labour, no longer the party of planning, was reluctant to attempt to direct developers to available sites or to seek to concentrate growth around existing 'hot spots' such as Milton Keynes or Ashford. Brownfield development had been one of Michael Heseltine's great ambitions, too, though he, unlike Labour, had the wit to establish powerful development corporations. He had been active in pushing the Greenwich Dome, and after the event instead of weeping he justified it as regeneration of a toxic site – though at nearly £1 billion it was hardly a model of cost-effective reclamation.

Labour had a vision of urban renewal for people as well as property, but its spending restraint cramped its style and its political caution forbade brave gestures. It commissioned the man whose Beaubourg centre had helped revitalize the Halles district of Paris – Lord Rogers of Riverside as he became – to dream of better cities. Rogers, not surprisingly after visiting Amsterdam and Barcelona, said cities were public entities that only worked thanks to huge and continuing investments in public spaces, public services and subsidized transport. He added that autonomous city government with real power and financial strength was also part of it. Under his influence, Labour talked up such ideas as 'home zones', streets where children can play in daylight hours which put pedestrians first (the UK had the second highest fatality rate in Europe for child pedestrians). He spoke of 'mixed-use' communities integrating different forms of housing with retailing, local services, transport and jobs. Labour's delayed response, in the urban white paper and Brown's pre-budget report, did offer some incentives and revised planning guidelines. There were tax credits to buy flats over shops in run-down areas, concessions on stamp duty ditto and £1 billion for cleaning up and conversions. Rogers had envisaged something altogether bolder: he became another of those fished from the pool of talent by Labour into taskforces, only to have their findings sidelined and their expertise squandered.

Yet Labour was mindful of how exclusion and inequality were concentrated in the cities and put huge administrative effort into urban regeneration. It followed policy largely invented by Heseltine, whereby local groups usually led by councils made bids for money from a central pot. The same model was used in dispensing new pots of regeneration money such as the New Deal for Communities and then, more ambitious still, the National Strategy for Neighbourhood Renewal, both described in Chapter 2. An older quango responsible for clearing sites for factories, English Partnerships, gave up some ground to the new Regional Development Agencies. Gordon Brown weighed in with his plans for 'social investment' to boost enterprise in the inner cities, as the focus of policy shifted from physical structures to the people who occupied them.

Many environmental questions rely on local councils to take action. Agenda 21 – a formula for local action adopted at the 1990 Rio environmental summit – had led to some councils making a bigger effort, such as encouraging households to recycle waste, which would cut the use of landfill sites and incineration. That was all going on under the Tories and it continued, but the UK was, after four years of Labour, just as poor a performer in European league green tables as before.

Here, as elsewhere, good intentions were never quite enough. The Environment Agency's website put up a searchable inventory

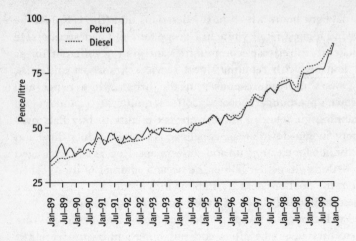

Figure 14: Average UK retail prices for premium unleaded petrol and diesel cash prices

Source: House of Commons Library

of polluting companies, but despite new legislative controls pollution fines were derisory: as ever, business was not to be affronted, not even to clean up its own filth. The large-scale sell-off of woods by the Forestry Commission ceased and new forest was promoted. The regime for sites of special scientific interest was strengthened. Labour introduced a string of measures small in themselves but vital for the more humane treatment of animals and maintaining the diversity of species: fur-farming was banned, so was shooting in sensitive wetlands, with new areas of special protection for fowl and new bird species protection plans.

As a party Labour had never been especially 'green'. It had bleated with the animal rights protesters in opposition but stood aside when Swampie and the tree-huggers were briefly joined by twinset and pearl protesters. A party born and bred in the industrial heartlands had not reinvented itself on this front: ask

Financial year	At 1999/2000 prices (£ billion)
1992/93	13.7
1993/94	14.9
1994/95	16.4
1995/96	17.6
1996/97	18.6
1997/98	20.5
1998/99	22.1
1999/2000	22.5
2000/2001	22.8

Figure 15: Net receipts of hydrocarbon oil duties

Source: House of Commons Library

most Labour MPs and in any contest the poor and economic growth come way ahead of greenery.

Blair tried to play two ends against the middle. It is unlikely that pollution control, safer food or above all reduction of carbon emissions can be had without the public having to make sacrifices along the way. Things will cost more. Governments everywhere hope that clever new technology or world prices will save them just in time from having to impose unpopular sacrifices on unwilling electorates. They could be lucky: if oil prices rise sharply that will lift greener alternatives such as wind and solar power into competitive viability, the mighty market solving everything. But if not, Labour did little to prepare people for a future of more expensive, less plentiful energy. In November 2000 the sight of fuel-protesting hauliers trying to drive their lorries through flooded York showed how little the public connected the use of fuel with environmental catastrophe.

10

Modernization

A prime duty of any Prime Minister in a democracy is to use the office to buttress public respect for government itself. In this Tony Blair failed. The people – ill-informed and apathetic as many were – had started with hopes of some newer, cleaner, brighter politics but Labour, 'new' as it called itself, all too soon looked like business as usual. Bernie Ecclestone's cash, Peter Mandelson's high-living on secret borrowings, tight controls and warped votes in Wales and London and civil war between the Brownites and Blairites – what was new about that?

Four years on, most measures of political attitudes towards politics had plunged below 1997's mark. There had been no recovery in voter turn-out for elections, and predictions for a 2001 general election were as low as 65 per cent. During their tenure the Tories had poisoned the wells, teaching the public to despise not only politicians but public works and fear government spending. In the years of Aitken and Hamilton, the Commons itself was devalued thanks to those brown envelopes. Labour's offences against the public's faith in politics were far less heinous but then higher standards had been expected of them.

But on the broader canvas Blair had recalibrated the relationship of the people of the UK with their Government. On his monument they will etch the permanent and profound change he made in Wales and Scotland and perhaps yet Northern Ireland too. Devolution does offer a prospect of democracy revived. But then Blair also had the strength to secure great and permanent change in the relationship between the people and the Westminster Parliament by introducing a voting system that would allow more proportional representation in the Commons. He

flinched and a once-and-for-all opportunity was frittered away
– a failure of nerve and imagination Labour (and the country)
will regret if ever a minority right-wing Conservative Party again
holds sway, as it did for eighteen years, 1979–97.

Under Labour nonetheless the constitution was reconstituted.
'Even today,' said Labour's National Policy Forum in 2000, 'the
scale of the changes to our democratic institutions is in some
ways underestimated.' If so, there are good reasons. Labour
could never quite weave a convincing tale about what it was
doing or why. There was no coherent pattern to the patchwork
of constitutional reforms, all of which had their own individual
rationale, none of which were stitched together to make much
sense, to 'tell a story'.

Lords reform was always going to be arduous but bold strokes
that might have cut a path through the jungle were not taken;
little effort was made to rouse the people against the peers. The
Human Rights Act, empowering citizens to check and sue the
state, would have been all the more of an achievement had it
been linked with measures to shore up the value of collective
action and the authority needed by a progressive state. Still,
no incoming Tory Government would ever dare afterwards to
reverse the reforms Labour did make. Government by ermine-
clad aristos is more or less gone for good – even if some of them
still cling on. Scotland's Parliament and Wales' Assembly are
permanent, but not a word was heard about the equally hereditary monarchy. The heir to the throne wanted to be defender of
faiths, he said, but in fact would become, if he succeeded,
Defender of the Faith, that peculiar title acquired by Henry
VIII but still emblazoned on the coinage. Tony Blair delivered
the national verdict on Diana's death in August 1997 but about
the institution she had forced into such public scrutiny he had
no public thoughts to offer. Constitutional change failed to touch
an established church to which (if Sunday weather was fine)
barely 3 per cent of the population went.

Modernization

As a theme tune 'modernization' wafted in and out of hearing range, audible when the forces of conservatism were being excoriated at Labour's 1999 conference, faint whenever it was seeking to pacify Middle England. Never explicitly defined, it shaded into democratization, meaning an effort to breathe new life into participative government by bringing its institutions physically or figuratively closer to the people, making them more accessible, accountable and intelligible. But Blair also wanted to govern effectively. That led Labour to cut local authority functions even further, to march a company of special advisers into Whitehall and to resist the clamour for public access to the private world of government information. All this it did not 'join up'.

It was constitutional reform in a fit of absence of mind. Looking at all Labour did, Professor Peter Hennessy declared that 'there is no precedent since 1688 for such a concentrated and deliberate rebuilding of the constitutional architecture'. But you have to ask, he said, 'why this extraordinary enterprise lacked the central position it deserved in the self-image of this most image-conscious of administrations'. The answer, perhaps, is that it suited many to keep quiet. Scottish Nationalists were not going to trumpet changes that, judging by opinion polls since devolution, have as intended killed Scots' appetite for independent statehood. For the sake of their English campaigning, Liberal Democrats needed to keep quiet about the extent of their coalition intimacy with Labour in Edinburgh and Cardiff. The Tories mostly held their peace out of fear that the new arrangements would indeed eventually enamour government to the people.

Proportional representation

Behind the scenes in the company of the favoured few, Tony Blair liked to lean back on the sofa, put his feet up on the coffee table and expansively talk of his dream for the new century. The twentieth was Tory, thanks to the freaks of first-past-the-post voting. Thatcher held sway with barely more than 40 per cent of the vote, while a majority of progressive forces (Blair's phrase) voted against her. Reuniting that century-old tribal split in the anti-Conservative majority was the big project. He was right: proportional representation was the fulcrum of realignment, possibly offering pro-Europe Tories a way of winning through, possibly offering the remnants of the far left a small chance of seats (Tommy Sheridan showed how in Scotland).

In opposition, talks with the Liberal Democrats had gone far; in the event of a smallish Labour majority in 1997 – up to fifty – maybe three cabinet seats would have been found for Paddy Ashdown and pals. PR was to follow. Early on, despite the scale of Labour's victory, that still seemed Blair's intention and his mentor Lord Jenkins was to be his way of realizing it. Jenkins would report and be 'free to consider and recommend any appropriate system or combination of systems in recommending an alternative'. In a further definition, which both sides fought over, he was to stick with 'broad proportionality, the need for stable government, an extension of voter choice and the maintenance of a link between honourable members and geographical constituencies'. Jenkins did the business, producing an elegant report and practical voting reform.

But Labour had no constitutional strategy, no broad picture of how power should be redistributed. Perhaps, the landslide having gone to his head, Blair believed he had ten years and could return to the turf – but of course there never is bright confident morning again. No connection was made between Commons reform, the Lords or the prospect of regional government for England or with Blair's wider thinking about trust in government. This was absence of joined-up thinking with a vengeance. By the time Jenkins produced his report in 1998, PR was clearly no longer a priority. A year after that, Prescott could without contradiction publicly promise to dump the Liberals and PR with them.

Blair was aware of his lack of courage – he subsequently said his failure to bring Paddy Ashdown into his cabinet in 1997 had been a great error; the price and the prize would have been PR. The Labour Party and some members of the cabinet were antagonistic but Blair in those early months was a master of the universe. The public were said to be bored by voting systems – a bad excuse since the many are rarely deeply engaged with any public policy, and when asked in polls did favour a more proportional system.

Yet PR was introduced when the Scots, Welsh and London electorates (for the Greater London Assembly) voted through the Additional Member System. The new Northern Ireland Assembly relied on the Single Transferable Vote and the Mayor of London was selected by Supplementary Vote. Regional lists ensured proportionality for the European Parliament election – though again Blair's insistence on a closed list system giving all power to party in selection of candidates soured enthusiasm. This was changed; next time open lists would let voters choose their representatives. Meanwhile the Scottish executive started to examine PR for local authorities north of the border. But John Prescott ruled it out for English local authorities, where it might have been a way of breathing life into single-party (Labour) rotten boroughs.

With the PR it did introduce, Labour was forced to concede power but in doing so introduced a new kind of government never before practised in the UK. In the elections of May 1999 Labour lost overall control of the new Scottish and Welsh Assemblies. The Tories, staunch opponents of PR then and since, were rewarded with eighteen Scottish Parliament seats for their 15.6 per cent share of the first vote. Coalition government resulted immediately in Edinburgh, after fifteen months in

Cardiff. Control freaks, as they were alleged to be in London, found almost at once that they could not control a Scottish Parliament intent, for example, on changing arrangements for university tuition fees.

Devolution

The promise to devolve had been inherited from Labour leader John Smith, necessary if Labour were to keep the Scottish National Party at bay. Whatever Blair's private sentiments, in office his commitment never wavered. The late Donald Dewar received credit for his perseverance but Tony Blair was devolution's midwife. From the referendum on 11 September 1997 to the Scotland Act 1998 and thence to the first elections to the Scottish Parliament in May 1999, Labour's promises were fully redeemed. On a turn-out of 62 per cent, Scottish voters said yes by 74 per cent to a Parliament and yes by 64 per cent on whether it could raise taxes (a bit). Similarly in Wales, though margins were narrower. There, turn-out on 18 September 1997 was only 50 per cent and the narrowest assent given to an Assembly by only 50.3 per cent; the nature of the Cardiff Assembly was more ambiguous.

Neither Parliament nor Assembly enjoyed a good press after their birth, but open-minded assessors noted the strength of the committee system in Edinburgh, the civilized nature of proceedings and the potential for representatives to subject the executive to scrutiny in a way Westminster MPs had never managed. The physical appearance of Scottish government certainly altered: 37 per cent of the Parliament's 129 members were women. New machinery was invented to secure coordination between London and Edinburgh. One, the Council of the Isles, sprang from the Good Friday agreement in Northern Ireland. Others, such as 'concordats' between Whitehall departments and the devolved administrations and various joint committees, secured practical power-sharing. The Scottish

Parliament repealed Section 28 (Clause 28), abolished the remnants of feudalism and forbade the forced sale of debtors' property.

The inauguration of a measure of self-government in Wales was marred by Tony Blair's never entirely explained decision to insist on Alun Michael as Labour leader over Rhodri Morgan after Welsh Secretary Ron Davies's famous stroll on Clapham Common. It was a big mistake. Labour, lacking a majority, governed in Cardiff on sufferance. Michael lost the Assembly's confidence and Morgan replaced him in February 2000. The press mocked an administration with a vegetarian Agriculture Secretary – missing the point that (excluding the ambivalent experience of the Stormont Parliament) the UK had never previously been able to compare parliamentary procedure and performance: maybe in the long run a few more vegetarians in post-BSE food and farming administration would not go amiss. John Reid, the Scotland Secretary (something of a non-job after July 1999), called devolution a process not an event. Rhodri Morgan capped the aphorism by saying people confused performance with existence. There is space between the two for new styles and new qualities of government. So did things get better? Polls in Scotland certainly suggest few would wish to return to the old way, though it remains to be seen whether devolution will enhance trust by the governed in their government. Press attacks on alleged extravagance (£400 million plus in total) in constructing new buildings at Holyrood and by Cardiff Bay did not help. But the experiment was necessary.

Northern Ireland

Blair's passionate determination to enter the history books as a peacemaker in the North of Ireland explains the huge investment of political time and energy he made in Ulster. The Good Friday Agreement of 1998 was a personal achievement. It led to the creation of a new multi-party executive; it also led to the explosion of a car bomb in the centre of Omagh in August 1998 and, with twenty-nine men, women and children killed and 220 injured, the biggest single death toll in thirty years of conflict and other murderous efforts. Labour's manifesto promises were vague. It inherited a 'peace process' stemming from the Forum election of May 1996. Northern Ireland Secretary Mo Mowlam affirmed Sinn Fein could enter the talks due to resume in September 1997 provided there was an IRA ceasefire, which was called in July 1997. The process was kept going after a courageous visit by Mowlam to persuade Loyalist prisoners in the Maze prison to sanction ongoing talks, under the chairmanship of former US Senator George Mitchell.

The result, after frantic negotiations, was the Good Friday Agreement, dated 10 April 1998, between the Northern Irish parties, Blair and Fianna Fáil Prime Minister Bertie Ahern. Its phrasing recognized that Northern Ireland would continue in the UK as long as a majority wished it. The constitution of the Republic of Ireland was to be amended to end its irredentist claims on the North. An elected Assembly was to be set up in Belfast after elections designed to give all parties a share of office. Joint bodies were to encourage consultation and new equalities and rights commissions were established. In a referendum in May, 71.1 per cent of Northern Ireland voters backed it and Assembly elections went ahead. To Blair and Labour belongs much credit, though ideological changes within both the Republican movement and Ulster Unionism played their parts, together with President Bill Clinton.

In principle, here was a platform not just for peace on the streets but for reform of relations within what historian Norman Davies christened the Isles – the pentagular system of states and governments across the Irish Sea and within the island of Ireland. But the agreement was hedged about with fatal ambiguity, especially on the core issue of the decommissioning of IRA weapons. Symbolic concessions were made to the nationalists. Lord Saville, a senior judge, was commissioned to inquire into the 'Bloody Sunday' events of 1972. But decommissioning did not happen. During 1999 Sinn Fein/IRA's insistence that the removal of guns and bomb-making equipment had to obey no timetable and the Unionists' insistence that decommissioning was the *sine qua non* of cooperative government in Northern Ireland were talked and bargained over without end.

Senator Mitchell was recalled to the colours and Labour asked the former Tory Party chairman Chris Patten to review the Royal Ulster Constabulary. His report, in September 1999, could be seen as mere modernization of the force, turning it into a community police operation. In the circumstances of Northern Ireland it was however deeply contentious. Labour's policy became maximizing concessions to the IRA/Sinn Fein for the sake of minimum levels of violence while hoping the Unionists would stay on board. By the middle of November – Mandelson's personal skills widely recognized – a temporary basis for the establishment of devolved executive government had been found, though one of its 'planks' was a commitment by David Trimble to resign if the IRA had not commenced decommissioning of its weapons by February.

Come February 2000 Mandelson had rapidly to push through legislation suspending the executive. Mandelson had to contend with an Irish Government taking an increasingly pro-nationalist line, misreading the pressures on Trimble. Like Mowlam before him, Mandelson's fate was to be bypassed by Blair since the dramatis personae believed (probably accurately) that they could get more out of last-minute summits involving Prime Ministers. From one of these, in May, emerged a formula for blindfolded 'inspection' of IRA weapons dumps by Cyril Ramaphosa, the former Secretary General of the African National Congress, and Martti Ahtisaari, former President of Finland. Trimble's political position crumbled, leading Mandelson to take the high risk of implicitly threatening Unionists with some version of 'joint rule' by London and Dublin if they did not back him. Decommissioning in the terms envisaged by the Good Friday Agreement did not happen.

But peace of a kind did hold – fewer soldiers but 'Real IRA' bombs (its personnel, methods and munitions known to the IRA proper), masked men firing weapons over tricolour-draped coffins and continuing local intimidation. Blair's achievement amounted to de-escalation, temporary or permanent, who knows. The larger goal he set himself – to establish a functioning devolved government for Northern Ireland embracing Irish nationalists and former terrorists – hung there unrealized.

The Commons

Blair did not seem to see that the imperative behind devolution also applied to the operations of the House of Commons. Labour MPs elected in May 1997 proved either too shell-shocked or too deferential to stir the muddy waters of Westminster. A modernization effort of sorts got going after Labour came to power. It led to better timetabling of bills, clearer explanatory papers to go with them and the publication of bills in draft to allow for earlier feedback. A new style of debate was staged in Westminster Hall (adjacent to the Commons chamber) for matters for which time could not be found in the chamber itself – though mainly this became just a means of MPs reading speeches into the public record to satisfy their constituents. A minor experiment in hours was launched, with the Commons sitting on a Thursday from 11.30 in the morning to 7.00 p.m. The top hat was retired: MPs no longer had to raise one to make points of order during divisions.

But Ann Taylor and Margaret Beckett, Chief Whip and Leader respectively, kept going the old myth that any change to Commons procedure had to have cross-party agreement, proving gender was no guarantee of radicalism. Blair despised the Commons and did all he could to prevent its improvement. Labour even slowed the technical re-equipment of a legislature that is still Victorian in habit and performance. Labour persisted with the stupid and insulting formula 'These are matters for Parliament rather than Government to decide' – when everyone knew the whips answered to the executive, not to some mystical corporation of MPs.

Blair had promised progress towards wiring up Britain, yet only a handful of MPs, and a good few of them Tories and Liberal Democrats at that, had personal websites. The pace at which they started using e-mail was glacial. Labour showed little interest in redefining the purpose of backbench MPs or the powers of select committees. A polite request from the Liaison Committee of chairs of these select committees for staff and new powers was repulsed. Most of all they wanted recognition by ministers that making law and policy should be a more consensual business, in which MPs are partners. Strengthening their committees was a chance to reinvigorate trust in Parliament, but what government volunteers to facilitate challenges to its own absolute authority? Not Tony Blair. Again, the absence of any bigger constitutional picture in which to site specific reforms was telling.

Prime Minister's questions was repackaged from twice a week to a single weekly session but too often still the Commons was a zoo. Studied inaction by Number 10 over the election to replace Betty Boothroyd as Speaker in October 2000 meant the forces of conservatism prevailed again – though commentators were quick to point out that by this stage any indication of Blair's preference would have been a kiss of death. The election of Michael Martin as Speaker saw that erstwhile radical Tony Benn writing articles for the *Daily Mail*, as if he in his dotage had come to believe the Tories cared two hoots for MPs' autonomy.

The Lords

It was a Labour Government that passed the 1948 Parliament Act which – it was thought – finally settled the question of how much legislative weight the second chamber should have. Visceral dislike of the hereditary principle had fuelled the Wilson Government's attempt at Lords reform, scuppered by that peculiar combination of Enoch Powell and Michael Foot. The Blairites here as elsewhere were Bourbons, remembering nothing and forgetting nothing. In their approach to the Lords, their refusal either to act boldly or to build reform on first principles proved their undoing. In half-abolishing hereditary peerages in a half-reformed upper chamber, Labour wholly deserved the mess it found itself in by autumn 2000 when the still-extant majority of Tories and 'crossbenchers' (mostly Tories by instinct and voting habit if not by name) thwarted the passage of critical legislation with a renewed sense of their own legitimacy.

Labour decided on its half-measures because it did not want to confront the key questions of whether the British constitution needed a second chamber and, if so, whether it had to be elected. The first question was barely addressed. The white paper *Modernising Parliament: Reforming the House of Lords*, published in early 1999, was vacuous. It merely toyed with options for reconstituting the second chamber, apparently unconcerned with the outcome. A trusty Tory, Lord Wakeham, moonlighting from his day job as PR for the newspaper interests (chair of the Press Complaints Commission), was asked to tour round the country collecting views on how a second chamber should be formed. Almost no members of the public turned up. He proposed a handful of elected peers revolving every fifteen years, the rest appointed.

The House of Lords Act abolished the automatic right of hereditary peers to sit and vote in Parliament, but the revolutionary significance of the measure was wrecked by the decision to allow the selfsame hereditaries to vote among themselves on which ninety-two should stay on, like zombies, to terrorize democracy from beyond the grave. This then was the 'transitional house'. No single party commanded a majority, though the cross-benchers threw power consistently to the Tories. Instead of the 1,100 peers in the old Lords, most of them Tory by conviction or declared allegiance, by autumn 2000 there were 232 Tory supporters overshadowing Labour's 182 peers – swamped in turn by the Liberal Democrats' fifty-four plus the

161 Tory-leaning cross-benchers. The Prime Minister had given up his right to veto nominations made by other political parties and his powers were further diluted by the creation of an Appointments Commission to nominate new unaffiliated cross-benchers. Things definitely got worse. The transition became a nightmare. Real reform remains to be done – the extirpation of all existing members and their replacement either by elected members or some mixture of elected and appointed.

The fundamental question remained unanswered – however they came to be there, should an upper chamber have the power to block and/or delay Commons legislation? If not, why bother with one at all? Blair already faced the prospect of never again having the kind of Commons majority by which radical reform of the upper house could be accomplished. His intention in all this was never clear.

The danger had always been a repeat of the Harold Wilson experience. If one firm model for the reformed Lords had been presented from the start, an unholy alliance of those who wanted no reform would have linked arms with those who wanted some other model. If the strange agreement to keep a sample of the old fossils had not been struck, the guerrilla war threatened by the old codgers could have lost a full year of Government legislation: Asquith's tactic of a mass emergency creation of peers was something Blair had promised not to adopt. The public's interest in these arcane matters was strictly limited, and a year-long all-out battle against the ermine might have seemed frivolous to those waiting for concrete change in schools and hospitals.

Labour and the machine of state

New Labour did not tamper unduly with the machinery of state it inherited from the Tories. Perhaps it should have done. Lord Phillips's BSE report exposed the narrowness of the civil service mindset and its failure to put a wider public interest before departmental imperatives. Ministers increasingly found their civil servants unable to think 'outside the box'.

But the biggest problem was Labour's own: it would not or could not devote time to modernizing the government machine. Blair revelled in the exercise of 'prerogative power' – the mass of discretionary decisions open to the Prime Minister with minimal external supervision and no basis in statute law. Labour saw no reason to make the centre any more transparent.

Nor did it seek to turn government on its head and put the brains and the civil service salaries into service delivery closer to real people. The ease and sure-footedness of Labour's arrival in power gave way to an enervating sense that the machine was not suited to realizing their priorities, but they no longer had the verve or confidence to reform it. In opposition Labour had bought heavily into Tory changes – executive agencies, managerialism and private sector contracts. Blair said he wanted to emphasize outcomes rather than the process of governing but did not grasp how much of a change in personnel and ethos this would require. He selected as replacement Cabinet Secretary (after Robin Butler's retirement) Sir Richard Wilson, who had manfully steered the Home Office through Michael Howard's tenure. Wilson's appointment guaranteed continuity but closed the door on radical reorganization. One of the few top civil servants with hands-on experience of dispensing services directly to the public, Sir Michael Bichard at DFEE, former chief executive of the Benefits Agency, was passed over.

Sir Richard Wilson produced a white paper, *Modernising Government* (March 1999), advocating better training of officials and ministers (who conspicuously failed to turn up to the courses subsequently laid on by the new Centre for Management and Policy Studies within the Cabinet Office). Tony Blair talked of the impact of new technology on government. By 2005 basic dealings with government, central and local, are to be conducted electronically. The impact of this edict was somewhat blunted when it was discovered civil servants were interpreting electronic to include the 120-year-old telephone.

The Blairites came to realize how the old baronial Whitehall departments made government rigid, but they did little to rearrange Whitehall's deckchairs. They kept MAFF, despite the relative unimportance of farming. No departments for Europe, children or women were founded. They created the jumbo Department of Environment, Transport and the Regions and the Department for International Development. It was not long, however, before DETR was regretted, as transport rose to the top of the political agenda. The need to placate John Prescott prevented dividing it up again.

An often-put charge against Tony Blair needs to be quickly settled. If he were as Napoleonic as his critics alleged, why did he not fight and win Whitehall battles? He did strengthen the Prime Minister's office but the Treasury under Brown was strong, too. But the much vaunted 'joining up' remained a goal rather than a reality. This was not 'politicization'; none of the protocols defining the boundaries of party and government were jeopardized, even after a kerfuffle in press and public relations where Alistair Campbell sat in the equivalent of a permanent secretary's chair. An innovation at Number 10 was the creation of the post of chief of staff, held by Jonathan Powell. Its 'innovativeness' was however somewhat diminished by the social fact that Mr Powell's brother Charles had been Mrs Thatcher's private secretary and political intimate, performing much the same function. When in September 2000 the polls suddenly showed a Tory lead, civil servants high and low were as able as in the past to contemplate switching to serve ministers of a different political stripe. Blair sought to strengthen the 'centre of the centre' and established new, intellectually alert units dealing with social exclusion and performance. These made an effort to reach out to universities, the voluntary sector, business and society at large to widen the source of information and ideas. Imaginative and effective government could not be done by civil servants alone.

Many more special advisers were brought in to strengthen the influence of ministers over their departments, and to act as political brains bridging the divide between departments and politics. For all the venom poured on them by the Opposition, and resentment at usurpation from within Whitehall, the best of them were good brains collating bright ideas from outside the narrow Whitehall loop. They were able to explain policy better than civil servants, they made government more open. Spending on special advisers rose from £1.9 million a year under Major to over £4 million – which paid for some seventy-four people. Blair had twenty non-civil-service people in Downing Street compared to Major's eight. The Committee on Standards in Public Life investigated and the Government accepted its recommendation that their numbers should be capped (Lord Neill suggested they could rise to 100), together with a code of practice on what special advisers did, including meeting lobbyists.

The press said 'cronyism' and were gratified when the Equal Opportunities Commission concurred, charging Lord Irvine with unfairness towards women applicants for the position of his special adviser. As an eighteen-year-long Tory establishment gave way to a new army, there were the inevitable Tory complaints as their people were replaced. The Commissioner for Public Appointments found Labour had appointed identifiable party supporters to 14.7 per cent of open positions on health trusts, advisory bodies and the like, compared with 3.4 per cent Tories and 0.9 per cent Liberal Democrats. But did that really signify party takeover of the state? Frank Dobson addressed the charge by pointing out that 8.9 per cent of appointees to public bodies were from ethnic minorities and 39 per cent were women. A study of the north-east found public jobs dominated by middle-aged white men but under Labour more women were appointed to health trusts and similar. The quango state was alive and well but there was little evidence that Labour had deformed proper procedure in making its appointments – if anything Labour had widened the pool from which Government was able to draw talent.

Labour's energetic review of policy by means of scores of advisory groups or taskforces was new and served to bring 'outsiders' into the business of government from the voluntary sector and local government as well as business. To employ David Mellor, the ex-Tory turned sports commentator, to head a football taskforce was pluralism of a kind the Tories themselves would never have contemplated. Yet little was done to clarify where quango responsibilities ended and those of elected politicians began: Dame Helena Shovelton fell foul of this ambiguity when she was forced out of the chair at the National Lottery Commission, after making a bungle of the choice between Branson's People's Lottery and Camelot.

Labour's attitude towards public sector workers, who had once been a key Labour constituency, was confused. What Labour did not seem to see, or if it did failed ever to say, was that better public services depended on attracting and keeping well-motivated and able public servants. That in turn required higher pay and also praise and encouragement for the virtues of public service. The latter, which cost nothing, the Blairites found oddly hard to do. While once public sector unions would have found a new voice when a Labour Government came to power, now market forces ruled. Public sector workers got annual increments but no re-assessment of the overall relation of their pay to earnings at large. The down-side to near-full employment for the skilled was that Labour discovered that would-be nurses, teachers and Whitehall economists had better opportunities elsewhere. To make up for the shortfall the Treasury had to suspend rules forbidding employment of non-UK nationals, leading to an influx of New Zealanders. Recruitment in London became particularly difficult because increasing allowances for staff could only be afforded by lowering them for staff in say, the north, where living costs were less. Unions were still strong enough to stop the breakdown in national pay-bargaining that might have let local pay rates solve local labour shortages. A pay 'explosion' in 2001 became a possibility as nurses and teachers sought increases in double figures. Their resentments might have been assuaged if Labour had done more to celebrate the public good. Carping came easier to Blairite lips than praise.

Beyond Westminster and Whitehall

Most public services are delivered locally. Labour had been seared by the loony left experience – not just Red Ken's GLC or Militant Liverpool but also Blunkett's Sheffield, its schools now having to be rescued by Blunkett's DFEE. Between the ambitions of ministers and the public at large stood local authorities, and in many deprived areas they remained the only reliable agency for public services. Logic said you either reform them or replace them. Labour sought to do both while often ignoring them completely.

Much political life takes place outside Whitehall on the back of appointment rather than election. Labour did not stint in the creation of new committees, including the regional development agencies, RDAs, many chaired by business types, mostly men. Local service delivery became, especially in poorer areas, a morass of partnerships and agencies. The manifesto had fantasized about directly elected regional assemblies, though 'only where clear popular consent is established'. RDAs were allocated money previously channelled through the regeneration quango English Partnerships, with some industrial assistance and training budgets to the tune of about £200 million, increased to £1.7 billion over three years to 2004. The regions – drawn on the basis of planning maps inherited from Harold Wilson's day – had enjoyed something of a renaissance under the Tories, as Government offices in Leeds, Manchester, Nottingham and Bristol had been rationalized and expanded. After four years, the English regions hung there as a constitutional possibility with Prescott fighting their corner against a sceptical Blair.

The Prime Minister was taken with another idea, first floated by Michael Heseltine – city states with their own directly elected executive mayors. Quite who these latter-day Joseph Chamberlains would be remained vague and Blair, typically, had not involved the Labour Party at large, the putative source of renewed local leadership. The limits of the idea were cruelly exposed in London, where only politicians stepped forward, not a new cadre of political entrepreneurs. The Greater London Act paralleled devolution to Scotland and Wales, though the powers granted to the new London Mayor and Assembly were circum-scribed, with a budget of only £3.25 billion a year. Only 34.6 per cent turned out to vote on whether to have a London Mayor and 72 per cent of those said yes (barely one in four adult Londoners).

Having learnt nothing from the antagonism stirred up in Wales by the machinations surrounding the selection of Alun Michael, Number 10 and Millbank cooked a dog's breakfast, humiliating the official candidate, Frank Dobson. Blair often seemed unable to understand the point of devolution. Ken Livingstone, serpen-tine but a sublime tactician, won the popular contest with a far from popular mandate: 32 per cent – 1.7 million voters out of a possible 5 million bothered to vote in May 2000 for Mayor and Assembly, which meant Livingstone got only 15 per cent of the London electorate's first choice votes. Democracy looked far from invigorated that day – and yet power relations between urban England and Westminster may profoundly change in consequence. The Local Government Act 2000 allowed people to petition their council for referendums to create an elected Mayor. Mayors who were directly elected by more voters than mere MPs might take on an unstoppable momentum.

Labour had promised the municipal unions to abolish compul-sory tendering of services, introduced by Heseltine in 1981. The Local Government Act 1999 invented a new duty of 'best value' for councils in providing services to their local communities. They were no longer forced to tender out services but would have to show good cause if the Audit Commission – which established a new army of inspectors – found their costs were higher than the next door council's. Councils complained that Labour was controlling their spending yet more tightly and removing more services from them. But they did win con-cessions, allowing them freedom to spend the proceeds of hous-ing sales under the Right to Buy. No longer would every council's spending be subject to capping by the centre, only those deemed to be spending excessively. But Whitehall refused to restore councils' right to levy rates on business, which had been taken under central command by the Tories. At least, having lost their empires in schools and social services, councillors were no longer saddled with unfair responsibility: the Local Government Act 2000 ended the anomaly by which a councillor could be personally surcharged for decisions taken in office, unlike any other elected official. Instead, councillors were to be answerable to a new standards quango which, if it found against them, could censure or disqualify them from office.

Freer information?

One easy hit for Labour would have been clear, unambiguous enthusiasm for freer access to official information, as promised in its manifesto. Instead ministers and their advisers were frequently to be found sneering that this was a minority issue, only of interest to a few *Guardian* readers – sneer again. Only later when the going got rough was this attitude of contempt regretted. Labour, like all its predecessors, had fallen in love with executive power. It showed no appetite for subjecting the often notoriously inefficient secret state to management disciplines or to opening the curtained windows of Whitehall and letting light shine in.

On taking office Labour tottered in a liberal direction as Blair issued a 'ministerial code' setting out what ethical obligations a minister's job carried. He moved swiftly to redeem an old promise by lifting the ban on trade-union membership at GCHQ, the intelligence communications centre. After that, however, the door swung on its hinges. Seduced by mandarins or simply weak-minded, Labour was persuaded that the state needed the same power of surveillance over the new e-world that it had commanded over snail mail since Home Secretary Sir James Graham opened the letters of that dangerous Italian Giuseppe Mazzini in 1844. His successors used age-old language:

'The powers crucial to keeping this country a safe place for everyone to live and work must remain effective in the face of the latest technological advancements.' Catching rampant paedophiles made a convenient scapegoat for e-intrusion. Blair put his weight behind what became the Regulation of Interception of Communications Act 2000. The UK, by going further even than the security-conscious Americans, was likely to retard the growth of e-commerce to which Blair had said he was passionately committed. But Labour did enhance individuals' rights to prevent personal data being accumulated for commercial gain. At least for the private sector there was a new law offering protection to whistleblowers. Two steps back, one step forward.

Despite the disclosure by renegade MI5 officer David Shayler that the Security Service held files on both the Home Secretary and Peter Mandelson, the Government made little effort to apply to its intelligence operatives the efficiency and effectiveness measures it said it believed in for other public services. The Secret Intelligence Service was allowed to move into an expensive refurbished Thames-side palace. Labour votes passed a new Terrorism Act which critics said extended definitions haphazardly and introduced a new offence of 'incitement', aimed at foreign-based groups or individuals living in Britain. Shayler claimed that in 1995 two MI6 officers paid £100,000 to Libyan plotters to kill Libyan leader Muammar Gadafi; they killed bystanders instead. Prosecuted under the Official Secrets Act, Shayler fled to France claiming he had only acted in the public interest. The Government, as if it had nothing better to do than protect the secrets of previous Tory ministers and unaccountable spies, went after him. In August 2000 he returned. His would become one of the first major test cases of the new Human Rights Act, if the authorities ever took him to court.

One clear liberal deed would have been freedom of information. But Jack Straw, belying his medieval namesake, weighed in on the side of the state's secretiveness. A bill had been promised in the 1997 manifesto and in the fresh dawn Blair vowed it would fundamentally change relations between public and government. You could add a list of inspirational quotes from Brown and Cook, even Lord Chancellor Irvine extolling the citizen's right to public information. But somewhere between a reasonable white paper, *Your Right to Know*, in 1997 and a draft bill in 1999, the machine made them see sense. Why, said the casuists of Whitehall, even democracy demanded secrecy, for unless a minister had the final right to veto the new Information Commissioner's decision on whether information should be disclosed, the will of the people would be usurped by an unelected official. This veto was only one of the fudges. No one was asking for the right to see everything, but the Government seemed to want to avoid disclosing anything: 'Information which in the reasonable opinion of a qualified person would prejudice the effective conduct of public affairs' could cover anything. The law passed, it was an improvement but it was so diminished and despised that Labour lost political support needlessly.

In opposition, Labour had linked the creation of an independent statistical service with cleaning up political life. Fundamental changes alone could ensure the integrity of official data on crime, waiting lists and prices, Blair said in February 1998. The reform scheme that eventually emerged did not satisfy the Royal Statistical Society but in creating an autonomous commission to oversee the Office of National Statistics, the public was at least given a proxy oversight of this critical work.

The law

If the powers of the state under Labour were only lightly reformed, some effort – though far from radical – was made to modernize the professions which, some would say, run the country as much as the elected Government. Labour sniffed at the accountants but decided 'self-regulation' would do. As for the law, change was to be carried by that ambivalent figure, Lord Chancellor Irvine. But first there was the matter of wallpaper.

Criticized in the press for the expense of refurbishing his office in the Lords, Irvine replied, 'As well as being a senior Cabinet Minister and the head of the judiciary, the Lord Chancellor has important duties as the Speaker of the House of Lords.' But that was the point: he was wearing too many hats, to say nothing of garters and breeches. Blair's modernization did not even ask how an official of the Lords who was also a cabinet minister and a senior politician could also be a judge?

Irvine was a reformer but like all lawyers a compulsive conservative. When it came to legal aid, his remit was political – cost savings. On jobs for judges – in 1998–9 he made some 634 appointments to the high court, circuit and district benches and tribunals – he repulsed the idea of a judicial appointments commission, neutral and expert. Instead he clung to what amounted to private selection by the Lord Chancellor's Department, though adverts were placed for the first time and judges were 'invited' to disclose membership of that other band of men in funny clothes, the freemasons. He did create a half-commission to 'audit' his work, attending occasional job interviews to check for bias. People rarely shake off youthful deference, and Tony and Cherie Blair deferred too much to their former boss and mentor: if appointments commissions were the right way to select new peers, how much more important might such transparency be for judges?

Irvine extended 'no-win, no-fee' (conditional fee) suits – not apparently giving much thought to what ambulance-chasing might do to the National Health Service, which faces some £2.8 billion worth of outstanding claims. If poor people could get lawyers to take their case conditionally then there would be less call on legal aid, which had been burgeoning. Another tactic was to cut legal costs of defence. A new Community Legal Service and Criminal Defence Service took over the £1.6 billion spent a year on legal aid. The former would seek alternative (i.e. cheaper) ways of resolving disputes; the latter was to contract with what Irvine hoped would be a better class of criminal lawyer. The 1998 white paper *Modernising Justice* proposed allowing all lawyers (even solicitors) to argue cases in the higher courts. In parallel with proposals made by Lord Woolf (Lord Chief Justice from 2000), Labour pushed faster-track processing of civil claims. But earlier, radical ideas on giving non-lawyers a bigger role in adjudication and home sale and purchase were not pursued. You did hear Lord Woolf acknowledging how the Human Rights Act would expose the way judges were trained and promoted, but few words on the subject from Labour ministers.

Enactment of human rights was a long-standing promise. The white paper *Rights Brought Home* in October 1997 promised not just incorporation of the European Convention on Human Rights into UK law but the spread of a 'culture' of rights within state and society. It would not touch on the economy since the Human Rights Act (HRA) applied only to 'public powers', which just about included the formerly nationalized utilities but not private companies. What this new rights culture implied was not spelled out then or later. It was another piece of patchwork sewn on without much thought about the overall pattern.

Under the HRA courts did not get to strike down laws they deemed incompatible with the various precepts on rights, but ministers would be under strong obligation to amend any legislation found to contradict the HRA. Labour resisted setting up a Human Rights Commission to undertake cases even if they did establish the Disability Rights Commission precisely to fight for the 'human rights' of people with disabilities. Reorganization of the 'rights' furniture is going to be needed soon.

Citizen, state and party

The press seized on the Ecclestone affair in the autumn of 1997 to argue that New Labour were as bad as old Tories. Taking money from Formula One boss Bernie Ecclestone smelled; whatever his aim in paying, he appeared to receive a commercial benefit over tobacco advertising. Across the West, parties needed to raise ever-larger sums to fight elections. The resulting sleaze destroyed Helmut Kohl's reputation and tarnished Al Gore's campaign. As long as power is sought by parties – and what other way is there of organizing democratic contests? – corruption can only be avoided by fixed and fair state financing.

At least Labour's Political Parties, Elections and Referendums Act did put parties on a legal footing for the first time. It set limits to spending during elections – £20 million per party is the new upper limit, with compulsory declaration of donations above £5,000. Labour had made its own funding transparent before the law passed, but the revelation of Geoffrey Robinson's bung made Labour seem too much like Hague's Tories, who hired themselves out to rich men as a matter of course.

The new act established an Elections Commission to take over the functions of the Boundary Commission with a statutory responsibility for educating voters. The need for which is surely great. A report from Professor Bernard Crick showed up deficiencies in preparing young people for civic participation – the group least likely to vote. In response Blunkett put citizenship into the national curriculum and urged more mock elections in schools. The trouble is that most political education takes place within a local context and local politics are rarely young and exciting. Experiments were carried out in the May 2000 local elections using mobile poll-booths and voting in supermarkets, which had little effect. Making it easier to cast absentee ballots did increase the vote, but it remained an uphill struggle.

Perhaps direct democracy is a way forward. By accident rather than design Labour had become the referendum party: in London, Wales and Scotland and – one day – joining the euro. Purists objected that referendums were a cop-out by politicians frightened to make hard calls. But they are now here to stay and Labour's Elections Act usefully regularized how they are to be carried out.

Lord Neill's Committee on Standards in Public Life which he chaired in succession to Lord Nolan evolved into a permanent if rather constipated organ of state. Neill did not like Labour's thinking on referendums, especially its idea that money would need to be spent by the Government on information about issues being decided. The point applied particularly to any referendum on UK membership of EMU. Our colleague Hugo Young called Neill's reservations preposterous. If the Government cannot express a view on such a vital issue – given the anti-Europe bias of three-quarters of the newspaper press – just what is public power for?

There is no doubting Labour's concern that legitimacy rested on participation. This was a focus of many, disparate policies. The New Deal for Communities depended, for example, on people getting together (on estates, in local groups) to make decisions. Ditto Labour's enthusiasm for transferring council dwellings to new not-for-profit landlords only if tenants assented in a ballot. But such decisions also downgraded the role of elected councils, which were at the same time being pressed to become more democratic.

There had been a plan, said the National Policy Forum of 2000, 'to build and sustain democracy through a connected series of constitutional reforms that put in place a new relationship between the citizen and the state'. Devolution was its most concrete expression of the policy, though Labour found it hard to adapt as a party to the demands of autonomy in Scotland, Wales and London. But then came human rights law, offering people a means of criticizing and diminishing the state in a culture of individual complaint hardly likely to endear government to people. But public sentiment about UK Government was ambivalent before Blair took office. His administration has to be credited with opening some windows and doors in the mansion of state. He can hardly be blamed if people do not like much what they see on looking in nor if, invited to participate more actively in rearranging the furniture, they do not take the opportunity.

Before House of Lords reform is completed in the next term – if there is one – there should be a great national constitutional convention to thrash out the growing contradictions about where power is to reside. It might not excite the public, but Labour's radical and haphazard ragbag of constitutional changes raised questions about the future shape of democracy that demand resolution.

11

Conclusion

On the eve of the 1997 election several about-to-be Labour ministers gathered at the end of a hard day's campaigning. Excitement was high in anticipation of victory. But after the first few drinks a sober mood settled upon them. They turned to us and one said, 'We will disappoint everyone. All this will wear off. Change takes time and people will get bored and impatient. Everyone will turn against us, that's the way it goes.'

Conversation took a darker turn. Labour Governments always disappoint because they – even New Labour – are out to transform society, no less. Labour carried eighteen years of historical expectations on its back; however hard it had tried to quieten the promises, however often it preached gradualism, too many people believed they were once again setting out in a charabanc on the road to Jerusalem. For party supporters who felt they had made so many sacrifices of principle and bitten their lips so often in the effort to get Labour fit for election, disappointment was hard-wired into personal and collective memory. The left expects disillusion.

As for the public at large, only a third of whom had actually cast their ballots for Blair back in 1997, what right had they to be disappointed when they clearly had willed either the status quo or minimal change? How could those fair-weather enthusiasts of 2 May dare to seem jaundiced after four years – during which things in general, jobs and incomes, had been pretty good?

Between the public and the partisans, where were the people of good heart, willing to give Tony and his crew the benefit of the doubt? The longer Labour held office, the more difficult it became to find anyone who would express admiration, let alone affection. Blair had no lovers, no passionate adherents. He was so very unlike Bill Clinton who, despite his lack of solid achievements, could call on profound reservoirs of affection among the black community and many others. Unlike Gerhard Schröder, who had sacked the man who said the heart beats to the left (Oskar Lafontaine), he commanded little of the mass respect a nation automatically gives a figurehead leader. How many Britons said 'our Prime Minister' with pride? It was not that Blair had committed some heinous offence, there was just a chilling indifference and detachment among those who were probably still going to vote Labour but without warmth.

The centre-left's disillusion, as keenly felt in the heartlands as in the salons of the metropolis, began with those pre-election taxing and spending pledges. Then came cuts in lone parent and disability benefit, blinding them to Gordon Brown's later largesse and to his odd fiscal radicalism on the corporate front. Instead they heard pro-business rhetoric and foot-dragging reluctance to rebalance relations between employers and bosses. Jack Straw sounded as if Michael Howard had never left office. House of Lords reform was half-cocked, leaving a newly empowered Tory majority in the hands of ninety-two old heredi-taries.

What were the emphatic points of Labour policy, its 'legend'? If Blair believed his fate was to remake Labour as a party Middle England would vote for, why did he not follow the logic of his own analysis and reform the voting system – destroying Labour's capacity for single-party hegemony, yes, but also creating the conditions for permanent progressive and liberal government?

What the people who voted Labour for the first time in 1997 cared about most was better public services. Expectations had been raised, only to be dashed when nothing much happened or, as with transport, things evidently got worse. Early trickery with figures undermined confidence. Winter crises in the NHS seemed as bad as ever. There were shady dealings too, Ecclestone and Robinson, Whelan and personality clashes made all the more puzzling because they did not relate to big, substantive differences on policy or spending. It looked like business as usual. How quickly went up the old cry, 'They're all the same.' Orchestrating it all, pumping up the cynicism, undermining the successes, there was the same old Tory press that had poisoned the public mind for most of the twentieth century. Controlling two-thirds of newspaper sales, setting the agenda for the broadcasters too, the defeated right could still throw acid every day. Historians of twentieth-century Britain have given too little weight to the political effects of ownership of the press by reactionaries.

Yet loss of faith in conventional politics is visible right across the Western democracies as wealthier generations loosen political allegiances and forget what government is for. Indifference and suspicion washed into the bus queues, wine bars, pubs – and was picked up with growing alarm by Labour in its own focus groups. Labour assumed it would inherit the same 'permissive consensus' among people at large that had buoyed previous governments. But during the 1990s indicators of dissent had started climbing. No longer was there any alternative to capitalism; we all lived in a world ruled by economics. John Dunn, the Cambridge political theorist, speculated that the politics prompted in the West in this post-socialist, post-Cold-War age was going to be 'irritable, reactive and myopic: endlessly saturated with *ressentiment*'. Was there a better way of describing what happened in September 2000 during the fuel protests?

While 48 per cent expressed 'quite a lot of confidence' in the Commons in 1985, by 1995 that figure had halved and has probably gone on falling. The proportion of people expressing attachment to a political party fell in the 1990s in seventeen out of the nineteen advanced countries for which data exist. Perhaps Blair, unluckily, ran into a new wave of democratic disaffection which would have washed over any leader of any government. Perhaps voters feel that representative institutions themselves are weakening: in a globalized world, it may just be harder to govern. We are losing confidence in government precisely because we no longer think we need it – in the economic realm above all.

This view may rest on a mistaken short-term perception that macro-economic problems have been 'solved'. Formerly the left wanted the state to intervene, help employees, correct failing markets and steer vigorously. The right resented government, but neither side denied its capacity or importance. Now, in our centrist age, that has been replaced by a kind of indifference.

In this book we confined ourselves to things done and things left undone. We tried to strip away the hyperbole, the claims and boasts, to look as coolly as we could at what Labour has achieved in four years. We needed a baseline on which to measure New Labour but none exists, dry and objective, to be taken down from history's shelf. Tony Blair was not the only centre-left leader in power in Europe in the latter years of the century and perhaps if he were marked alongside Lionel Jospin, Massimo D'Alema, Goran Persson and Gerhard Schröder he would shine. But voters do not make such comparisons, especially in the contemporary climate of Euroscepticism the Blair Government did so little to disperse. The fairest judgements must be based on what New Labour itself promised.

Manifesto prose does not get us very far. But behind what was said in 1997 lay something else, a historic capitulation by Labour to fiscal conservatism for the sake of winning power in post-Thatcher Britain. Was Labour right to defer extra spending in its first two years? With hindsight, no, it only delayed the massive programme of infrastructural improvement – from broken rails to leaking classrooms – universally recognized as necessary. Electoral calculators say Labour would still have won even if Gordon Brown had not made his promises on tax and spend, albeit with a smaller majority. Or at least that is what psephologists say now. Then, in early 1997, Labour still walked in the valley of the shadow of '92. Remember that the prognosis was for an economic downturn to start in the last quarter of 1997 – Eddie George at the Bank of England was one of those financial physicians who positively relish telling patients they are at death's door. Brown had to convince the markets. All the talk about his affair with Prudence was meant to be seductive. Without binding himself in Tory chains of fiscal masochism he might never have engendered the City confidence that made Labour's victory and Brown's first budget such unremarkable events in the life of the FTSE. Fiduciary trust was what Gordon Brown won and for it Labour sacrificed much. Even a Labour Party which had jettisoned most of its egalitarian or transformational policies still had to ingratiate itself, or run the risk of capital flight or destabilizing speculation. Hence Brown's disavowal of his mentor, John Smith.

Labour's ship sailed into Downing Street on a rising tide: many said at the time that whoever won in 1997 might be in power for twenty years, so good was the economic outlook. By mid-2000 the OECD gave Britain's economy a glowing report – 'enviable', it said. Employment soared, money flowed into the Treasury, debt was repaid, the economy grew above trend, inflation plunged. But how much of this was economic weather, how much the result of deliberate decision? The answer is probably 60:40, but the golden goose would not have laid if Gordon had not been such a gentleman, who gave up his monetary policy seat to the Bank of England and pledged never to borrow except to invest for the long term.

The tax pledge was intended to anchor the trust of those voters without whom – 1992 again – Labour could not win. It did. Brown had not promised not to raise taxes, as motorists discovered. But eschewing income tax as a way of adjusting demand, he became the golfer lacking a driver, having to putter around with irons.

By the time of his pre-budget statement in November 2000 Brown's coffers were overflowing with money he could not spend, because the independent Bank threatened to raise interest rates if he did. Refusing to tax more, he had no way of dampening consumer demand to compensate for the public spending needed so obviously. But this was a government of mixed message: did Labour want to spend, anyway? The 1 per cent income tax cut that astonished in the 1999 budget seemed like an impudent joke at the time, leaving the Tory benches gasping. But what did it say about Labour existentially? It cemented the idea that the public could expect to have better public services and pay less too. It did nothing to educate people on the balance between revenues and outlays, nothing to remind them that the UK's poor transport, health and education were the direct result of low taxation, too low to meet the long-term aspirations of a prosperous country. When people travelled elsewhere in Europe and wondered why the trains and streets, hospitals and schools were all brighter, cleaner, better, there was no political leadership to tell them these things were bought at an average 8–10 per cent more GDP devoted to public purposes.

Labour undermined its own potential long-term support by failing to draw the ideological line between themselves and their opponents. As the numbers of mega-rich soared, there was no one to advocate that they shoulder a fairer share of the burden: fat-cats over-paid and under-taxed were never asked to contribute a little more in a society still growing more unequal in its extremes under Labour.

Brown was a chameleon Chancellor. He had a genuine obsession with social policy, concerning himself with details of what works in getting unqualified youth into jobs or nursery education for poor children. If redistribution from the rich was off his agenda, then at least distributing most of the available money to the poor was his mission. He was a formidable brain, a rock-steady pillar. Yet he lacked the insights and instincts also essential for the job and the story of his tenure of the Treasury was also one of serious political miscalculation. Immured with clever aides and their calculators, he devised brilliantly well-targeted benefits and tax credits. But they were hard to understand and complex to administer. When these generous increases for the poor needed to be emblazoned on Labour's shield, who told the story? Who helped ordinary people follow, say, the translation of Family Credit into Working Family Tax Credits, to be transmuted in its turn into Integrated Children's Tax Credits, partly paid via employers into the pay packet, partly returned as before into direct payments into mothers' handbags?

The clamour for higher basic pensions came in part from incomprehension of the better principle of his pensioners' minimum income guarantee. He lacked the political flair to sell good ideas.

He also lacked the antennae to know when the clouds were gathering, when to bend with the wind and when to stand iron-firm. If Tony Blair was too pliable, Gordon Brown bent too little. A cannier politician would have ducked the lone parent and disability benefit cuts: he forced good soldiers out to fight for things not worth the candle. Harriet Harman paid the price. Frank Dobson was sent on a suicide mission against Ken Livingstone to win Londoners over to partial privatization of the tube. John Prescott did much harm to his own credibility, obliged to defend even the privatization of air traffic control – none of it financially necessary, more a point of pride with the Chancellor. How casually Brown set aside transport for urgent repair in the first years. The health service could not be frozen for two years without crisis erupting – it never can. The petrol rebellion which rocked the Government might have been forestalled. How did he never see what the 75p pension meant politically?

Most serious of all, he lost trust by his devious accounting in the July 1998 Comprehensive Spending Review. It took time for pundits to unravel what he had done, multiplying spending over three years as if it were three times as much. Of all his errors, this was the most permanently disabling for Labour. They only began to confess to this error when Peter Mandelson ventured a *mea culpa* in a lecture at the end of 2000. 'Not yet chastened by the sheer hard work and grind of government, we were all a bit guilty of letting some of our sense of the possible get out of sync with the pace of change on the ground.' But by then iron had entered the soul: it sounded, in Mandelson's mouth, like another blow in the perpetual Blair–Brown battle.

If Brown seemed to walk away unscathed from political calamities of his own making, that is because after four years his custodianship left the economy in better shape than for a long,

long time, the only Labour Chancellor ever to reign four years without having to contend with a crisis. (Few Tory Chancellors have either.)

In this book we have eschewed personality, resisted the temptations of the grand soap opera of Westminster, the rows and jealousies that preoccupy political reporters to the exclusion of what is and is not happening to change policies, spending and beyond them real people's lives. And yet characters and their interplay matter, for the two great players on the stage are inextricably linked, in war and peace.

Blair and Brown shared so much, especially the scars of defeat. Recovery from the loss in 1992 made them but unmade them too. It left them scared, fearful of the people of this country. Control-freakery was just another sign of insecurity, that twitchy finger on the pager of every MP. If the Tories and their bully-boys in the press had an outraged sense that Labour was a usurper, the new monarch had a sneaking sense they might be right. A majority of voters might have chosen Labour, but Blair and his pollsters wondered if all they wanted was a kinder, gentler Tory administration: better health and education, a strong economy, more jobs, more law and order and no more income tax. Blair detected little yearning for great liberal or constitutional reforms and, truth to tell, there was none. New Labour had said time for a change, not for a revolution. The reformed party's promise was safe and clean hands, optimism and improvement, tempered with caution and prudence. And that was pretty much what the people got.

Blair remained a mercurial figure, slipping away from clear definition, the very embodiment of the Third Way. There were those who swore he was at heart a conservative. Others believed he had a radical vision but played a long game, letting the line out and reeling it back until the time was right to land the fish. But was it a sprat or a shark? Trust me, he would say to us liberal types, but coming out of his room at Number 10 we glimpsed in the antechamber a columnist for the *Daily Mail*, also to be sincerely reassured. Crafty or vacillating? Smarmy or sincere?

Blair was a believing Christian, but was his faith a weak man's crutch or the guarantor of moral rigour that would sustain a mission for social justice? One thing was clear – whatever his long-term strategy, he was too often blown off course by fear of the people. When he should have dared to lead opinion, he too often ducked and chose to follow behind – prompting the question, what was he in power for?

Like others who wished for progressive government and so welcomed Labour in 1997, we found ourselves on a zig-zag course in our columns and editorials. Conversations with colleagues, friends and ministers argued back and forth the true nature of New Labour. The low moments were very low. Cheap populism on law and order damaged an honourable determination to deal with crime effectively and enlighten the public about what works. The *Daily Mail* and *Sun* too often drove the agenda. Unctuous committees on family policy delivered unwelcome hollow homilies. Even as the right-wing press turned on them, Downing Street often stooped to lick the bullies' boots. Long after the *Daily Mail* had turned to devoting itself daily to trashing Labour, its editor and his wife were to be found at an intimate Downing Street dinner. Even he asked on that occasion why Tony Blair bothered: 'I will always be a Tory.'

In opposition Blair and Brown had learnt passionate admiration for business – as an idea as much as a corporate reality. All that zeal for private-sector solutions was part of a 1990s mindset they never escaped, still fighting long-dead wars when the unravelling of rail privatization should have stopped them in their tracks. With work/life balance issues pressing on a country working the longest hours in Europe, the Government caved in to the employers despite all the hand-wringing over family life.

Most serious of all was Blair's failure of nerve on the two milestone questions – Europe and the century-old split in the centre-left. Still needlessly insecure in the first years, he dared not throw his immense political capital behind a quick referendum to join the euro. It would have resolved the UK's future trajectory, instead of prolonging the enervating debate: the majority of voters think joining inevitable, Europe is our destiny. Instead, a nasty English nationalism has flourished alongside anti-Europeanism and for the time being, the opportunity looks lost.

Paddy Ashdown's diaries were not needed to show how close Blair came to forging coalition with his Liberal Democrats. In opposition he had told all and sundry how he meant to end the tribal rift between the parties of the centre-left in order to keep minority Toryism from again holding sway. He would make the twenty-first century safe for progressive forces. That was the Project. He junked it. Proportional representation as a matter of principle should have been delivered by a party strong and secure, not (as may now happen) as a by-product of some last-minute scuffling between Labour and Liberal Democrats in the event of a future hung parliament. Blair was the man, after all, who had confronted his party over Clause 4; why did he not go on to open UK politics permanently to its post-socialist future?

It is hard at the end of the day to compile a single balance sheet – the illiberal government which ended discrimination against gays in the armed forces, a government which showered small businesses with tax credits but also made a stab at abolishing child and pensioner poverty. Zig-zag. On the plus side must be counted devolution, human rights, London government. Of course it depends what the Scots and the Welsh and Londoners make of their varying degrees of self-government, but Labour must be credited with bringing people into closer touch with their collective destinies in those places. A start has been made on the House of Lords; new voting schemes are in use throughout the UK; valiant efforts have been made to settle the governance of Northern Ireland. Small things, too, count: Labour's restoration to the Aberfan disaster fund of money abstracted to contribute towards the cost of removing the waste tip which had ruined the village; some justice for Japanese prisoners-of-war; remarkable apologies by the Queen and Blair for sins in the British past.

The social account is full: the principle as much as the practice of the New Deals, that nobody is going to be left out of the labour market; Sure Start for poor young children; the greatly augmented incomes of poor families with children; devoting money for pensioners not as across-the-board increases but, first, increasing the incomes of the poorest. Schools have been given a focus and, despite Chris Woodhead of Ofsted, teachers are moving up to where they belong in public esteem. At work Labour established the minimum wage and gave all workers their first formal right to belong to a trade union. Abroad, the UK has become identified, however falteringly, with the Good: over arms sales, human rights, the protection of minorities. On the most selfish level, economic growth and price stability have made everyone better off. Labour deserves a decent share of the credit for that.

On the other side of the ledger we have to note the way the Government almost celebrated punishment and prison, its authoritarianism, and the way it fell into executive-mindedness, and watered down its initially generous attempt to diminish the cult of secrecy in British government.

This book is of course an interim judgement. The great spending increase announced in July 2000 has yet to come on stream. Not only the outcome of so many projects, but the party's true long-term plans are yet to be made entirely clear. Blair liked to point out how little Mrs Thatcher did in her first term: she had not even thought of privatization then. What we came to call 'Thatcherism' was an accident of office. So, too, is Blairism a work in progress. Once, Blair talked of ten-year schemes; his first term was about constructing earthworks, solid and prudent, on which great things were later to be built. Now, we wonder if this is as good as it gets – a modest, competent, unambitious government, over-given to high-flown rhetoric while trimming its sails to every wind. Perhaps, after all, it suits the nature of these times and a British public seemingly so volatile.

'Wait and see', Blair used to say. Indeed as the first term wore on and a general election drew closer, Labour seemed to be acquiring a sharper ideological profile – more spending slugged it out with Tory tax cuts, means-testing to secure payments to the poorest v. universal benefits, an aspiration towards internationalism against Europhobia.

The Third Way was a convenient fog and a second term would need new clarity of message. Things did get better. They could get a lot better still but not unless Labour confronts the ghosts of the Tory past and announces itself as the party of the public weal, higher taxes included. Without a far bolder stand on where the boundary between public good and private possession is to be placed, those great promises to abolish child poverty or make health and education the best and transport tolerable are likely to stay just that – promises.

New Labour, New Laws

1997

Education (Schools) Act
- abolished assisted places

Finance (No 2) Act
- windfall tax on utilities, pension fund tax changes

Firearms (Amendment) Act
- banned private ownership of handguns

National Health Service (Private Finance) Act
- empowered health trusts to enter into PFI deals

Referendums (Scotland and Wales) Act
- legal basis for referendums on establishing a Scottish Parliament with tax-varying powers and a Welsh Assembly taking over the functions of the Welsh Office

1998

Bank of England Act
- transfer of operational responsibility for monetary policy to Bank

Competition Act
- Competition Commission, tightened rules on mergers

Crime and Disorder Act
- created anti-social behaviour and new parenting orders and curfews

Criminal Justice (Terrorism and Conspiracy) Act
- powers to arrest and detain people suspected of terrorism overseas

Data Protection Act
- extended individuals' right to inspect data held in their name

European Communities (Amendment) Act
- incorporated Amsterdam Treaty

Fossil Fuel Levy Act
- 'climate change' tax on energy use by companies

Government of Wales Act
- established Welsh Assembly

Greater London Authority (Referendum) Act
- provided for vote on new London arrangements

Human Rights Act
- incorporated the European Convention on Human Rights

Landmines Act
- banned sale of mines-related material and joined Ottawa convention

National Lottery Act 1998
- created National Lottery Commission

National Minimum Wage Act
- established minimum payments in employment

Northern Ireland Act
- established devolved assembly, north–south council, etc.

Public Interest Disclosure Act
- protected 'whistleblowers' at work

Regional Development Agencies Act
- established business-led agencies in England's regions

School Standards and Framework Act
- established 'action zones', allowed more central intervention

Scotland Act
- gave Scotland an elected parliament and tax-raising powers

Teaching and Higher Education Act
- established General Teaching Council, reorganized teacher training, student fees

Wireless Telegraphy Act
- authorized the auction of radio spectrum

1999

Access to Justice Act
- changed legal aid, allowed 'no fee' litigation

Disability Rights Act
- set up Disability Rights Commission with powers to help disabled people

Employment Relations Act
- gave unions statutory right to be recognized and various new rights at work

European Parliamentary Elections Act
- allowed 1999 and subsequent EP elections to be conducted on 'regional list'

Food Standards Act
- set up Food Standards Agency with the aim of protecting public health

Greater London Authority Act
- established the GLA through elections for Mayor and Assembly

Health Act
- abolished GP fundholding, established primary care trusts and Commission for Health Improvement

House of Lords Act
- ended automatic right of hereditary peers to sit and vote in Lords

Immigration and Asylum Act
- tightened rules on entry, required applicants for visas to provide financial security

Local Government Act
- councils to operate 'best value' regimes and compulsory competitive tendering abolished

Protection of Children Act
- childcare organizations to refer names of individuals considered unsuitable to work with children to a central list

Tax Credits Act
- brought in Working Families' Tax Credit

Water Industry Act
- prohibited the disconnection of supply for reasons of non-payment

Welfare Reform and Pensions Act
- stakeholder pensions, changed pension rights on divorce

Youth Justice and Criminal Evidence Act
- allowed courts to refer young offenders for non-custodial programmes

2000

Care Standards Act
- created commission regulating homes and council to oversee training of social workers

Carers and Disabled Children Act
- councils to support those caring for people with long-term illness or disability

Children (Leaving Care) Act
- councils to continue support for children previously in their care

Countryside and Rights of Way Act
- walkers' rights of way over open country

Criminal Justice and Court Services Act
- new law on sex offenders and reform of Probation Service

Electronic Communication Act
- allowed e-signatures and other commercial uses of the internet

Financial Services and Markets Act
- set up the Financial Services Authority and compensation scheme

Freedom of Information Act
- new rights of access to official documents

Fur Farming (Prohibition) Act
- banned keeping of animals for their fur

Government Resources and Accounts Act
- introduced resource budgeting, expanded remit of National Audit Office

Learning and Skills Act
- set up new Learning and Skills Council and new youth service, Connexions

Local Government Act
- executive mayors and other changes in council business

Police (Northern Ireland) Act
- changed name of the Royal Ulster Constabulary

Political Parties, Elections and Referendums Act
- established new elections commission to oversee contests

Postal Services Act 2000
- converted Post Office into a plc owned by the Government

Race Relations Amendment Act
- made police and other public authorities subject to race equality law

Regulation of Investigatory Powers Act
- reworked powers of security services to intercept messages sent via internet

Representation of the People Act
- allowed voting experiments

Sexual Offences (Amendment) Act
- lowered age of consent for homosexual sex to sixteen

Terrorism Act
- extended terrorism measures outside Northern Irish context, removed need for annual review of counter-terrorism law

Transport Act
- set up Strategic Rail Authority, privatization of air traffic control, congestion charges

Utilities Act 2000
- created Gas and Electricity Authority to regulate energy

Scotland

Abolition of Feudal Tenure etc. (Scotland) Act 2000
- abolished vestiges of old property forms

Ethical Standards in Public Life etc. (Scotland) Act 2000
- set up codes of conduct for councillors and public appointees

Books and Selected References

Barker, Anthony, *Ruling by Task Force*, London, Politicos, 1999.

Coates, David, and Lawlor, Peter, *New Labour in Power*, Manchester, Manchester University Press, 1999.

Crewe, Ivor, and others, *Why Labour Won the General Election of 1997*, London, Frank Cass, 1998.

Fairclough, Norman, *New Labour, New Language*, London, Routledge, 2000.

Gaffney, Declan, and others, *Funding the London Underground: Financial Myths and Economic Realities*, Listen to London (Unity House, 205 Euston Road, London NW1 2BL), 2000.

Gould, Philip, *The Unfinished Revolution. How the modernisers saved the Labour Party*, London, Abacus (paperback edition), 1999.

Hennessy, Peter, *The Prime Minister. The Office and its Holders since 1945*, London, Allen Lane, 2000.

Jowell, Roger, and others, *British Social Attitudes*, London, Sage, 2000.

Labour Party Manifesto, 1997.

Labour Party National Policy Forum report, 2000.

Lapping, Brian, *The Labour Government 1964–70*, London, Penguin, 1970.

Little, Richard and Wickham-Jones, Mark, *New Labour's Foreign Policy*, Manchester, Manchester University Press, 2000.

Macintyre, Donald, *Mandelson and the Making of New Labour*, London, HarperCollins (paperback edition), 2000.

Mandelson, Peter, and Liddle, Roger, *The Blair Revolution. Can New Labour Deliver?*, London, Faber, 1996.

Pharr, Susan, and Putnam, Robert, *Disaffected Democracies*, Princeton NJ, Princeton University Press, 2000.

Rawnsley, Andrew, *Servants of the People*, London, Hamish Hamilton, 2000.

Sassoon, Donald, 'Convergence, continuity and change on the European left', in Kelly, Gavin (ed.), *The New European Left*, London, Fabian Society, 1999.

Stationery Office, The Government's Annual Reports, London, 1998–2000.

Vincent, David, *The Culture of Secrecy*, Oxford, Oxford University Press, 1998.

Websites

Audit
   www.audit-commission.gov.uk
Arts Council of England
   www.artscouncil.org.uk
Association of Directors of Social Services
   www.adss.org.uk
British Medical Association
   www.bma.org.uk
Cabinet Office
   www.cabinet-office.gov.uk
Centre for Economic Performance
   http://cep/lse.ac.uk
Charter 88
   www.charter88.org.uk
Centre for European Reform
   www.cer.org.uk
Centre for Transport Studies
   www.cts/cv.ic.ac.uk
CIPFA
   www.cipfa.org.uk
Commission for Racial Equality
   www.cre.gov.uk
Countryside Agency
   www.countryside.gov.uk
Day Care Trust
   www.daycaretrust.org.uk
Disability Alliance
   www.disabilityalliance.org
Equal Opportunities Commission
   www.eoc.gov.uk
Fabian Society
   www.info@fabian-society.org.uk
Federation of Small Businesses
   www.fsb.org.uk

Government
   www.ukonline.gov.uk
Health
   www.nhsdirect.nhs.uk
   www.hmso.gov.uk/acts
Industrial Society
   www.indsoc.co.uk
Institute for Fiscal Studies
   www.ifs.org.uk
Institute for Public Policy Research
   www.ippr@easynet.co.uk
International Institute for Strategic Studies
   www.iiss.org
Joseph Rowntree Foundation reports
   www.jrf.org.uk
Kings Fund
   www.kingsfund.org.uk
Labour Party
   www.labour.org.uk
Legislation
   www.hmso.gov.uk
   www.parliament.the-stationery-office.co.uk
Low Pay Unit
   www.lowpayunit.org.uk
National Association of Citizens Advice Bureaux
   www.nacab.org.uk
National Centre for Social Research
   www.natcen.ac.uk
NHS Confederation
   www.nhsconfed.net
Office of National Statistics
   www.statistics.gov.uk
OECD
   www.oecd.org
   www.open.gov.uk
Police Foundation
   www.police-foundation.org.uk
Public standards
   www.public-standards.gov.uk

Royal College of Nursing
  www.rcn.org.uk
Runnymede Trust
  www.runnymedetrust.org
Scotland
  www.scotland.gov.uk
Social exclusion
  http://sticerd.lse.ac.uk/case
World Health Organization
  www.who

Index

References to figures are given in italics